KENNEDY'S AVENGER

Also by Dan Abrams and David Fisher

Lincoln's Last Trial
Theodore Roosevelt for the Defense
John Adams Under Fire
Alabama v. King (with Fred D. Gray)

DAN ABRAMS
AND **DAVID FISHER**

KENNEDY'S AVENGER

ASSASSINATION, CONSPIRACY, AND THE FORGOTTEN TRIAL OF JACK RUBY

HANOVER
SQUARE
PRESS

**HANOVER
SQUARE
PRESS™**

Recycling programs
for this product may
not exist in your area.

ISBN-13: 978-1-335-46952-6

Kennedy's Avenger

First published in 2021. This edition published in 2022.

Copyright © 2021 by Dan Abrams and David Fisher

Hanover Square Press
22 Adelaide St. West, 41st Floor
Toronto, Ontario M5H 4E3, Canada
HanoverSqPress.com
BookClubbish.com

Printed in U.S.A.

For Emilia Pesenti Abrams, born February 18, 2021.
We are thrilled to welcome you to the family.

CONTENTS

INTRODUCTION

Delving into any aspect of the November 1963 assassination of President John F. Kennedy is an ambitious and even perilous endeavor. So much has been said and studied: thousands of pages of scientific evidence, hundreds of witness accounts including some that have evolved over fifty-plus years, numerous government investigations and literally thousands of books. It has long been difficult for so many to believe that Lee Harvey Oswald, who had previously defected to Russia, killed Kennedy acting alone and that less than two days later, Jack Ruby, with his loose ties to the Dallas underworld, also acting alone, so easily killed Oswald. Dozens of conspiracy theories about who "really" assassinated JFK have abounded and become a booming and seemingly limitless business. After all, an angry and broadly anti-government Oswald pulling off the assassination of the century isn't nearly as intriguing as the Mafia, CIA, FBI, Fidel Castro, the Russians or even Lyndon Johnson leading the effort.

In almost every single Gallup poll taken in the decades since

Kennedy's death, a majority of Americans, across all demographic and political lines, were convinced that Oswald was part of a broader conspiracy to kill the president. Of course, if Oswald was part of any orchestrated plan to kill Kennedy, it also significantly increases the probability that Jack Ruby was involved in the assassination, as well.

The intrigue has been exacerbated by the fact that some significant information connected to the case still remains under seal. In 2017, as required by a law passed twenty-five years earlier, more documents and information were finally released. But like everything Kennedy assassination related, the new material presented as many questions as answers. For the first time, the public saw a memo apparently dictated by then FBI director J. Edgar Hoover the night of Oswald's death: "The thing I am concerned about…is having something issued so we can convince the public that Oswald is the real assassin."

But was that an effort to convince the public that there was not a "scintilla of evidence" of a conspiracy as Hoover claimed publicly, or something more sinister? We also learned that someone called a news service in Cambridge, England, twenty-five minutes prior to the Kennedy assassination, urging a reporter to call the American Embassy in London "for some big news and then hung up."

In that same memo, Hoover mentioned a specific threat to Oswald's life: "Last night we received a call in our Dallas office from a man talking in a calm voice and saying he was a member of a committee organized to kill Oswald," Hoover wrote. "We at once notified the chief of police and he assured us Oswald would be given sufficient protection. This morning we called the chief of police again warning of the possibility of some effort against Oswald and again he assured us adequate protection would be given. However, this was not done… Oswald having been killed today after our warnings to the Dallas Police Department was inexcusable."

About Jack Ruby, who had been arrested instantly for killing Oswald, Hoover said, "We have no information on Ruby that is firm, although there are some rumors of underworld activity in Chicago."

For many, understanding Jack Ruby, his background, travel and associates became the key to blowing open the conspiracy. For example, one author and former high-ranking official in the administration of Richard Nixon has said that in 1982 Nixon recalled hiring Ruby as an informant for the House Un-American Activities Committee when Nixon was a member of Congress. The official, who believes Lyndon Johnson was the architect of the assassination, claimed Nixon said he hired Ruby at the behest of LBJ, one of "Johnson's boys." A document presumably from a congressional staffer in 1947 even sought to prevent Jack Rubenstein (Ruby's given name was Rubenstein) from having to testify in front of the committee in public. "It is my sworn statement that one Jack Rubenstein of Chicago noted as a potential witness for hearings of the House Committee on Un-American Activities is performing information functions for the staff of Cong. Richard M. Nixon, Rep. of California. It is requested Rubenstein not be called for open testimony in those aforementioned hearings."

Putting aside the paucity of support for any theory that Johnson was somehow involved, some dispute the authenticity of the document; others more persuasively argue that the Jack Rubenstein referred to in the document was a prominent young communist of the same name who later became a labor union official. But perhaps most importantly, the source of the supposed Johnson connection came from a former Nixon official named Roger Stone, who was convicted, and then pardoned by former President Donald Trump of a host of crimes including lying to Congress. But this sort of conspiracy rabbit hole is familiar terrain for many Kennedy assassination buffs.

Even those with mundane intentions can get caught up in

the desire to find that tantalizing Ruby connection that could break open the case. There would be no more certain way to do so than by offering proof of a connection between Oswald and Ruby who according to every official account did not know one another. Texas Judge Brandon Birmingham, an expert on the Ruby trial, had access to many of the original documents and pieces of evidence in that trial, which were stored at the Dallas courthouse. He described digging through the files as part of an effort to find and preserve evidence for a local museum. There, he made a startling finding: "One day, I found a transcript of a tape-recorded conversation between Lee Harvey Oswald and Jack Ruby from days before the assassination.

"I nearly had a heart attack."

If this transcript was authenticated, it would have proved that these two critical figures, who supposedly had each acted alone and did not know one another, were actually part of a larger conspiracy to kill the president. "For about 30 minutes, I thought I'd uncovered a single piece of evidence that would have rewritten the history books."

It certainly would have done just that. Alas, it was not meant to be. He "realized it was a part of a movie script written in the '70s. In my defense, it did look like an official transcript, numbered margins and all."

In retrospect, it is fair to say that the official and often underappreciated 888-page Warren Commission report, which ruled out any possible conspiracies, missed some details and got certain facts wrong. The FBI and CIA were partially responsible since both had Oswald on their radar—though not as a threat to the president—and sought to minimize that fact. But did the report whiff on the ultimate question of whether Oswald and then Ruby acted alone?

That question certainly was in our minds when we decided to further examine one of the most interesting and often overlooked trials of modern American history. A forgotten trial somehow few have focused on despite the fact that it served as the genesis or launching pad for many of the conspiracy theories. Sometimes in the form of testimony, and many other times with questions left unanswered. And while the trial wasn't about a possible conspiracy, the issue was forever lurking within the halls of the courthouse and the courtroom itself. Both sides sought to use the possibility of there being "more to the story" for strategic advantage.

It has even been alleged that the defense team was involved in the conspiracy, that Ruby's lead attorney, Melvin Belli, then considered the nation's greatest legal showman, was part of an effort to ensure that Ruby was actually convicted. Neither David Fisher nor I take that seriously, but we did differ on the strategy employed by the defense. This was not an easy case, but I believe Belli did Ruby a disservice with the defense he chose and yet David felt Belli generally made a compelling case. So keep an eye out for the subtleties in our agreed upon characterizations of the defense and decide for yourself.

This is our fourth book together, where we have tried to tell the story of an overlooked trial while tracking the evolution of the American legal system, from the Boston Massacre trial, to defense attorney Abraham Lincoln and defendant Theodore Roosevelt, to *The State of Texas v. Jacob Rubenstein*. By the time this trial took place in 1964, the once streamlined trial system had expanded to include a great variety of different legal paths, from pretrial hearings through appeals. More than just stories about trials with great repercussions, these books have been an exploration of the American legal system, in all its glories and complexities.

In the end, when examining this trial and Jack Ruby's role, remember that fate played a role. If Oswald had not paused to put on a black sweater over his shirt before being transported that fateful day, or if Ruby had not agreed to wire $25 to a woman who worked in his club, history would have been changed forever.

"That's the prisoner, wearing the light sweater; he's changed from his T-shirt. Being moved out toward an armored car. (Pause) Being led out by Captain Fritz.

"There's the prisoner. (Shouting:) Do you have anything to say in defense?"

(Sound: A shot.)

"There's a shot! Oswald has been shot! Oswald has been shot! (Pause) A shot rang out...mass confusion here. (Pause. Background clamor.) All the doors have been locked. Holy mackerel. A shot rang out as he was... A shot... There's mass confusion here...rolling...fighting... As he was being led out, no, he is being led back... Looks like he was thrown to the ground. The police have the entire area blocked off. (Yelling:) Everybody stay back. Everybody stay back is the yell."

To an unidentified man: "Did you see it?"

"Yes, I did." (Indistinguishable)

"(Repeating:) The dark stocky man with the hat on...put the gun right in his belly. One of the wildest scenes I have ever seen... The man rushed up and jammed the gun right into Oswald's stomach and fired one shot. Oswald was carried back in the hallway..."

—Ike Pappas, *CBS Radio News*, November 24, 1963.
Dallas, Texas

CHAPTER ONE

Dallas was booming. It had become the financial capital of the American Southwest. The availability of affordable air-conditioning had brought year-round comfort to an already rapidly growing city. Prestigious companies like Texas Instruments and LTV had established it as the nation's third largest high-tech region. The Dallas Market Center, which grew out of the mammoth Home Furnishing Mart, had become the world's largest wholesale trade center. The Dallas Petroleum Club, founded in 1934, had enabled the city to become the financial heart of the state's oil industry. The insurance industry had settled there, making it the insurance capital of the Southwest. It was one of the nation's leading manufacturer of women's apparel. Even the defense industry was moving in with factories and plants popping up on previously undeveloped lands. Like vast concrete spiderwebs, highways were being built to connect the sprawling suburban developments to the city. They were even singing about "Big D" on Broadway; "my, oh yes," where "every home's a palace…" and "there's oil all over your address."

As it moved confidently into the future, Dallas was trying to leave its past behind; taking steps to reinforce its image as a modern city welcoming to all, a good place for growing businesses to find an educated workforce, affordable land and available housing. It slowly had begun integrating public facilities in 1961, opening up lunch counters, civic services and even a limited number of schools to African Americans. Vice President Lyndon Baines Johnson, a Stonewall, Texas man, had helped burnish that image, leading passage of two important civil rights bills while serving as Senate Majority Leader.

But other forces, powerful forces, envisioned a significantly more conservative Dallas. Texas oilman H. L. Hunt, reputed to be the richest man in the world, was a founding member of the John Birch Society, an anti-communist, anti–civil rights organization that had been actively campaigning against Catholic president John F. Kennedy. He had been joined in that organization by oilman Clint Murchison Jr., the founder and co-owner of the NFL's new Dallas Cowboys franchise. Radicals had fostered a hateful political climate in the city; among its leaders was General Edwin Walker, who had been relieved of his command by the army for attempts to indoctrinate troops with Birch Society beliefs, and subsequently had been arrested for organizing riots in Mississippi to protest the admission of Black students. General Walker, whose outspoken extremism was rumored to have inspired the character of crazed General Jack D. Ripper in director Stanley Kubrick's anti-war movie *Dr. Strangelove*, had become a national spokesman for the Birchers.

Although the state of Texas remained firmly Democratic in the 1960 presidential election, Dallas County had strongly supported Republican Richard Nixon, giving him 62 percent of the vote compared to Kennedy's 37 percent. Four days before that election Lyndon and Lady Bird Johnson had been jeered, pushed and spit at by a small group of wealthy women, a "Mink Coat mob," when they campaigned there.

Winning Texas remained essential if Kennedy and Johnson were to be reelected in 1964. To encourage voters, a campaign trip was scheduled for November 22, 1963; it was to be part of the Kennedy charm offensive, highlighted by the appearance of the president's glamorous young wife, Jackie. The opposition's political extremists intended to take advantage of this visit for its own purposes. In October, UN ambassador and twice-Democratic presidential nominee Adlai Stevenson had spoken in the city—and was greeted by protestors who hit him with a "Down with the UN" placard and spit on him. While city officials apologized, General Walker hung an American flag upside down—the sign of distress—in front of his house and said, "Adlai got what was coming to him." Citing this reception, Stevenson suggested to Kennedy that this trip be postponed, advice that was ignored.

As Kennedy's visit approached, mug shots of the president, captioned "Wanted for Treason," were circulated among the crowd waiting along the planned motorcade route. On the morning of the twenty-second the *Dallas Morning News* printed a full-page advertisement bitterly "welcoming" the president while accusing him of "going soft on Communists, fellow-travelers and ultra-leftists," "scrapping the Monroe Doctrine in favor of the 'Spirit of Moscow,'" and allowing the CIA to arrange "coups and having staunch Anti-Communist Allies of the U.S. bloodily exterminated," among a long list of grievances.

Dallas's leading citizens, a powerful loosely knit group of businessmen known as the Citizens Council, were justifiably concerned about Kennedy's safety. Texas Governor John Connally supposedly had also tried to dissuade Kennedy from coming. But the charismatic young president had barely won Texas in the 1960 election and desperately needed its twenty-four electoral votes in the 1964 campaign if he was to win reelection, and the obvious political benefits of tens of thousands of spectators cheering the president and his wife were impossible to resist.

At 12:30 p.m. Central Standard Time, as the motorcade proceeded down Elm Street into Dealey Plaza, twenty-four-year-old Lee Harvey Oswald, hiding behind a wall of cardboard boxes on the sixth floor of the Texas School Book Depository, fired three rifle shots at the president. One of them ripped into Kennedy's skull, killing him instantly.

Texas Governor John Connally, who was accompanying the president, was also shot and seriously wounded, although he made a complete recovery.

In the chaos Oswald slipped away. Less than an hour later, when police officer J. D. Tippit, an eleven-year veteran of the Dallas PD, confronted Oswald on a Dallas street, Oswald pulled out a handgun and killed him. With various witnesses attempting to follow him, Oswald then raced into a nearby movie theater where the film *War Is Hell* was playing. It was there, after punching a police officer, that he was finally captured.

As all of this was happening, Jacob Rubenstein, or Jack Ruby as he had become known, was five blocks away at the offices of the *Dallas Morning News*, placing his regular weekend advertisements for his two local nightclubs. In addition to doing his business, Ruby talked, as he was known to do, and then talked some more with Don Campbell and John Newnam, the advertising department employees responsible for taking the details of the advertisements. Ruby covered a variety of unrelated topics ranging from the financial challenges his clubs were facing to his physical prowess in handling unruly customers. One thing Ruby did not mention was the presidential motorcade passing right near them.

As news of the shooting broke, Ruby and other *News* employees quickly moved to another room with a television set to watch the coverage of the tragedy. They later described Ruby as "ashen" and "shaken." Ruby borrowed an office phone and placed calls to his sister Eva Grant and an employee of his Carousel Club to discuss closing for the night. He then turned to John Newnam and mysteriously declared "John, I am going to have to leave Dallas."

For the next two days the world paused. Tens of millions of people sat in front of black-and-white TVs watching as America buried its president. The Nielsen ratings organization estimated 93 percent of homes with television sets watched the funeral. NBC spent seventy-two hours covering it; CBS assigned eighty journalists to its coverage. The entire country was on edge. Emotions boiled over. In Sioux City, Iowa, for example, a man named Vaschia Michael Bohan was watching with his mother as President Kennedy's body was being moved to the Capitol. When Bohan's sixty-eighty-year-old stepfather, Stephan Sikerachi, entered the room, he apparently cursed Kennedy. In response, Bohan picked up a pair of scissors and stabbed his stepfather six times, once in the mouth and five times in the chest. Sikerachi died at a local hospital an hour and a half after Oswald. Bohan plead guilty but his sentence was suspended because, explained the judge, "the entire nation was under stress and strain from the tragedy."

In Dallas, reporters raced to uncover any information about the assassin: He had been a Marine sharpshooter and received a hardship discharge from the service. In 1959 he had defected to the Soviet Union and had attempted to become a Russian citizen. He was married to a Russian woman, and in 1962 he and Marina Nikolayevna Oswald returned to the United States and settled in the Dallas-Fort Worth area. They had two girls, one a newborn. Although no one made the connection at that time, it was later proven that a bullet fired from the same rifle Oswald had used to assassinate Kennedy had ripped into General Walker's home seven months earlier, barely missing Walker.

But Dallas itself also was being blamed for the tragedy. Newspapers across America described it as "The City of Hate," several of them reporting that fourth-grade students in a wealthy suburb had cheered news of the assassination. One resident reported seeing someone throwing his "sombrero" into the air with joy when told of the killing. News stories describing that type of response often pointed out the power of the John Birch Society in the city.

Many millions of Americans were still absorbing the loss, sitting in front of their TV sets on Sunday morning, November 24, to watch live coverage of Oswald being moved from a cell in the Dallas city jail to the county jail. NBC was the only network broadcasting live from the basement of the Dallas Municipal Court Building. CBS's coverage that morning focused on what eventually would be 115,000 mourners passing slowly through the Capitol rotunda to pay their respects.

Authorities had permitted reporters and cameramen into the restricted basement so Americans could see for themselves that the assassin had not been mistreated by the Dallas PD. About fifty journalists lined the ramp leading from a door to the waiting armored car, a distance of less than one hundred feet. The armored car was being used, according to Dallas police chief Jesse Curry, because "Our squad cars are not bullet-proof. If somebody's going to try to do something, they wouldn't stop him."

The garage ceiling was too low for the armored car, so Oswald had to be hustled out through the basement. He was flanked on either side by detectives, his hands handcuffed together with his right wrist shackled to one detective and his left held by another. Reporters shouted questions to him. Flashbulbs popped. Men jostled for a better position. Suddenly a burly man burst out of the crowd in the lower right of the screen, stuck a .38 revolver in Oswald's stomach and fired once.

Oswald collapsed. "There is Lee Harvey Oswald. He's been shot," shouted NBC correspondent Tom Pettit, "Lee Oswald has been shot. There is a man with a gun. It's absolute panic, absolute panic here in the basement of Dallas Police headquaters." Detectives leaped on top of the shooter. An ambulance raced Oswald to Parkland Memorial Hospital, the same place Kennedy had been brought two days earlier. But nothing could be done to save him. Two hours after being shot, Lee Harvey Oswald was pronounced dead.

NBC was able to cover the shooting almost as it happened, while CBS took a few more minutes to begin broadcasting its own taped coverage. Millions of eyewitnesses had watched a murder being committed. Many millions more saw the scratchy kinescope or the still photograph on the front page of every newspaper. Officers had grabbed the shooter's hand and wrestled him to the ground. The man, a local strip club operator believed to have low-level Mob connections, was identified by officers on the scene, many of whom had known him for years. There could be no doubt about the killer's identity: Jack Ruby.

"You know me," the shooter had apparently screamed as police officers tackled him, "I'm Jack Ruby." Jack Ruby was a man of average stature—five foot nine, 175 pounds—but big dreams. He was one of those likable characters who always had a smile and a scheme. He had owned and operated striptease clubs in the city for more than a decade, places he liked to describe as "fucking classy joints" in which cops and newspapermen were always welcomed. Ruby was a street-smart guy who was tough enough to protect his interests and his "girls," but was also known as a soft touch when someone needed a hand. People also knew he was volatile; on occasion he would lose his temper for brief periods of time and overreact, sometimes violently, but no one who knew Jack Ruby believed him capable of the cold-blooded murder of a manacled man. Within minutes of the shooting, people were asking the question that would resonate through history: Why?

Rumors sprung up faster than oil derricks in East Texas: Ruby had been paid by the Mob or wealthy supporters of the Birch Society to silence Oswald, who had been hired by the Mafia or the Communists to kill Kennedy. Several police officers had been involved, which explained how a civilian carrying a loaded gun was able to get inside a highly protected facility. Ruby himself was a Communist and had traveled to Cuba to meet officials of the Castro government to discuss the plot to assassinate the president. But the most prevalent rumors were those linking Ruby and Oswald. On the day Oswald was killed, an illusionist known professionally as Bill DeMar, who had worked at Ruby's club, told the Associated Press that he had seen Oswald at the club a week earlier: "I have a memory act," he recalled. "I have twenty caller-customers call out various objects in rapid order. Then I tell them at random what they called out. I am positive that Oswald was one of the men that called out an object nine days ago." The story got circulated nationally but when the FBI caught up with DeMar, the man with the "memory act" could not recall any details and denied saying he was "positive."

The *Dallas Morning News* reported, "Officers say that FBI and Secret Service agents believe they have confirmed the report that Oswald and Ruby were neighbors." Yet another newspaper headline blared: "Police Told Oswald, Ruby seen in Waco." For investigators and prosecutors these rumors were only the beginning of what would be an avalanche of tips and even confessions.

Almost immediately the *New York Times* reported that, according to detectives, "Ruby had been impelled to kill President Kennedy's assassin by sympathy for Mrs. Kennedy... He did not want her to go through the ordeal of returning to Dallas for the trial of Oswald."

The killing had been broadcast on live TV. There were more eyewitnesses to this killing than any crime in history so there could be absolutely no doubt about the shooter's identity. This was a capital crime; if malice could be proven, under Texas law defined as a voluntary act without justification, it was potentially

PICTURELUX/THE HOLLYWOOD ARCHIVE/ALAMY STOCK PHOTO

"There is Lee Oswald," described NBC News correspondent Tom Pettit as Oswald appeared. Suddenly, tens of millions of viewers heard a single shot, and after a long pause, Pettit reported, "He's been shot. He's been shot. Lee Oswald has been shot. There is a man with a gun. It's absolute panic, absolute panic here in the basement of Dallas Police headquarters."

punishable by death. But only after a fair trial. This became one of the greatest challenges ever faced by the American legal system: how to make certain that Jack Ruby had his day in court before an impartial jury. Was it possible to find twelve people in the city of Dallas who had not seen or heard the evidence and formed an opinion? More than this nightclub operator, more than the city of Dallas, it was the American legal system that was about to be put on trial before the entire world. Dallas County district attorney Henry Wade said flatly that in this proceeding "The whole system of justice is at stake."

While there was no doubt Jack Ruby had committed a heinous act in front of several million witnesses, the question remained, precisely what crime did he commit? Could the shooting have somehow been justified? Long before any trial might be held, the formalities of that system had to be followed; adherence to procedure theoretically guaranteed he would be treated no differently from any of the other eighty-one men and women indicted by the Dallas County Grand Jury that week.

On November 26, Wade, who would lead the prosecution, presented the evidence to the grand jury. The pugnacious, cigar-chewing Wade was a bulldog in appearance and demeanor; he had been the city's district attorney since 1951. People in Dallas knew and respected Henry; maybe he spoke a little slow and was known to find his down-home drawl when he needed it in front a jury, but when he got his teeth into you he didn't let go. He liked to brag that he'd asked jurors for the death penalty twenty-four times—and got that verdict twenty-three times. Wade was well-respected in town; he was a former FBI agent who had been Governor Connally's roommate at the University of Texas and had served with him in the Navy during World War II. There were whispers floating around that maybe, just maybe he was considering taking a stab at a higher political office; convicting the man who had damaged the entire city's reputation would make for a great campaign ad.

It took the grand jury two hours to return an indictment, a formal charge: "In the and by the authority of the State of Texas, the Grand Jurors, good and lawful men of the County... (do present that Jack Rubenstein alias Jack Ruby)...did then and there unlawfully, voluntarily and with malice aforethought kill Lee Harvey Oswald by shooting him with a gun...against the peace and dignity of the State."

Within hours of the shooting, five trial lawyers had arrived at the courthouse volunteering to represent Ruby. Among them was Tom Howard, considered one of the city's top defense attorneys. He had been contacted by Ruby's partner in one of the various nightclubs he had owned or operated in the previous years. Howard had a storefront office across the street from the courthouse. "A dapper dresser, inclined to wide-brimmed hats," according to the *Morning News*, Howard was also pure Dallas, having practiced there for more than a decade. If you committed murder in Dallas, Tom Howard was the man you wanted defending you. He had represented more than fifty accused murderers, more than half of them facing the death penalty, and not a single one had been executed.

Jack Ruby had known Tom Howard for several years, and didn't so much officially hire him as he did simply accept him as his lawyer and spokesperson. Howard was a respectful man and tended toward quiet, but when necessary he could make his point heard loud and clear. During one case early in his career, for example, he'd started throwing punches at the DA; another time he'd been put in jail briefly for shouting in a courtroom.

Tom Howard embraced his role—and the mammoth publicity that came with it. Howard's strategy from the beginning was to try this case with the odds; he made the assumption that the courtroom was staffed by good men on both sides and on the bench, men who knew each other well and had worked in harmony countless times to bring justice to the good people of Dallas County. As he told reporters, "This is just another... murder case."

As Mr. Howard had done many times in previous cases, he would claim his client had been overtaken by the passion of the moment and had committed a murder without malice, a crime punishable by no more than five years in prison. It appeared that verdict would satisfy a lot of people in the city; newspaper polls taken in the days after the murder indicated about half the population believed Ruby should receive no punishment at all, and in a poll of over two hundred Dallas residents, of those who felt he had to be found guilty, by a seven-to-one margin they supported a light sentence.

Being in the calm center of the hurricane, Howard had less appreciation for the incredible response to the Kennedy assassination already sweeping the country. Dallas had a colorful criminal history; Bonnie and Clyde had set out from there to shoot their way across the Southwest. Butch Cassidy and the Sundance Kid, along with the rest of the Wild Bunch, kept their headquarters in a hotel over a grocery story in nearby Fort Worth. Sam Bass, "Texas's Beloved Bandit," and his gang had robbed trains and stagecoaches, including the Union Pacific "Gold Train" before being killed in a shoot-out with the Texas Rangers. And Ben Long, the former two-term mayor of the city, had been shot dead in a saloon by a man angry about his bar bill in 1877. But the city had never experienced anything like the whirlwind that was about to storm through the country.

No one had. With the exception of the occasional salacious scandal, like Harry K. Thaw's Girl on the Swing Murder or the 1954 trial of Cleveland neurosurgeon Sam Sheppard, who had been convicted of bludgeoning his wife to death supposedly to be with his mistress, crime reporting mostly had been limited to a regional audience. Recently though, the new medium of television had knitted together the entire country. People in California could watch what was happening in New York as it took place. San Francisco State University professor S. I. Hayakawa predicted the spread of TV was as revolutionary as the invention of the printing press, telling thousands of students at a civil rights conference, "The impact of nationwide networks enables [all Americans] to laugh simultaneously at the same joke, thrill at the same adventure, detest and admire the same good guys and bad guys yearn for the same automobiles [and] dream the same dreams…"

And few events enthralled Americans more than a great courtroom battle. Great orators dueling in a courtroom with lives at stake. While throughout history Americans had always considered trials a source of great local entertainment, the legal system suddenly had become a font of popular culture. The award-winning 1955 Broadway show and subsequent movie *Inherit the Wind*, the story of the 1925 Scopes trial, had secured lawyer Clarence Darrow's place in history. *Perry Mason*, the first weekly one-hour series in TV history, had remained an award-winning top-rated show since its debut in 1957. After debuting in 1961, courtroom drama *The Defenders* had won three best dramatic program Emmys. Courtroom-set movies like *Witness for the Prosecution*, *12 Angry Men*, *Compulsion*, *Anatomy of a Murder* and *To Kill a Mockingbird* had made trial lawyers glamorous figures. Trial lawyer Louis Nizer's 1961 memoir *My Life in Court* had stayed on the *New York Times* bestseller list for seventy-two weeks.

The trial of Jack Ruby instantly became the new national sensation. Within a day of appearing for Ruby, filing a petition with the criminal district court demanding his client either be brought before a magistrate to be legally arrested or released, Tom Howard received numerous phone calls from media outlets clamoring to buy the exclusive rights to his story. "*Saturday Evening Post, Life* and several others have been calling," he said. "But I just can't do it." And then he added, "At least not for the time being."

Howard's desire to keep the case "among us Dallasites" soon was overwhelmed as reporters from around the world flooded into the city. Ruby's brother Earl and his sisters, Eva Grant and Eileen Kaminsky, quickly determined that he should have a far more high-profile defense lawyer, believing Howard lacked sufficient experience in major cases to lead the defense. In addition to his courtroom fisticuffs from his early days, Howard had also once been fined and suspended from the practice of law for six months after failing to file tax returns, an issue that could become magnified in this sort of high-profile trial.

With the case in the headlines everywhere, many lawyers

were eager to offer their services but the family wanted one of the emerging "superstar" attorneys, high-powered lawyers willing to travel anywhere in the country to participate in the most complex or highest-profile cases. Men as adept at navigating the intricacies of the legal system as they were dealing with the demands of reporters. A man who was comfortable in the limelight and in the headlines. The decision to bring in an outsider did not "set" well with the local legal establishment; Assistant District Attorney Jim Bowie pointed out, "They forgot that even though Tom Howard defends whores and pimps he does it damn well."

The Ruby family, primarily Earl, Eva and Eileen, making decisions in consultation with their brother, informed Howard of their decision and asked him to help with the search, assuring him that he would remain a critical part of the defense team. Howard and the Ruby family considered or contacted several of the best-known trial lawyers in America. Houston's Percy Foreman, whom *Time* described as "The biggest, brashest, brightest criminal lawyer in America" turned down the case for reasons never clearly explained. Famed defense attorney Jake Ehrlich, whose celebrity clients included Errol Flynn, Billie Holiday, Howard Hughes and poet Lawrence Ferlinghetti (charged with obscenity for selling Allen Ginsberg's book *Howl*) and who had been rumored to be the inspiration for actor Raymond Burr's Perry Mason as well as a second legal drama, the NBC show *Sam Benedict*, supposedly was encouraged by that network to defend Ruby. The family finally decided against retaining him; the speculation was they didn't want to bring a Jewish lawyer into the case to defend this Jewish defendant.

Finally the Ruby family settled on square-jawed, silver-maned, impeccably groomed Californian Melvin Belli, arguably the most famous lawyer in the country. Belli, who was credited with bringing medical science and intricate displays into the courtroom in personal injury cases, had been awarded record-setting monetary judgments in more than a hundred cases. Mel Belli was a master performer in the courtroom, among the first lawyers to appreciate the value of publicity; once explaining, "You have to ring the bell in order to get people into the tabernacle." Belli's courtroom antics were already legendary: he once brought in a pickled brain for a jury to examine. He was known to display artificial limbs and even assembled a section of a San Francisco cable car in front of the jury to prove his client had been injured by a defective gearbox. He would have his crippled clients stumble across the courtroom to demonstrate the damage a defendant had caused. When the New York Giants baseball team moved to San Francisco he bought season tickets, then sued the team for fraud and breach of warranty because, he said, its Candlestick Stadium effectively became a frozen wind tunnel at night. After delivering his closing argument in a winter parka and boots, a jury ruled the team owed him over $1,500; when they were slow in paying, he convinced the sheriff to serve a writ of execution on Giants' property—specifically on centerfielder Willie Mays, who he claimed to own a piece of until the judgment was paid. "Even Texas has never seen a performance that can match Belli at his best," warned an editorial in the Knight Newspapers chain. "The urbane Belli, with his cowboy boots and Savile Row suits is the greatest actor since Barrymore."

His flamboyant lifestyle reinforced the image: he had, he admitted, "A zest for life, a penchant for all good things bright and beautiful, kinky and flawed, for good wines, great tables, wide travels and beautiful women." While living in Europe he and swashbuckler Errol Flynn made headlines enjoying the best Parisian delights. He boasted he'd been to every country in the world other than Tibet. He drove a Rolls-Royce. His San Francisco law office mostly resembled a nineteenth-century bordello; with mahogany paneling, Persian carpets, floor-to-ceiling bookshelves explored on a velvet-covered ladder, lavender tinted windows and four crystal chandeliers suspended from a gold-trimmed ceiling. It included a mahogany bar, a huge brick fireplace, red velvet drapes and upholstered chairs, an antique safe and rolltop desk and assorted Victorian pieces.

The office was decorated with items he picked up on his travels. Prominently displayed were demon masks from Katmandu, a buffalo hide from Nigeria, a skeleton, a cuckoo clock from Germany's Black Forest region, numerous apothecary jars from his grandmother's drugstore in Sonora including one labeled "The great ghonorrhea and fleet remedy. Prepared only by Penn Drug Co. inc. Price $1.50." A cannon on the building's roof was fired and the pirate flag, the Jolly Roger, was hoisted to celebrate each of his legal victories.

His personal fashion also was classically stylish, or at least memorable. Judge Joe Brown described Belli as "my notion of a grandee of Italian extraction." He was known for wearing expensive European-cut suits with a vest, both lined with bright scarlet silk, a gold chain draped loosely across the front, his hand-made pastel shirts set off by Byronesque ties, and high-heeled, polished black boots. When appropriate he wore a Chesterfield overcoat with a fur collar and almost always carried his legal papers in a red velvet carpetbag.

In court though, to emphasize his respect for the system, he wore a gray suit—an expensive gray suit, the finest fabric cut and sewn by the most-skilled tailors on the continent—but still a gray suit.

Beneath the show, fifty-six-year-old Melvin Belli was as brilliant as he was controversial. "The King of Torts" as he had been dubbed had revolutionized personal injury law. Among the eighteen books he had published were several highly respected texts, including *Medical Malpractice* and the six-volume set *Modern Damages*. He had waged a continuous battle with the stuffy American legal associations, who discouraged his courtroom flamboyance—the American Trial Lawyers Association, which he had cofounded, once barred him from speaking at a convention to maintain propriety. But no one, absolutely no one, doubted his ability in front of a judge and jury. During a trial he was always charming, extremely well-prepared, and knowledgeable about the nooks and crannies of the law. When a restricted California neighborhood tried to enforce a covenant prohibiting Belli's Chinese client from living there, for example, he found an obscure 1854 State Supreme Court decision that ruled under California law the Chinese actually were American Indians because Columbus believed he had landed on an island in the China Sea "which washes India," and therefore named the inhabitants Indians. The claim became moot before the jury had to make its decision, as his client divorced his wife then temporarily moved into Belli's house and together they opened an exotic restaurant, Fong's Iroquois Village. (Featuring dishes ranging from strawberry omelets to boiled cabbage O'Fong.)

While Belli's reputation had been earned primarily representing plaintiffs in just about every conceivable type of personal injury case, from brain concussions to severed toes, during his career he also had been involved in a great variety of criminal cases. He'd represented the gangster Mickey Cohen who was accused of murdering infamous mobster Bugsy Siegel; he defended comedian Lenny Bruce multiple times on obscenity charges and renowned stripper Candy Barr in a drug possession case; he represented the legendary comedienne Mae West and his friend Errol Flynn. After Flynn's sudden death, he represented Flynn's teenage girlfriend Beverly Aadland, who applied for a share of Flynn's estate claiming unsuccessfully that he had involved her in "immoral debauchery and sex orgies and taught her a lewd, wanton and wayward way of life."

In addition to high-profile clients, Belli also took the case of a San Quentin inmate accused of stabbing to death another inmate, winning an acquittal by arguing self-defense. To prove to jurors that the defendant's life was in danger in the prison,

Belli "accidentally" tripped in the courtroom, causing a boxful of knives and sharp objects taken from other prisoners to scatter across the floor. During World War II he represented God, or at least the leader of a religious cult who claimed to be God and was facing one hundred years in prison for encouraging sailors not to fight in the war. Describing the man as a harmless "crackpot" in his summation, he won an acquittal by pointing out the government had waited more than a year to bring charges—and as a reward, his client named him "Second Typical God" rather than paying him.

Defending Jack Ruby seemed like a perfect fit. The trial would generate worldwide headlines, which was always good for business, and it was a seemingly hopeless case: an estimated ten million witnesses had seen Ruby murder Lee Harvey Oswald. He really couldn't lose. No one would blame him if Ruby was convicted, but if he could get an acquittal…

For the publicity-loving lawyer, the lure of "worldwide attention" could not be ignored. And that might translate into money: in addition to his $50,000 fee, which the Ruby family believed could be raised by selling Jack Ruby's story, Belli also planned to profit from a documentary he would assist with about the trial and was confident the enormous publicity eventually would result in a book deal. He arrived in Dallas accompanied by a writer to assist him with the book and a documentary filmmaker.

But he told reporters that the money was not a factor in taking the case. The Ruby family, which was spread around the country, could not possibly pay his normal fee upfront. He took it, he said, because it was a great legal challenge: "Here was the first time in the history of man and the law that anyone was going on trial for murdering another man on live television with a national audience…

"Ruby deserves a fair trial. On television, no one could see Ruby's state of mind… This was a big trial that could focus worldwide attention on mental health and its unsatisfactory, archaic relationship to the law."

On December 10, Belli arrived in Dallas with the fanfare of a hired gun riding into an old western town. But rather than a celebrated gunslinger, prosecutor Henry Wade cast him as a dangerous city slicker come to pick the pockets of the good folks of the city. "Mr. Belly," he said, emphasizing that pronunciation with his down-home twang, "is an interesting man. He just made a trip to Roosha."

The implication was clear: Belli was a world traveling subversive, maybe even a Commie. One thing he most surely wasn't, was one of "us." Belli responded by giving Wade a copy of his recently published book, *Belli Looks at Life and Law in Russia*.

The lawyer's associate on the defense team, a mountain of a man named Joe Tonahill, welcomed him with a warning. The motel in which he was staying was known for its attractive young waitresses. Don't get caught alone in a room with one of them, even innocently, he said, because it might be a setup: "You'd be hog-tied before you knew it," he told Belli. "Don't let the friendly surface fool you. They play rough down here."

During that December visit, Belli met his client for the first time. Jack Ruby, the son of impoverished Polish immigrants, had been raised in the Maxwell Street area of Chicago. He had been a tough kid, counting among his closest pals Barney Ross, the fabled world champion boxer and World War II hero. Ruby had moved to Dallas after serving as an airplane mechanic in the Army Air Corps during the war and had owned or operated several dance halls, nightclubs and striptease joints. The Carousel Club, which he owned at the time of the shooting, was known for more tease than strip—risqué, more than scandalous. He was one of those street-smart guys who was always promoting some type of legal hustle; everything from selling punch boards, in which people paid a few bucks to push out a slip of paper that might reveal a monetary prize, to attempting to sell war surplus jeeps to Cuba's Castro government. But despite his nightlife associations, Ruby didn't drink or smoke and he hated drugs. Sitting in his cell he was not what Belli—who was intimately familiar with Ruby's world—expected. "In my imagination he would have been fat, oily, with polished nails, wearing a sharp, shiny suit with rings on his pudgy fingers."

Instead, "He had a face like a ferret, he was clean shaven and fanatically neat, and his thinning black hair was combed straight back. There was something odd about his eyes. They shone like a beagle's." But at that first meeting Belli reached a conclusion. "Something was mentally wrong with Ruby."

While Ruby had killed the assassin of the president of the United States, murder was a state rather than federal crime so this case would be tried under Texas law. Each of the fifty states maintains its own legal system, which governs the application of the law and the conduct of a trial. While the basic rules are similar, the details differ, having grown out of each state's unique needs and history. Gun laws, for example, were different in the former frontier states, where people once lived distances apart and needed to protect themselves, than in the eastern urban centers. An out-of-state attorney like Belli would have to learn quickly how things were done in Dallas.

Long before even the pretrial motions would be heard decisions had to be made. The court had already received almost four hundred requests for press credentials from "all the major nations of the Free World." To handle this, Judge Joe Brown had asked one of the city's civic leaders, Sam Bloom, to serve, without pay, as his press representative. He became, as Belli complained, the first judge in the history of jurisprudence to have his own public relations adviser. Although Sam Bloom held no city office, he was representing the interests of the city. It was his job to help protect Dallas's reputation. The trial itself was initially scheduled to be held in Judge Brown's small courtroom, which would give Bloom power to influence reporting by handing out seat assignments, but the demands for media access were so high that the trial was moved to an older but far larger courtroom, capable of seating more than two hundred spectators, and a new public address system was installed.

A far more modern problem was whether or not to televise the trial. The Sixth Amendment had forever enshrined the right of a defendant in a criminal prosecution "to a speedy and public trial," but how public that might be had never been conclusively defined. The presence of TV cameras in a courtroom was controversial; no one knew how that might affect the trial. The technology necessary to broadcast a live trial was relatively new, and different states were already experimenting with it. In fact, only eight years earlier the first televised criminal trial in American history had taken place about one hundred miles down Highway 77 in Waco. Helen Weaver had been murdered by a car bomb and her former son-in-law, Harry Washburn, was accused of planting it after being cut out of the family fortune. Washburn's trial initially had been scheduled to take place in San Angelo, but his attorney had argued successfully for a change of venue because there had been so much pretrial publicity. The four-day trial was broadcast gavel-to-gavel without commercial interruption on KWTX in December 1955 with the approval of the defendant who decided, "Let it go all over the world." Witnesses including barmaids, strippers, a female wrestler known as "Nature girl" and thugs riveted the viewers at home, making the broadcast so popular, according to a local newspaper, that when court was in session you "could have shot a cannon down Austin Avenue...and not hurt a soul."

Washburn was convicted and sentenced to ninety-nine years in prison. The single TV camera and three strategically placed microphones had not appeared to influence the outcome. That experiment had proved successful. In this case, apart from the television networks themselves, it was Judge Brown who most strongly favored permitting cameras in his courtroom. Belli

DAN ABRAMS AND DAVID FISHER

was publicly ambivalent. But Henry Wade and other town leaders, as well as the state bar, were against it. They believed live television already had done enough damage to the city. Judge Brown pleaded with Bloom, reportedly asking, "Sam, couldn't you give me just one camera?" Finally Judge Brown reluctantly ruled there would be no television cameras, radio equipment or still photography allowed in his courtroom while the trial was in session.

That decision could not dampen the public's interest in the case. America's newspapers were filled with any tidbit about the murder and the forthcoming trial. The National Life & Accident Insurance Company announced it had paid Marguerite Oswald, the assassin's mother, $863 on a life insurance policy she had taken out almost two decades earlier. Fort Worth police estimated more than ten thousand people had visited Oswald's guarded grave in a month. Meanwhile, Dallas officials were still trying to figure out how the shooting had happened. It seemed incredible that police would permit an armed man to stroll into the basement of city hall at exactly the moment the president's assassin was being moved. To combat those rumors of police involvement, several Dallas police officers had voluntarily taken and passed lie detector tests. But these were issues that undoubtedly would be raised at the trial.

By the end of the year, 1963, the pieces were all in place: The trial of Jack Ruby for the murder of Lee Harvey Oswald was scheduled to begin in February 1964, slightly more than two months since the incredible event had been seen 'round the world.

CHAPTER TWO

In January 1964 the Rolling Stones began their first American tour as the headline act, while The Beatles reached the top of the charts for the first time with their single, "I Want to Hold Your Hand." In Florida, brash twenty-two-year-old boxer Cassius Clay, still two months away from becoming Muhammad Ali, was in training for his heavyweight championship bout with Sonny Liston. New president Lyndon Johnson, in his first State of the Union address, announced his War on Poverty, a massive investment in America's inner cities that would provide new opportunities for the underclass. On Broadway, Carol Channing's *Hello Dolly!* premiered in the first of its 2,844 performances. *Bonanza* remained the top TV show, while Clint Eastwood's spaghetti western *A Fistful of Dollars* and Stanley Kubrick's anti-war satire *Dr. Strangelove* debuted in movie theaters. But for millions of people, news about the assassination of John F. Kennedy, the murder of Lee Harvey Oswald and the coming trial of Jack Ruby dominated their attention.

PAUL SLADE/PARIS MATCH VIA GETTY IMAGES

Flamboyant Melvin Belli would run the Jolly Roger up the flagpole outside his San Francisco office and fire blank cannonballs when he won a case, but he also was a widely respected lawyer and the author of numerous legal texts. Here he is dwarfed by his cocounsel, Texas native Joe Tonahill.

While the trial was being promoted in the media as a legal shoot-out between the flamboyant Mel Belli and down-home prosecutor Henry Wade, in preparation for the trial both men had added impressive firepower to their legal teams. Tom Howard remained on the defense, though in a significantly reduced role as Belli hired his longtime friend Joe Tonahill. Tonahill was the prototypical Texan, everything about him was big, from his highly shined boots to his booming voice that could cut through courtroom clatter. At six foot four, and slightly south of three hundred pounds, people said Joe was so big that even when sittin' down he was still looking down on you. In some ways he was the local version of Belli, a very smart, publicity-savvy lawyer who had done so well in his personal injury practice that his offices were located in Jasper, Texas's Tonahill Building.

To guide the defense through state trial procedures, Belli also hired Phil Burleson, who only a year earlier had been heading the appellate division of Dallas's district attorney's office. The thirty-year-old Burleson had earned a reputation as a student of the system; a man who understood local courtroom traditions, the rules of evidence and sometimes complicated points of state law. Perhaps most importantly, he was known as "Mr. Appeal," having represented the state in more than seven hundred appellate cases while literally writing the go-to manual for appealing criminal convictions.

Henry Wade also was busy building a fine team. That included Bill Alexander, a former FBI agent who might have been cast as the legal hatchet man in an episode of *Perry Mason*. Tall and rail thin, his face was pockmarked, his eyes were slits and if he had ever smiled warmly in a courtroom no one in Texas had heard talk of it. But he was a sharp take-no-prisoners prosecutor. During his fifteen years in the Dallas DA's office, "The Burner," as he was nicknamed, had been involved in every major criminal trial. He had also been the lead lawyer overseeing the questioning of Oswald the weekend after he was captured and before his death. The police worked for many hours unsuccessfully trying to get Oswald to confess and desperately attempted to gather any information about a possible conspiracy. Oswald answered many questions about his life, his background and his whereabouts that day but despite increasingly overwhelming evidence against him, consistently denied any involvement in the killing of the president or Officer Tippit. Bill Alexander was there advising on how far the interrogators could legally go with their questioning and as needed, even joined officers in the field serving search warrants in a frantic effort to gather more information. And while his rough style was said to sometimes rile up jurors, he was well-respected for his ability to speak plainly and cut to the heart of a case. Alexander was known to carry a concealed handgun in the courtroom, although after learning Belli intended to use it as an example of "Texas justice" he left it home.

Wade's "book lawyer" was Assistant DA Jim Bowie. In Texas's Old West days, Bowie would have been the God-fearin' rancher while Alexander would have been the rustler. Bowie was well-liked and greatly respected by the Texas bar for his calm courtroom demeanor and his legal knowledge, and served to smooth the prosecution's rougher edges.

The case would be presided over by Joseph Brantley Brown Sr. or, as he supposedly was known in the Dallas legal community, "Necessity" Brown, because "necessity knows no law." People liked Joe Brown. He was a ruggedly handsome white-haired man who bore a perpetual smile; people said he was a fair judge, but noted that he had his own peculiar way of running a trial. Like all judges in Texas, he had been elected to his position. Brown had not been a practicing lawyer and had never tried a case. According to local reporters, he admitted watching TV's *The Defenders* "so I can study how judges act." As one attorney who had argued before him colorfully described him, "With Joe Brown it's like playing handball with a football, you never know which way the ball is going to bounce."

Brown had been taking his turn supervising the grand jury in a four-judge rotation when Oswald, and then Ruby, was indicted, so he automatically would try the case. Although he claimed that he wasn't at all anxious to sit in judgment, in fact he held on to the high-profile role tighter than a bronc rider. Joe Brown liked the spotlight—he never turned down a request for a picture or even an autograph—and he was up for reelection in the fall of 1964. He was a polite, good-natured man who just naturally couldn't resist answering any reporter's questions.

He had crossed paths several years earlier with Belli during the trial of Juanita Dale Slusher, a popular striptease artist, adult model and 8 mm soft-core porn performer better known as Candy Barr, who had been sentenced to fifteen years in prison just for possession of marijuana. The prosecutor in that case had been Bill Alexander. During a recess in her trial, Judge Brown had invited her into his chambers, where the two of them happily posed for pictures—fully clothed. When cash bail had been set at $15,000, Belli had sent Brown a telegram asking if his friend and sometimes client, the infamous gangster Mickey Cohen, would be allowed to post it. That request was refused and Barr, who also was a casual friend of Ruby's, spent three years in prison.

Judge Brown ran a casual courtroom; during the proceedings he'd slouch in his chair, chewing reflectively on a cigar, occasionally depositing the results in the green spittoon next to his chair. At other times he clamped down on one of the two hundred pipes in his collection. He permitted others to smoke in his courtroom as well, which led to a semipermanent cloud hanging over the trial. He wasn't a stickler for procedure; when an attorney had something to say he generally let him say it. Things moved along when he was on the bench. "I own forty gavels," he once said, "and I never used one in my life."

In preparation for the trial, the defense had filed a series of motions, legal points that would help shape their case. Belli couldn't claim his client didn't commit the act; not with literally several million eyewitnesses. But as the law had developed through the centuries numerous types of extenuating circumstances had been folded into it; the issue was no longer simply a matter of guilt or innocence. For several hundred years, juries had been allowed to consider the why of a crime. Was the act committed in self-defense? Or was it done in the white heat of passion? Might it have been revenge for an earlier crime? Or does the person who committed it suffer from mental problems? Was he or she incapable of understanding the difference between right and wrong or the consequences of their actions?

So while the person may have done the deed, there were different degrees of guilt, which carried penalties ranging from acquittal to execution. Texas law had its own peculiarities, which grew out of frontier justice, where a man was required to protect himself, his kin and his property. As Judge Brown once wrote, "In Texas, you can kill a man if you catch him in the act of adultery with your wife, but only if you kill him at that instant. You may pursue him if he runs and kill him so long as you don't lose sight of him. You may kill in defense of your own life or the life of another. You may kill to protect your property if you can demonstrate that the killing was force reasonably required. You may kill an invader in your own house, but not a person who has merely invaded your yard." But there was little codified in the state law about a man's mental condition.

The first order of business for the defense was to request that Ruby be released on bail until the trial began. Under Texas law, that was generally considered a right for defendants who are always presumed innocent, but often it was not quite that simple. There were exceptions including for capital offenses "when the proof is evident" and it was hard to imagine a case where proof was more evident than this one. So the defense team, which now had swelled to five lawyers, was well aware that the chances of Jack Ruby attending to his club or strolling the Dallas streets pending trial was essentially nonexistent. But there were potential strategic gains to be had from these proceedings. The prosecution would have to call at least a few witnesses to support its case against bail, thereby providing the defense with a peek inside the state's case and a record of statements that might be useful during the trial.

The first bail hearing took place on December 23, 1963, less than a month after Oswald was killed. The world was mesmerized with the story. Every detail was being scrutinized, analyzed and discussed, and this would be the first time Jack Ruby, as an accused murderer, would appear in public. While at times the hyperbolic media coverage made it feel like the trial itself was about to begin, the actual bail proceeding was a fairly low-key and standard one. Henry Wade called two police detectives, direct eyewitnesses to the shooting, including Detective James Leavelle who had been shackled to Oswald when he was shot. They had seen Ruby up close and even helped subdue him while trying to protect Oswald. There was no doubt in their minds that the man now sitting at the defense table was the same man they had seen pop out from the crowd with weapon in hand.

The defense then called three witnesses to try to show that the shooting was not planned or premeditated. For the defense, a pre-trial proceeding like this, with no jury present, can also provide an opportunity to observe how their witnesses fare under cross-examination. It poses certain risks since that testimony could be used against them later but when shaping a defense, knowing how strong or definitive a witness may be is critical. The witnesses all offered testimony as to the timeline: Oswald was shot at 11:21 a.m. and Ruby, according to the defense, happened to be at a Western Union just over one hundred yards from the police station sending a money order stamped only four minutes earlier. If Ruby had, on impulse, decided to walk over to the police station to see Oswald being moved because he just happened to be in the area, it certainly would support a defense that the incident occurred in a moment of heated anger or passion.

The highlight of the hearing, however, may have been when defense attorney Joe Tonahill made a motion seeking to have both sides stipulate, or legally agree that Oswald had acted alone in shooting President Kennedy and that Ruby and Oswald had no prior relationship. Henry Wade responded flatly: "We ain't agreeing to nothing."

The nation was asking the same questions. Had Oswald and Ruby known each other? Was reporting on their possible connections accurate? Were they players in a larger conspiracy to assassinate President Kennedy? These questions would continue to permeate the proceedings both inside, and outside, the courtroom.

At the conclusion of the short presentations of evidence, Judge Brown denied Ruby bail "for the present" but called for additional evidence at a second hearing.

While the legal maneuvering was slowly grinding into gear, life began returning to normal in Dallas. In early December Governor Connally finally left Parkland Hospital to return to the state capitol in Austin. At the Cotton Bowl, 29,653 fans watched in dismay as the visiting New York Giants came back from 13 points down in the fourth quarter to defeat the Cowboys 34-27. As Ruby sat in his cell meeting with lawyers, his Carousel Club had reopened for business under the direction of his friend Ralph Paul, although, reported the *Times* "the strippers have been back on the job, what zest they had for their work somewhat muted. Till 1:30 A.M. Little Lynn, a shapely and artificially gray Texan of about 20, paraded saucily in pink heels and matching G-string among the customers lining the bar. Most of the tables were empty…with dancers, musicians, waitresses and bartenders going through the motions in what seems to be a state bordering on disbelief that their generous and boisterous employer had perpetrated such a slaying."

It was at that next legal proceeding, nearly a month after the first one, that the conspiracy theories would be further fueled with another question left unanswered. The defense put an FBI agent on the stand to ask if the bureau had found any evidence Oswald and Ruby were connected, but before he could respond Wade and Alexander objected loudly, and that key question was left hanging in the smoky courtroom air. For a public starving for any morsels of information about who else might have been involved in the killing of the president, these pretrial hearings were tantalizing but hardly satisfying.

But it also was at this second bail hearing that the case of the *People of the State of Texas v. Jacob Rubenstein* really began to take shape. This time all the evidence was presented by the defense and rather than focusing on lack of premeditation or uncontrolled passions as everyone had expected, Belli appeared to be pursuing a very different type of defense, a psychological one. Ruby, Belli said, "remembers going down the ramp and seeing Oswald" but nothing else until the officers subdued him. The doctors who testified called it a "fugue" state. Belli intended to prove Jack Ruby suffered from a rare form of epilepsy and had been legally insane when he killed Oswald.

Judge Brown was apparently as surprised as everyone else by this new strategy and, after a day of dense medical testimony from the defense, recognized that more psychological tests needed to be conducted. The defense agreed and withdrew its bail motion. Now, in addition to Ruby being examined by experts who would testify on his behalf, Judge Brown named three doctors, designed to be neutral observers, who would oversee testing.

No trial lawyer in America was better suited to dissect medical testimony than Melvin Belli. During several hundred trials, he had become expert in forensic medicine. He had spent time with the leading pathologists in the world, literally putting on surgical pajamas, participating in autopsies and observing procedures ranging from amputations to cosmetic enhancements. He had fought and won cases involving almost every conceivable type of medical malpractice, from the loss of a penis to the amputation of the wrong leg.

He had also gained a particular expertise in insanity pleas. In his very first case, he successfully argued that a man who had helped hire a hit man to kill his girlfriend's husband was insane; in addition to the results of psychiatric tests, he suggested his client had to be insane to have fallen in love with a profane, unkempt, unattractive woman. The man was committed to an institution, avoiding prison. In another murder case, the jury deliberated only three minutes before declaring his client not guilty by reason of insanity. Ruby's case would be considerably more difficult. Jack Ruby had been a functioning adult, he had run several businesses, he had friends, he had a real life. People might testify he was a little strange, maybe he was a character, but insane?

When Belli announced his defense strategy, many suggested he might be the crazy one. But he had fought enough battles in enough courtrooms to remain confident he could convince a jury Jack Ruby was a sick man and not in control of his senses when he had committed what would ordinarily be considered murder. By laying out his approach in the bail hearing, he had now provided prosecutors with an early road map of the case to come. But Belli also felt that disclosing his defense in advance could help in the court of public opinion, the venue from which the jurors in this case would be selected. In fact, the defense had commissioned J. Clements, a marketing research firm, to poll Dallas residents about whether they believed Ruby was sane: in December 66 percent answered yes, but after intense coverage of the two bail hearings, the firm asked the same question again and this time only 40 percent responded that they thought Ruby was sane. Belli's gambit appeared to have paid off.

Despite that seeming success and what could potentially be a receptive jury pool, his next big move was to try to have the trial moved out of Dallas. Belli filed for a change of venue, arguing that Dallas, the Kennedy assassination and the murder of Lee Harvey Oswald were so inexorably entwined that it would be impossible to find twelve people who were not concerned about the reputation of their city jury, precluding Ruby from receiving a fair trial.

Different attorneys use pretrial motions for a variety of strategic reasons. Sometimes it's used for publicity, or to establish a courtroom presence, or to send a feeler to the prosecution to see if a good deal for a client might be negotiated. Most often lawyers know even before making their motion what the outcome will be. In this instance Belli believed he would succeed in having the trial moved out of Dallas. Over and over the defense repeated that Dallas was on trial too and the world was watching. Ironically, the *Dallas Morning News* reported in bold headlines that the defense contended Ruby's life was in jeopardy "because of a conspiracy in Dallas to deprive him of a fair trial, because of a highly emotional situation in the city and because the news media covered the case so much more thoroughly in the city."

The concept of a change of venue, moving a trial to ensure publicity and local prejudice does not deprive a defendant of a fair hearing, dates back to the reign of Scottish King James VI, who ascended the English throne in 1603. As Sir William Blackstone wrote in his 1765 *Commentaries on the Laws of England*, to "prevent a defect of justice...it will sometimes remove the venue from the proper jurisdiction (especially of the narrow and limited kind) upon a suggestion, duly supported, that a fair and impartial trial cannot be held therein."

Change of venues were not unusual in eighteenth and nineteenth century America, even though news spread slowly and local people were loath to give up the entertainment of an especially salacious trial. One such case was the sensational 1844 trial of Polly Bodine in rural Staten Island. "The witch of Staten Island" was accused of murdering her sister-in-law and baby niece then setting fire to their house. Edgar Allen Poe and P. T. Barnum were among the celebrities who wrote about the trial. After a local jury failed to reach a decision, the trial was moved across the river to Manhattan, where Bodine was convicted. But after that verdict was overturned, the trial moved to Newburgh, New York, where she finally was acquitted.

In 1915 the former president Theodore Roosevelt was granted a change of venue from Albany to Syracuse, New York, after claiming he could not receive a fair trial in the state capital when the leader of the New York Republican Party sued him for libel.

More recently, the 1954 Cleveland murder trial of Dr. Sam Sheppard had been marred by extensive newspaper coverage, which defense lawyers said had helped create a circus-like atmosphere. An appeal of the guilty verdict based on the claim Sheppard did not get a fair trial was slowly wending its way through the legal system to the Supreme Court while Belli made his case.

Belli was adamant that the city would turn Ruby's case into a show trial in order to protect its reputation, telling reporters, "Dallas wants to cleanse itself of blame in the [Kennedy] assassination by giving Ruby a 'fair trial,' and then sending him to the slaughterhouse."

Texas Governor John Connally disagreed, saying, "I feel the people of Dallas would give him a fair trial," then equivocated, adding, "As fair as he could get anywhere in Texas. If I were in trouble I'd be as happy to face a jury in Dallas as anywhere."

And then he added, in defense of the city, "Lee Harvey Oswald was not a native of Dallas. He had been in Dallas only a few weeks. This tragedy could have happened anywhere."

Most pretrial motions are dealt with quickly by the presiding judge. But the hearing on the change of venue motion was conducted as a sort of minitrial; Judge Brown would decide the outcome. Both sides would call witnesses and there were plenty to choose from. The defense subpoenaed almost two hundred of Dallas's most important and prestigious residents and leaders in the hope that even they would admit that it would be difficult for Ruby to get a fair trial in the city just months after the assassinations of both Kennedy and then Oswald. It had been said that if you didn't get a subpoena to appear at the Ruby change of venue hearing, you were nobody in Dallas.

That hearing began on February 10. That same morning the defense team received four stuffed folders with the final J. Clements polling report showing that less than half of Dallas residents now believed Ruby was sane. It was a typically busy day in Dallas courts; a jury was fixing the penalty of Johnny Grant, who had signed a statement admitting he had killed his wife. In a civil action a group was demanding a neighboring farmer whose cows were polluting the air with "unpleasant odors" remedy the situation. In the courtroom set aside for domestic relations cases, Judge Hughes was scheduled to hear as many as twenty divorce actions. In the Commissioner's Court, which handled local government business, county judge Lew Sterrett presided over a contentious hearing about renewing the beer and wine licenses for two nightclubs Jack Ruby had owned or managed; even though he was no longer legally involved with the Carousel Club or his other called Vegas Club, the Liquor Control Board had turned down the applications charging Ruby with "not being a peaceful and law-abiding citizen." The clubs were denied a license pending a hearing to determine legal ownership of the clubs to be held in Austin.

Judge Brown's courtroom was unusually hot and humid for a midwinter day when the change of venue hearing began. The defense made its case first. "It may seem [as if we are] attacking the integrity of a fair lady, the city of Dallas. I don't mean to do so...this great American city has all the integrity to hold her high amongst the...cities of the world." He continued to laud the city, pointing out only that it was not the proper place to try this particular case.

Finally, Henry Wade had enough sweetener. "Judge, we object to all this."

He instantly was echoed by Bill Alexander who said with irritation, "Let's get on with the hearing before us."

Belli faced the prosecutors as he responded, "I am apologizing because of the activities of a particular counsel. On November 27th...the stage was set to make it impossible to have a fair trial when [here he quoted an article from the *Dallas Morning News*]

DAN ABRAMS AND DAVID FISHER

'Mr. Wade said he regarded Ruby's trial as one of the most important in Dallas history… Our whole judicial system will be on trial. This trial will determine whether Dallas has a government based on the orderly process of law or a government in which an individual can take the law into his own hands.'" Belli continued reading: "'Wade said he will ask the death penalty with full confidence a Dallas County Jury will return the correct verdict in this case.'"

As Belli began reading another article, this one quoting Wade's colleague, Bill Alexander expressing disgust at "The shooting of a manacled man in cold blood…" Wade stood and objected, suggesting the court let the evidence speak. Belli did what a great attorney does, attribute motive to his opponent. "Because the District Attorney is ashamed to have this spoken in open court is not reason…not to have it entered in the record."

Brown, in his casual manner told Belli, "If you are going to read everything that has been in the newspaper since November 27th, we will be here for the next twenty-five years."

Belli slipped through that opening. "If it takes that long to prevent this man from being hanged, I intend to stay here for the rest of my lifetime, Your Honor, to prevent it." When the judge suggested he simply enter the newspapers into the record, Belli responded, "Well, Your Honor, you can't absorb these by the process of judicial osmosis. These have to be read and have to be digested."

After this exchange Belli made the first of many motions, asking Brown to rule from the bench for him, reminding him about a recent decision in the trial of Texas swindler Billy Sol Estes, whose fraud case was moved five hundred miles from Reeves County to Smith County after the court received eleven thick volumes of press clippings that showed the case had "national notoriety."

"The court will overrule your motion," Brown responded.

Great attorneys are actors on the courtroom stage, becoming whatever character will most benefit their client. Belli was an acknowledged master of this; but anyone who believed he might adapt a conciliatory manner to ingratiate himself with the court was almost immediately disabused of that thought. Belli had come to fight. When Alexander then tried to explain in a friendly way to Belli how things were done in Dallas—"local customs," he called them—Belli shook his head. "That's about as false as any of the other statements Mr. Alexander has made."

This was about an hour into the hearing.

Judge Brown resisted, Belli persisted: unless he was permitted to read all the articles "in open court...we are not getting a public hearing...and I respectfully submit under the constitution..."

Eventually Joe Tonahill spoke up. "Judge, he [Belli] offers it into evidence and Jim Bowie says 'We will have it all in evidence.' And then Mr. Alexander and Mr. Wade reach into their pocket, get their bowie knife and proceed to cut our tongues off, and Your Honor's ears off, so that you can't hear or see evidence that Your Honor must have before you to pass upon." Then he wondered aloud, "Why are you afraid of that, Judge? You can't afford to be afraid."

Both sides found ways to toss nasty remarks at their opponent. When suggesting the judge needed to read specific articles rather than the entire newspaper Belli said, "We don't want Your Honor to read all of the corn ads or cotton ads...unless they are enlightening to the District Attorney."

Belli eventually wore down Judge Brown, who agreed to let him enter specific portions of pertinent articles into evidence. Defendant's Exhibit #1 was an article from the *Fort Worth Star-Telegram* headlined "Dallas to go on Trial in Ruby Hearing."

He then cited an article from the magazine *U.S. News & World Report*, which described a powerful coalition known as the Dallas Citizens Council as "the group that really runs Dallas." Belli paused to differentiate it from other White Citizens' Councils, which had been formed in other Southern cities to oppose racial integration. He continued reading. 'This is a group of top-bracketed men... The Council is made up of men, about 250 in number, who are chief officers of important companies... The Citizens Council, which actually runs Dallas, is a benevolent oligarchy...'

"'The assassination was Dallas' darkest hour. Afterwards there was what one Dallas businessman called "a period of self-examination." When life resumed its regular rhythm there was general agreement that the actions of two maverick gunmen, the alleged assassin and his slayer, would not impede the dynamic growth of Big D.'"

With that the defense called its first witness in this pretrial hearing, Frederick Carney, an associate professor of Christian Ethics at Southern Methodist University and a former full-time pastor. Joe Tonahill questioned him, asking him if he had been in the city when "President Kennedy was ambushed by the Communist Lee Harvey Oswald..."

"We object to all this," Wade interrupted.

Judge Brown sustained it, and a puzzled Tonahill pointed out, "Well, I think you are supposed to assign some intelligent reason for an objection, Your Honor, so that we will be in a position to attack the record. He just says, 'I object.' I don't think we're supposed to be gagged just because the District Attorney would like to gag us."

When Brown told him a bit more directly to just ask his question, he instead embellished it again. "Were you here on November 22nd when that Lily of the Valley, Lee Harvey Oswald, murdered President Kennedy." The prosecution objected again, and was again sustained, so Tonahill wondered bitterly, "Have you ever heard of President Kennedy?"

Yes, he had. And what, Tonahill asked, was the reaction of "the community as a whole to the assassination," and to the subsequent shooting of Oswald? Shock and embarrassment, said

Carney. As a result, the professor had written, mimeographed and distributed a paper he titled, *Crisis of Confidence in Dallas.*

The defense offered a copy as evidence, thus allowing the prosecution to question the witness about it. Alexander established that very few copies of this pamphlet had been distributed in Dallas, making it very unlikely it influenced any potential jurors.

But Carney also testified that the events had caused "a real soul-searching element" that was put aside while citizens rose "to the defense of the city of Dallas." The message supported by the oligarchy was this, he said, "Dallas should not be held responsible in a direct and causal sense for the assassination of President Kennedy." All of it based on the economic need to "Preserve the image of Dallas."

As with any experienced attorney, Tonahill's questions were chock-full of information. When speaking about a CBS News special several days after Kennedy's assassination, he asked, "Did the clapping of the children [in a fourth grade class in a North Dallas elementary school] when they learned of the assassination of President Kennedy indicate that the right-wing extremism existing here in Dallas had permeated into the lives and hearts and spirits of their children?"

The prosecution's objection was sustained, so it was not answered—but there was no real need for an answer. The purpose of the question was to point out that the atmosphere in Dallas was already too highly charged for the killer of Kennedy's assassin to receive an unbiased trial.

During further questioning, the witness spoke highly of the Citizens Council, which had, he said, "done everything possible to make President Kennedy's visit here a great success." As he repeated that sentiment in different ways throughout his testimony, it became obvious Dr. Carney was walking a tight line: When this trial ended, he still would be living in Dallas and the words he spoke in the courtroom would continue to reverberate. If the trial remained in Dallas, each witness would have to consider the impact of his or her words against their future in the community. Considerations the defense team should have been attuned to as well in the event that they lost this motion and the jurors were all Dallas residents, many of whom would have been following at least some coverage of these proceedings.

Tonahill made it clear that such concern was a real factor, that there was danger in speaking the truth. Citing what happened to the schoolteacher who had reported the cheering children, he asked, "Following that, was it necessary for he and his family to be given police protection and held incommunicado and taken to other places, so they could protect him from the threats he was receiving?"

"He was given police protection, yes."

The questioning of this first witness continued through the morning. Over and over Tonahill tried to make the same point: "The decision…goes to the saturation of the mentality of the community… The only way to reach that is to…get into the minds, and the motivations and the attitudes and the defenses and the thoughts and idea of the image that exists here; and the feelings, the embarrassment, the chagrin and shock, the extreme regret, the consciousness of it that is what show the fact that Dallas is not an indifferent community to this case that is on trial.

"That's why we are dwelling upon it."

It came down to this: "Do you feel that there was a situation of hate prevailing here in Dallas on November 22nd, 1963, the right-wing hate or any kind of feeling of hate, that was unusual for this community?"

"There was considerable intolerance, yes." Still backtracking though, Carney explained, "The Dallas oligarchy's concern for some of the intolerance that exists in this community, and attempt to rectify the situation, was the very fine way they went about the reception of the president here."

That Citizens Council oligarchy, the defense brought out

through its questioning, exercised complete control over the social and economic affairs of the city. It was the oligarchy that decided that Dallas would be peacefully integrated. And it was the oligarchy's realization that its bitterness toward the Kennedy administration had hurt the city; for example, that was one reason NASA had landed in Houston rather than Dallas.

The defense was creating the image of an all-powerful ruling class, a group of business leaders who would decide Jack Ruby's fate and let it be known so that their will could be carried out.

When the prosecution again objected to a portion of an article being read aloud, the defense team's "book man," Phil Burleson spoke for the first time. "If the court does not have anything but a portion of the exhibit before it…then the court will not be able to exercise its judicial discretion…based upon the facts…

"…Then the court will have commit reversible error, and anything that is done will be a nullity from that point on." His words, which were largely ignored, would much later become significant.

As in a trial, the prosecution had the opportunity to cross-examine the defense witness. Henry Wade cut immediately to the quick. "Let me ask you…you don't know of any combination of citizens that are trying to prevent him from getting a fair trial, do you?"

"No," Carney replied, "I don't." He added he knew of no reason that Ruby could not get a fair trial in Dallas, although still maintaining his balance he said, "I am not trying to judge this question."

Casting shade on the defense, Wade got the witness to admit that Tonahill had asked him to bring with him to court as many as forty or fifty additional copies of his paper, then suggested they were to be distributed to the news media, further inflaming an already tense situation.

When the prosecution finished, Tonahill picked up his thread. Carney admitted he'd had previous conversations with the prosecutor's office. Both Wade and Alexander rose and screamed their objection. Tonahill responded by revealing some fascinating news. "Judge, I hate to say this but there has been a brief-case tampered with in one of the Defense organization rooms, and I would like to get this all out into the open, without objection from the state."

Carney insisted he had gotten no instructions from the prosecutors, no advice, claiming he actually had initiated the meeting to make certain his paper was not misrepresented.

Belli eventually introduced an article from *Life* magazine into evidence, beginning with the sentence, "Dallas, perhaps more than any American city, worries about and promotes its image," it revealed much of the soul of the city disguised as compliments. About the Citizens Council, the article continued, "There is scarcely an aspect of the city's existence in which they do not have the final say...they 'advise' the city government and invariably the government pays attention..."

As for the character of the city, "Anything less than straight patriotism would have to be viewed as subversive..." and everyone, it seems, is armed, "carrying pistols in pockets and glove compartments of cars." The article concluded by quoting Stanley Marcus, owner of the renowned department store Neiman-Marcus, who had called for the city to examine its attitudes, adding, "Mr. Marcus's acts require courage because he is Jewish, a faith not popular among the Hard Shell Baptists..."

The defense then continued calling its witnesses, each of them guardedly critical of the city. A. C. Greene, the editorial page editor of the *Dallas Times Herald* agreed with Tonahill that everybody was talking about the case and expressed concern about its effect on the city. In an editorial Green had written, "The Dallas community is on trial... (it) is under the inspection of dozens of writers, commentators, social scientists at this moment... The truth as they see it may be harsh on Dallas...

"We are on trial."

The two shootings, he explained, "put the spotlight of world attention on us."

Tonahill's approach was friendly, confiding. "You've read where if you're from Dallas you come from the City of Assassins, haven't you? That has pretty much been stated everywhere, hasn't it?... And people outside Texas have commenced calling the great football team...the Dallas Cowboys, they've started calling them the Dallas Assassins...even though they lose all the ball games."

Wade's objection was sustained, although he made clear he objected because the question was immaterial rather than it being a comment on the NFL team.

Next up was Ray Zauber, publisher and editor of the *Oak Cliff Tribune*, which reached about a third of Dallas residents. He had printed a column on December 2 quoting Henry Wade, in which the prosecutor said that due to the inflamed public feeling it would be highly unlikely that Jack Ruby could get a fair trial in Dallas until about mid-February. Zauber was a reluctant witness, sometimes remaining silent, but repeating in various forms that Wade had told him the situation would have calmed down sufficiently by mid-February for Ruby to be tried fairly. Belli then reminded the court as it was only the tenth of February it still was not possible for the trial to proceed. Many agreed with Belli about the timing. In fact, the prosecutors had expected the defense to seek a continuance, or delay in the trial. There was no question that Dallas had been shaken, that its citizens needed some time to recover. But Belli wasn't asking for time, he was asking for the trial to be moved out of the city.

Zauber said Wade told him that "the preponderance of newspapers, television, radio and magazine coverage at this time" made a fair trial impossible. But now, this was Zauber stating his own opinion. "I think Jack Ruby has a much better opportunity to get a fair trial now..."

Belli had long been admired as a trial lawyer who rarely

missed an opportunity to bring a witness to his point. He asked Zauber, "Is that because there hasn't been anything in the newspapers?"

The editor shook his head. "The newspapers are still full of it."

Belli had what he wanted: "Then if the newspapers are still full of it, still there is the inflamed feeling of a reason for it, isn't there?"

Normally Belli liked to roam around a courtroom, leaning on benches, approaching the jury, making side remarks, but physically demonstrating a level of comfort and control. But even given his casual demeanor Brown ran an orderly courtroom. While permitting participants and spectators to smoke, for example, he demanded lawyers stayed seated or stood relatively stationary at a podium when questioning witnesses. That was difficult for Belli, who loved to roam around the courtroom, making emotional contact with the jurors, when making his case. Now he leaned forward on the defense table as he reminded Zauber that he had written, "'While some news media have come staunchly to the defense of Dallas and the police department, the overwhelming majority of commentators and editorial writers are literally crucifying Big D.'... Did you think that would stop, that crucifixion of Big D, about the middle of February?"

Belli barraged Zauber with stories his paper had published making false claims about Ruby: He and Oswald were neighbors. He had been investigated by the House Un-American Activities Committee. That he was a member of the Communist party. That after killing Kennedy Oswald may have been headed for Ruby's home. The paper had even pointed out that Chief Defense Counsel Belli "had exhibited an unusual interest in Russia." Zauber shrunk in his seat, admitting, "I do not have that information," "I have no information they knew each other," and "I doubt if I have that much influence."

It is odd for an attorney to ask questions about his own statements, but Henry Wade was in that awkward position. When he got the witness he asked directly, "I never did say that he couldn't get a fair trial, did I?"

"Never once," Zauber agreed.

That began a parade of witnesses, each of them in their own way trying to protect the city's reputation. *Dallas Morning News* reporter Harry McCormick admitted he had heard many rumors; there was a connection between Ruby and Oswald, and "Ruby shot Oswald to shut his mouth." And that the FBI had a witness to the Kennedy assassination in protective custody.

Belli shifted gears. The reporter had been at the jail when Oswald was shot. As many as three thousand people had gathered outside in hopes of getting a glimpse of the assassin. "Did you hear the crowd cheer when the news [that Oswald had been shot] was flashed to the crowd?" He didn't hear the cheers, McCormick claimed, but rather heard that those people had cheered the news.

The defense was painting a bright portrait of a city consumed by the two killings. To counter that impression, the prosecution focused on the fact that while sitting in a prison cell Jack Ruby had done extensive interviews for a nationally syndicated article entitled *The Story of My Life*, which had been published in newspapers throughout the country. According to McCormick, the rumor was that Ruby had been paid $28,000 for the story and the money was "in a lock box in a Los Angeles bank."

But when Wade asked him the key question, could Ruby get a fair trial, the witness frowned and made a telling statement. "Who knows what a fair trial is?"

There was only one way to determine if Ruby could get a fair and impartial jury in Dallas, suggested the next witness, Justice of the Peace Pierce McBride, who had signed the arrest warrant for Ruby after the shooting, "That's to try to get one."

The defense did everything possible to emphasize the unique aspects of this trial: Several witnesses confirmed they knew of no other case in which the Court had to have a public relations representative. Others agreed that this was the first time reporters covering the trial had to be assigned seats.

Houston Post reporter Lonnie Hudkins denied that Wade and Alexander had leaked a story to him headlined "Oswald Rumored to be U.S. Stool Pigeon." Tonahill defended this line of questioning by telling the court, "It may be very pertinent if they're [the prosecution] planting stuff in the paper that isn't true...the planting of it certainly prejudices Jack Ruby's opportunity to get a fair trial in Dallas County." Nevertheless, the prosecution objected to every question and Judge Brown dutifully sustained each objection.

In his cross-examination Wade made the point that Ruby's story had not been printed in any local newspaper, then asked McCormick the key question, did he believe "the defendant, Ruby, and the state of Texas that we represent, can both get a fair and impartial jury to try this case in the County of Dallas."

"That he could."

The final witness of the day was Deputy Sheriff W. W. Mabra, who was used to make the point that should the case remain in Dallas, jurors would be deliberating in a room from which "the spot where the president of the United States was assassinated" could be seen. In fact, that wasn't accurate. Wade asked one question: "Standing in the jury room there's not any way to see where the president was shot, is there?"

"No, Sir." It turned out that the portion of Dealey Plaza visible from a window in the jury room actually was about fifty yards from the spot where Oswald killed Kennedy. That actual spot was hidden behind a building, which blunted whatever point the defense was trying to make. Court adjourned for the day without Ruby saying a single word. He'd sat impassively, occasionally glancing around the room, but seemingly more a spectator than a participant. But silently he was reveling in the spotlight.

CHAPTER THREE

There was something slightly "off" about Jack Ruby, those people who knew him agreed. He was "different," they would say, often without specifics. Maybe it had something to do with his background, they speculated. Ruby had grown up on the streets of Chicago. His Russian-Polish father, "The Cossack," they called him, was an alcoholic. Ruby would hide under the bed when he came home drunk. Ruby's mother was a paranoid schizophrenic who at one point was institutionalized for several months. Ruby left home at twelve, living in Jewish foster homes and eventually dropping out of school. He did whatever work he could find, from selling fireworks to scalping sports tickets. For a while, he told Belli as they sat together in the prison, "I was a partner of William Randolph Hearst. Working in circula-tion!" Meaning he sold subscriptions door-to-door. Like his pal, boxing champ Barney Ross, he earned a reputation as a scrap-per but unlike Ross he didn't take it into the ring. Instead, he got involved in the scrap-iron and junk handlers union organizing activities, a good place for a guy with a short fuse and a big temper. The work was dangerous; his best friend was killed and Ruby suffered several concussions.

After serving stateside in the Army Air Corps during World War II he settled in Dallas, to be near his sister, Eva, and got into "show business." Among other ventures he ran a nightclub and managed a twelve-year-old African-American kid who could sing and dance. In the late 1950s he and Eva opened a rock and roll dance club and managed a seedy striptease parlor. The cops got to know him; he liked to do favors for the guys walking a beat, and if they didn't especially like him, they at least tolerated him. Hugh Aynesworth, a *Times Herald* reporter who knew Ruby well, claimed the FBI actually tried, unsuccessfully, to recruit Ruby eight times in 1959: "They wanted him as an informer on drugs, gambling, and organized crime, but every time they contacted him, Ruby tried to get his competitors in trouble. 'Ol' Abe over at the Colony Club is cheating on his income tax… Ol' Barney at the Theatre Lounge is selling booze after hours.' After a while the FBI gave up on the idea."

There were some women in his life, and he was once engaged but never married. Most of the women who worked in his clubs seemed to like him, although he liked to give the public impression that he was closer with them than was true. Up until 1961 he lived in his sister's apartment. In November 1963 he was a fifty-two-year-old, but still a tough guy, working as his own bouncer in his clubs.

And if there was one thing everybody knew about him, it was that Jack Ruby liked to be noticed. Nobody ever accused him of being shy. He wasn't one of those guys who stood in the background when people were taking pictures. He loved attention; he was loud and he was pushy. And now that he had a platform, now that he was somebody, he was going to use it.

In January 1964, just a week after he was denied bail, newspapers throughout the country published Ruby's syndicated feature, *My Story*. "I, Jack Ruby," he supposedly wrote, "shot and killed the murderer of our President, John F. Kennedy." Although millions of people "regard me as a hero," he continued, he did not believe as some others did, "I be given the Congressional Medal of Honor." His opinion of the city of Dallas couldn't be discussed, he explained, because he was about to go on trial for his life, but wanted it known he was a not a "small time operator" or a millionaire, "but I have always kept my word and honored my obligations…

"I am not, nor have I ever been a gangster, a racketeer, a hoodlum or an underworld character… I am also not a white slaver, a panderer, a homosexual, a sex deviate or a narcotics user." While it was later revealed that Ruby had cooperated only indirectly in the piece, with his family and Joe Tonahill providing much of the information and quotes based on discussions with him as well as from his notes, the piece was written in his "voice" and was widely accepted throughout the country as his written testament.

The second installment touched on the day of the killing, with Ruby describing a diet pill he took that morning called Preludin: "when I take a drink with Preludin, I get nasty." He recalled that when he saw Oswald later that morning, "He looked like a creep. But he didn't look like he could have killed our President all alone."

In the first article, Ruby had responded to the conspiracy claims that already were becoming widespread, stating flatly he was not a Communist, that he had not known Lee Harvey Oswald and he had not "been employed by anyone to 'silence' Oswald." The public was ravenous for any details coming from the mouth of the assassin himself. But his protestations came too late: the Kennedy conspiracy industry was already in operation.

The chain of events leading to this trial seemed implausible; a lone gunman acting entirely on his own had assassinated the president from over 250 feet away and then been murdered while in police custody by another lone gunman who simply walked into the police station. As a result, rumors were rampant. They began at the first bail hearing when Wade refused to stipulate that Oswald had acted alone and had no connection to Ruby. Oswald's mother suggested to a reporter that her son had worked for the FBI or even the CIA. Ruby supposedly was connected to known mobsters like Miami's "Handsome" Johnny Roselli, causing some to wonder if organized crime had hired Oswald to kill the president and then hired Ruby to silence him. Others speculated that the Dallas Police Department was in on it too, which was why Ruby had been allowed to slip so easily into the heavily guarded garage with his pistol.

The rumors and claims grew more bizarre. A reporter suggested to Belli that Oswald and Ruby, who actually looked vaguely alike, were the illegitimate half brothers of the same father.

To deal with the rumors, on November 30 President Johnson announced the creation of a fact-finding commission, headed by Chief Justice Earl Warren, to investigate the assassination. Initially the chief justice had refused the assignment, but finally accepted it after Johnson told him, "When this country is threatened with division and the president of the United States says you are the only man who can save it, you won't say no, will you?" The seven-member Warren Commission met for the first time on December 5, charged by the president to "satisfy itself that the truth is known as far as it can be discovered." But by then the seeds of conspiracy already had been planted.

While Ruby was silent during proceedings in the courtroom, he was practically rambunctious speaking to the media. He gave daily press conferences before the sessions began, at every break and when done for the day. It was astonishing that even after the events in Dallas the media was allowed almost unimpeded access to a man on trial for his life. Belli and Tonahill permit-

Jack Ruby remains an enigma, the street-smart nightclub owner who became the central figure in America's enduring mystery: Was there a conspiracy to assassinate President John F. Kennedy?

ted their client to speak, but urged him to hold back. "Just give your name rank and serial number."

But Ruby couldn't resist. Finally, people were paying attention to him. He spoke about reading the Bible in prison and with tears welling in his eyes said, "I am trying my best to forget the things I was involved with on the outside."

In response to a question from a French reporter who translated a letter of support he'd received, Ruby said, "I think after being incarcerated as long as I have, I know that most people don't know how small is the minority of people in the world who create hatred." Later, he added about these hate groups, "They are the cancer on our free society. So many of our great people have been hurt by them."

And he made a point of praising Sheriff Bill Decker, calling him "a great human being… I consider him a friend and hope he accepts me as his friend."

Jack Ruby had become a celebrity. Spectators began lining

up outside the courthouse at 4:00 a.m. to get a seat in the court-room. Security for those people was stringent; in fact, that first morning of the change of venue hearing, according to the *Morning News*: "Sheriff's deputies found a pistol in the handbag of a woman spectator at the Jack Ruby trial—a water pistol.

"It wasn't loaded." The embarrassed woman explained she'd taken it away from her son at church the previous Sunday and forgotten it was in her purse.

When the second day of the change of venue hearing began, the defense called Stanley Marcus to the stand. As the president of the prestigious upscale department store Neiman-Marcus, the lifelong Dallas resident was among the city's most respected businessmen—although the fact that he was Jewish did set him apart. He was quite clear about his personal feelings on holding the trial in Dallas. "I have great reservations as to whether either the defense or the prosecution can get a fair trial...it is more likely that he could get a fair trial some other place then here."

The parade of defense witnesses filled the morning. Clayton Fowler, president of the Dallas County Criminal Bar Association said that, in his opinion, "I think it would be most difficult" for a jury to judge Ruby fairly while, as Tonahill pointed out, "the State, the Nation and the world judge Dallas."

The attorney used Fowler to suggest other underlying bigotry against his client that might exist in the city, asking him if he was aware that Ruby was indicted as "Rubenstein," a name he legally changed in 1947, and if he felt that might raise an issue of anti-Semitism.

Fowler adamantly denied it. "In Dallas I doubt very seriously it would, Sir."

Tonahill laid out the defense claim repeatedly. "By virtue of the fact that...the Dallas image is at stake in this trial..." He emphasized the difficulty the Court would have finding twelve men and women in Dallas who had not formed an opinion about the case.

Prosecutor Jim Bowie turned that around, asking the witness if he thought jurors "would seek an image of Dallas with being prejudiced, with hatred and bias to the extent they would refuse to give Jack Ruby a fair trial?"

That led to a series of outbursts from the defense and the prosecution over whether Ruby would take a lie detector test, or had been offered to take a lie detector test, until both sides were quieted by Judge Brown, who sustained everybody's objections "so we can go on."

The defense also pointed out that Judge Brown had hired a public relations man, a highly unusual step that spoke to the city leaders' concern with its image. The prosecution tried to explain that, asking if the witness had ever heard of a situation in which three hundred newspapermen competed for seats in a courtroom that fit less than sixty. But that only reemphasized the fact that this trial had attracted worldwide attention. When the prosecution rejected the idea that Judge Brown had hired this firm to "build up on his own image," Tonahill agreed in a tone as serious as he could manage, "The judge's image can't get any greater than it already is!"

When the prosecution persisted, Tonahill put the situation in perspective, asking Mr. Fowler, "Did you ever hear of Blackstone or anyone else that had a public relations officer to control the press at a trial?" Blackstone being Sir William Blackstone who published the first of his four volume *Commentaries on the Laws of England*, an overview of the history and application of English law, in 1765.

"Never did, Joe," the witness replied. Within a few years, as media interest in trials and means of broadcasting them increased, PR advisers and media experts capable of handling the inquiries and controlling the narratives would become quite common.

The next witness, Costine Droby, chairman of the board of directors of the Dallas County Criminal Bar Association, told the Court, "From what I've heard over-all it seems to be the consensus of opinion that Jack Ruby couldn't get a fair trial in Dallas County...that Jack Ruby must be convicted to clear Dallas' name, in plain English."

The courtroom remained absolutely silent as he testified, loudly and clearly so there could be no mistaking his anger. He described the situation as so dangerous that, when it appeared he himself might represent Ruby, anonymous callers had made threats on his life. He wasn't alone. Later a minister would testify that as a result of portions of his sermon questioning the character of the city, his life too had been threatened and he had been placed under police protection.

The prosecution hammered away at Droby, who was well-respected in the city, trying to chip away at his testimony. But he wouldn't be moved: "I think the spotlight is on Dallas because the president was assassinated here... I'm just telling you what I heard and I think it boils down to the fact that they think the only way to vindicate Dallas is to convict this man. That's what I've heard from numerous people."

Attorney Sam Donosky, another respected man in Dallas, said the same thing. "The image of our good city has been besmirched... Get us out from under the spotlight." Donosky agreed with Jim Bowie that it was possible to get a jury that had not been tainted by publicity or a desire to protect the city—but it was improbable. He admitted he himself had seen only limited television coverage because "My set just gets channel 4," but was well aware of the interest in this trial, adding in exaggeration, "I'm sure probably Telestar..." the new communications satellite, "has it in the foreign countries."

The prosecution was taking a beating, so Bowie retreated, suggesting to several subsequent witnesses that one guaranteed way to find out if it were possible to seat a fair jury was to try to seat a fair jury. The bias, the prejudice, the ability to keep an open mind would all come out in voir dire, the process of the questioning of potential jurors.

It wasn't simply the adverse publicity, the defense contended, but that the prosecution had taken deliberate steps to ensure Ruby could not get his fair trial in the city. Ruby's lawyers intended to show that their opponents had tried to damage the defense.

Ed Mahar, a respected member of the Citizens Council for almost fifteen years, also was chairman of the board of Parkland Hospital. The hospital had refused to conduct tests on Ruby when Judge Brown had ruled that he should be examined by court-appointed psychiatrists to determine his mental state. Belli wanted to know why. "Did you talk to the district attorney about whether you would take in Mr. Ruby for an examination?"

Wade and Alexander were on their feet, screaming that this question had no bearing on this hearing, shouting a barrage of objections.

Belli ignored them. "And the District Attorney told you not to take him in?" The question was never answered as Brown upheld the objections. But Belli had gotten what he wanted, knowing his words were going to be published in hundreds of newspapers and quoted on broadcast news programs. "We offer that if they cannot even examine him in a community because of his reputation...how can we get a fair trial?" Belli finished with this witness by quoting Judge Brown's remarks to a reporter about the hospital's decision, to put them in the court record. "'They told me they didn't intend to have anything to do with Ruby.'"

The defense continued to put the most powerful people in the city on the stand. Earle Cabell, who had resigned as the mayor of Dallas only a week earlier, was next. Cabell did a fine job bobbing and weaving, refusing to admit much of anything, even something so obvious as the fact that all of the residents of the city were aware of what had happened there. "I would hesitate to say that."

"That might be possible."

"I can't speak for majority opinion…"

"I couldn't say that definitely."

"I couldn't answer that with any degree of accuracy."

Through the two days of change of venue hearings, the animosity between the prosecution and defense grew as each side maneuvered for an advantage. When the prosecution, supported by Judge Brown, claimed that jurors might hold an opinion about a case until they are sworn in, at which time they take a vow of neutrality, Belli drew on the great history of the law, including Supreme Court Justice Charles Hughes. "Impartiality is not a technical concept, it's a state of mind for ascertaining of this mental attitude of appropriate indifference."

"They must be indifferent," Belli emphasized. "They must be unknowledgeable; they must be unappreciative; they must know nothing about the case in order to give a fair trial!"

The witnesses came faster now, reinforcing previous testimony but adding interesting touches; columnist Tony Zoppi, who covered the nightclub scene for the *Morning News* said singer Tony Bennett had called him. Bennett, who loved Dallas so much he worked there for half of what he was paid in other cities, was dismayed by the killings. "I can't believe this happened in Dallas," he said. "This is unbelievable that a thing like this could happen in Dallas."

Zoppi testified that the city was being vilified around the country, according to his contacts. When a prominent manufacturer going through customs said he was from Dallas, "People looked at him like he was some kind of a freak." In Los Angeles people he knew "were abused, told to get out of restaurants, when they learned they were from Dallas."

Again and again Belli found ways to reinforce his contention that Dallas was on trial as much as Ruby. He read from an article quoting a "young Republican pediatrician, 'All I know is that three distinguished men visited Dallas in three years. All three were treated violently, the last one was killed. I think all kinds of nuts can thrive in the boisterous political climate we have had here.'"

Eventually the defense went after the media, which supposedly had so soiled Ruby's reputation as to make it impossible for him to be judged solely for his actions. Conspiracy theories had been growing fast in the press. A drummer in Ruby's Carousel Club band, Bill Willis, had heard a TV commentator cite a report that Ruby was a Communist and Oswald had been in the club. That was ridiculous, he told Tonahill. Jack wasn't a Communist, then he added weakly, "I told him that I didn't definitely think I could have seen Oswald there... Well, there was one guy sitting in there and maybe that's who Bill (the illusionist who said he saw Oswald there) thinks he was."

Willis was firm about this. "If the public communications media had not said this in the first place, I rather doubt it would exist now as a popular theory, which it does...a city of half a million people have all come to the independent conclusion that Jack Ruby had something to do with the Communist element." And that association would, he believed, prevent Ruby from getting a fair trial in Dallas.

Once it was hinted that Ruby was a Communist with previous connections to Oswald, that possibility took hold. It was revealed that Ruby had visited Castro's Cuba in 1959. Supposedly he had been invited by a friend trying to promote a casino. That friend asked him to bring along Tony Zoppi, who might write about it for the *Morning News*, but Ruby ended up going alone. Outside the courtroom Ruby explained to journalists that Cuba was "a new country opening up" and that while he had discussed trying to export fertilizer and jeeps to the Cuban government, "I never got to first base...I wanted to get out of the beer business, to be honest with you." But others noted suspiciously that Mafia boss Santo Trafficante had been on the island at that same time. It all fit nicely into the growing theory that Communists were involved in JFK's assassination.

The hearing had already displayed the great variety of opinion present in the city's business and legal community, but the next witness, attorney Ben Henderson, brought a novel point of view to the stand with him. He had "heard and read" many rumors that Ruby had a connection to Oswald, that he was a Communist and even that he should receive a medal for the murder, he testified, but then he floated his own theory: that the only way Ruby could be convicted would be to prove Oswald was an innocent man; "I know of no offense," he told the court, "when you kill the tyrant."

During its cross-examination, the prosecution began to raise what certainly was going to be a novel issue to resolve: Could anyone who had seen Ruby shooting Oswald live or on film serve as a juror? Was it possible to have witnessed a killing and judge it fairly? After Bill Alexander pointed out Ruby's face had never been seen on the screen, Henderson likened it to the mayhem of a football play, "the way someone goes to an opening and then moves toward it and then goes into the enemy's backfield."

Perhaps believing he had an agreeable witness, Alexander asked, "So nobody could truthfully identify Ruby from what he saw on television, could he?"

"Well," the witness reminded the court, "nobody ever accused anyone other than Mr. Ruby of firing that shot of all the people that were there."

When Alexander suggested it would not be difficult to find twelve jurors drawn by chance among the 425,000 eligible people, the veteran attorney Henderson revealed an uncomfortable truth. "The way some of these jurors would reappear here, over such a variety of time elements," had made him aware that "I frankly fail to see a recurrence as often of the people who vote a defendant innocent as those who vote him guilty back on the panel."

Tonahill immediately called for a grand jury investigation of that charge. Alexander tried to clean it up, claiming again a jury panel was drawn by lot but the witness persisted in claiming that's what he saw.

Looking for any potential opening, the defense called Judge W. L. Sterrett who had jurisdiction over the courtroom in which the case was scheduled to be tried. The trial was causing all types of disruptions; while the influx of media pouring into the city would have a major impact on the hotel and restaurant businesses, the county had been forced to scramble to find adequate facilities. Initially it was proposed witnesses would be kept in a building across the street—until the company insuring that building objected, threatening to cancel its million dollar policy. And the courtroom itself, said Tonahill, "Is such that it's very difficult to ventilate, cool or heat and because safety measures must be taken to keep the windows down..."

It was a problem, Judge Sterrett agreed, and everyone knew the city needed a new courtroom. When the prosecution objected to the whole area of questioning, Tonahill rose to his feet and explained, "If Dallas is on trial as we allege, then the District Attorney is defending the image...in not wanting this case moved to a larger jurisdiction or...larger courtroom where the image of Dallas can actually be aired out in the eyes of the world...

"It denies [Ruby] a fair trial because of the feeling and demand that says Dallas first must be preserved and protected... This man cannot get a fair trial here because everything is too limited. The sense of fairness is limited here, and can't be helped."

The prosecution countered by asking the judge if he was comfortable. "Is the climate too hot or too cold...the weather isn't affecting your ability to testify here today or the conditions in the atmosphere, is that right?"

That was right, Sterrett agreed.

While this hearing was in progress, young boxer Cassius Clay was training in Miami Beach for his February 25 heavyweight championship bout against Sonny Liston. Even this early in his career, before he had changed his name and become known as Muhammad Ali, his antics had changed boxing. He turned pre-fight weigh-ins into events, mocking his opponents with rhyming predictions, creating grudges that fans believed would play out in the ring. His extraordinary boasting, his vibrant personality, his dime-store poetry brought new attention and energy to the staid, scandal-plagued world of boxing.

That message, confrontation brings attention and attention brings results, also was playing out in the courtroom in Dallas. Throughout this hearing the prosecution objected regularly and their objections were almost always sustained. Often Wade or Alexander didn't allow the defense to complete its question before shouting an objection. In a preview of what was to come when the trial began, Tonahill told the judge, "Never in my life have I ever seen such rudeness by prosecuting attorneys. I don't know whether it's rudeness or a desire to suppress the truth. I think it's a combination of both. And you're the only one who can do anything about it."

The chastised judge replied, "All right. Go ahead."

When Bowie objected to Tonahill's next question, he added, "And I apologize if I appear to be rude."

Sarcastically, Tonahill replied, "I accept your apology."

If Judge Brown used a gavel, he would have banged it right then and there. He wasn't going to allow that kind of discourtesy in his courtroom. No, sir! He was sick of those sidebar remarks. "That's gonna cost you twenty-five dollars Mr. Tonahill. Go pay the clerk!"

Tonahill asked the judge if he could borrow the money. The judge turned him down. But the stage was being set.

By late afternoon the hearing was finally winding down. Jack

Ruby's nineteen-year-old next-door neighbor had testified she doubted he could get a fair trial. "I know that the newspapers are prejudiced against him because they put things in the paper that I didn't say and they are supposedly quotes." She guessed far more people were against him than supported him—but few of them didn't hold tight to an opinion already. The courtroom was silent when she said firmly, "I think when a man's life is at stake, he ought to have every chance that he can get. And I think it [the trial] should be moved to another city."

Ed Carroll was the office manager for a radio advertising business and also wrote country songs. He had become friends with Jack Ruby through Fort Worth native Fess Parker, the actor who had become famous playing Davy Crockett on television and owned a record label. Carroll's best song, "The Gila Monster," had been recorded by a singer named Joe Johnson, who performed at Ruby's club. Carroll knew a lot of people, he said, but he hadn't met one person who didn't have an opinion about Jack's guilt or innocence. Although he added that most people he knew weren't sure if Jack was of sound or unsound mind. He didn't hesitate though when asked by Alexander, "Do you think you could give the defendant a fair trial?"

"No."

Alexander tried hard to get the next witness, housewife Edna Knight, a longtime friend of Jack and his sister, Eva Grant, to admit that there was no place in the entire country that had not seen the killing or felt the impact. When she explained, "There's been so much publicity I…" Alexander interrupted, "Well, the publicity has been everywhere in this state and nation, has it not, ma'am?" And perhaps even more in other places, he suggested.

Knight summed up the defense argument perfectly. "But their town isn't on trial. Our town is on trial."

Alexander pushed back, trying to regain lost ground by emphasizing that Ruby was on trial, not Dallas, and that the rules of evidence would protect the defendant and didn't she think the people of Dallas would be fair? "Well, of course," she agreed, "they are just average housewives like myself." But before the prosecutor could take a relieved breath she continued, "And I think they feel the same as I, that Jack was temporarily insane at the time it happened."

While that response would certainly indicate a willingness to entertain the defense argument, Alexander still persisted, probing for any opening to poke a hole in her testimony. Texas was on trial too, she agreed with him, but not as much as Dallas. Finally, frustrated, he wondered, "Don't you feel that the entire system of jurisprudence of the United States is on trial in the eyes of the world in this case?"

"Yes, Sir, I do," she agreed, ending her appearance.

The change of venue hearing continued into a third day, lasting as long as many actual trials. Dozens of sweating reporters waited in the hallway outside the small courtroom and whenever there was a break they would pile into the room and barrage the participants with questions. It was a bizarre spectacle: a man who was on trial for killing an accused killer in the midst of a large crowd was surrounded by a large crowd with no security. Judge Brown, as well as all of the attorneys, patiently answered questions and posed for photographs. And while Jack Ruby sat silent when court was in session, when reporters surrounded him during these breaks he seemed thrilled to be the center of attention. The defendant was in good humor, they wrote, but he asked reporters to call him Mr. Ruby rather than just Jack. And he got very serious, reportedly on the edge of tears, when asked if he felt he had brought shame on the city. "I love this city," he replied in a choked voice. The owner of tawdry nightclubs and strip clubs added, "Because there is so much culture here..."

District Attorney Wade was furious about these impromptu interviews and asked Judge Brown to stop them. It was strange, he said, that Ruby was so outspoken while his attorneys were complaining that too much publicity might influence potential jurors. "His statements amount to unsworn testimony."

Tonahill dismissed those complaints, reminding reporters that his client hadn't been convicted of any crime and "still has the constitutional rights of free speech."

Like the overture to a grand opera, the hearing reached a crescendo as the lawyers settled in for a long and contentious conflict on the third and final day. The first witness was the court's PR man, Sam Bloom, who admitted he was also a member of the Citizens Council. Bloom was a large lump of a man; Belli described him as "lugubrious… Frog-like, with heavy-rimmed glasses over his bulging eyes." Soon after arriving in Dallas, he and Tonahill had spent several hours with Bloom trying to understand his role representing the court. He found that Sam Bloom was a man who spoke slowly but thought quickly. He had mastered the public relations skill of talking a lot without saying anything of importance. It became obvious that he was the public voice of the city's decision-makers on the Citizens Council.

On the stand Bloom insisted he had volunteered his assistance, rather than having been recruited and directed by the council to protect Dallas's image. His job, he said, was limited to making recommendations for media credentials and seating and providing adequate phone and telegraph lines. The defense suggested an ulterior motive. His voice rising, Belli said, "We believe there is a conspiracy, no matter how sophisticated or subtle it may be…to make an image" for Dallas.

Belli spent two hours trying to attack Bloom as the representative of the entrenched power structure. Bloom was unshakable. When Belli raised his voice, Bloom warned him, "Don't bark at me."

"Well, don't snap at me," the lawyer responded.

Frustrated at his inability to pin down Bloom, Belli finally asked, in a serious tone, "After the President was shot did you hand in a report of the warm welcome Dallas had afforded him?"

In an equally serious tone, Bloom replied that he had not done so.

The defense next put *Dallas Morning News* reporter Carl Freund on the stand, hoping to show his coverage had further poisoned the well of public opinion. Freund had written extensively about supposedly secret psychological tests given to Ruby, one of his many stories had claimed "Laboratory tests given Ruby at a Dallas clinic showed no significant evidence of brain damage…"

Belli contended this prejudicial reporting had made it impossible to seat a fair jury in Dallas. Those "inflammatory" stories, Belli shouted, were deliberate lies intended to undermine the defense. To prove that the reporter had his own strong opinion, Belli asked him, if he believed "Ruby had brought trouble down on Dallas."

"Yes," Freund said, "I do." But he didn't back down, challenging the attorney, "If you have evidence it [my story] is false, I will be glad to write a story in the morning."

Belli spent considerable time contending the information about those tests was false, then transitioned easily into trying to find out where Freund had gotten the tip. He knew that the reporter did not have to—and would not—reveal the source of his information, but he used Freund's answers to infer the prosecution was leaking potential evidence to journalists in order to groom potential jurors. It was a strong charge to make and, at one point, Alexander jumped to his feet, faced Belli and threatened, "If the court won't keep him in line, he'll be on his own."

Asked about his relationship to Sam Bloom, the reporter said he barely knew him, even though they'd shaken hands when they'd met in the courtroom. That wasn't surprising Belli said. "You and he are on the same side."

This time it was Jim Bowie who objected, accusing Belli of "a full day of fishing and nothing caught."

Belli denied that, perhaps referring to his grilling of Bloom earlier when he said, "Oh, I caught a big one this morning, Mr. Bowie."

Without hesitation Bowie looked at the massive Joe Tonahill and said, "You can keep Mr. Tonahill." The entire courtroom burst into laughter.

Oddly though, when Freund reported on the hearing in the *News* the following day, he neglected to even mention that he had appeared as a witness.

Throughout the rest of the day the defense put witness after witness on the stand to cite all the possible reasons Jack Ruby could not get a fair trial in Dallas. The attorneys continued to use legal arguments to attack the opposition; lawyers are not supposed to launch personal assaults on their opponents, but both sides came perilously close to doing exactly that. When respected Dallas lawyer Harold Berman testified he did not think it was possible to seat an unbiased jury, based on his conversations, Alexander commented, "You are closer to the people in the city than the peasants out in the country."

Belli immediately was on his feet, defending the peasantry. Minutes earlier he had described Alexander's courtroom attitude as "insulting and disgusting." But this was an "insidious" remark, he fumed, which he certainly hoped voters would remember when District Attorney Wade was on the ballot.

Throughout the day it seemed the defense was trying to put every lawyer (and a large cross section of Dallas residents) on the stand to repeat the same mantra: Ruby could not get a fair trial in this city. Attorney Laurel Bates talked about "the subconscious desire to punish Ruby" for what he had done to the city. Bank executive W. M. Beavers said, "You can't see a man shot down with his hands tied without forming an opinion." Attorney Thomas K. Irwin Jr. wondered, "I don't know where you can find 12 people in Dallas County who can get in the jury box and cast aside their opinions." US Attorney Harold "Barefoot" Sanders actually agreed with the prosecution, admitting it would be difficult to find twelve impartial people, but believed the only way to find out was to question members of the panel and see if it was possible before making any decision.

The defense appeared willing to put an endless stream of witnesses on the stand. Twenty-eight-year-old law student James Buchanan had been standing in the corridor, hoping to get a seat in the gallery, when he was asked to testify. On the stand he agreed with Sanders, he didn't think it was possible to seat an impartial jury but the best way to find out was to question panelists. Another law student called to testify, Searcy Ferguson, generally agreed with that, but was firm in his belief, "Anyone who commits murder is insane."

As the third day of the hearing came to a close, the defense claimed it could call an additional 150 witnesses who would support its motion to move the trial but believed that point had been made. Instead they rested.

Rather than presenting any witnesses, District Attorney Wade filed affidavits from thirty-eight Dallas residents swearing Ruby certainly would get a fair trial. It was a clever move; Belli couldn't cross-examine an affidavit.

Judge Brown announced his decision the next afternoon. Rather than ruling on the motion, he said, "The true test of whether the state and defense can get a fair trial rests on the prospective jurors. The decision rests until examination of jurors."

The judge also revealed that the trial would be switched to a significantly larger courtroom in the building, allowing more than two hundred reporters and spectators to view the proceedings. Responding to that, Tonahill sighed and said, "I guess Judge Brown didn't understand me correctly. I asked him to move the trial 200 miles and instead he moved it 200 feet."

As it later became known, Judge Brown did not want to move the trial unless he went with it. This was the case of his career, and he was not going to give it up. Apparently he had repeatedly told Belli privately he intended to move the trial, then changed his mind after speaking to the presiding judges in other districts and learning they would not allow an outside judge to sit on the bench at their courthouses. While the prosecution had won this argument for now, the defense had also laid down a strong record for any possible appeal if the judge did not ultimately move the case from Dallas.

As the hearing concluded, the prosecutors had developed larger concerns about the defense team, believing their court-room antics and strategies might actually be creating an envi-ronment where a fair trial for Ruby could be in jeopardy. While Belli was seeking, thus far unsuccessfully, to move the trial out of Dallas, he was doing so by impugning the city's residents in and out of the courtroom, thereby making it that much more difficult to find an impartial Dallas jury. And why wasn't he seeking to delay the trial, at least for a while, to allow passions to cool? They also were stunned that rather than pursuing Tom Howard's far safer strategy of admitting guilt and claiming Ruby had acted in a moment of intense passion—which could have had him out of prison in two to five years—they were preparing to argue that he was legally insane, a far more difficult case to win. Wade's concern about Belli in particular was so great, that he informed his team to seek to halt the proceedings if neither of the Texas based defense lawyers, Tonahill or Burleson, were present in the courtroom.

It was with this friction and antagonism that the parties began what was arguably the most important phase of the trial. The world had served as witness, and now the lawyers had to some-how find twelve people untainted by the mountain of public-ity that surrounded the case, prepared to ignore the impact on Dallas, and solely focus on evidence presented in court. Belli and Tonahill did not intend to make that easy.

CHAPTER FOUR

Reporters from newspapers and magazines around the world had flocked to Dallas. No trial in history had received this level of international attention. The courtroom benches, reported the *Morning News*, "were filled by reporters from virtually every major newspaper in the world." They had come from the English-speaking countries, from Spain, Italy, France, Germany, even Bulgaria. Still photographers and film cameramen, barred from the courtroom, waited impatiently in hallways and hotel lobbies to catch a meaningful image of the participants.

The public relations man Sam Bloom, representing the Citizens Council, embraced this opportunity to use the gathered media to restore Dallas's soiled image and perhaps introduce a new and exciting city to the nation, and the world. To accommodate media demand, and perhaps to derail a threatened lawsuit from journalists not provided access, the trial had been moved from Judge Brown's cozy courtroom into Judge J. Frank Wilson's considerably larger space. Judge Wilson had initially declined to give up his courtroom for the trial, saying he had his own trials that would be taking place at the same time. That problem was solved when the chief judge gave Judge Wilson what clearly was a surprise two-week vacation. The media had been provided workspace in a courtroom down the hall from the larger courtroom where the case would now be tried. Telephones and Western Union teletypes had been installed, and each journalist was provided space for his typewriter.

The trial would take place on the second floor of the Dallas County Criminal Courts Building. The eleven story "skyscraper" had cost almost $675,000 to build and had been opened in 1915. In addition to courtrooms on the first two levels, this "state-of-the-art" model for the "administration of justice" had included both men's and women's segregated jails—steel bars were thoughtfully installed inside the cell windows to make the building less threatening seen from the street—capable of housing as many as five hundred prisoners, including several padded cells for "insane" prisoners, jailer's and matron's quarters, a chapel, a hospital and operating room, four electric elevators, a barber shop and, on the top floor, a hanging room.

The building had a colorful history: Bonnie's Clyde Barrow had spent time in a cell there, the gambler and killer Benny Binion had been there as had Harvey Bailey, "the dean of American bank robbers." Until 1923 condemned prisoners were hanged on the top floor, perhaps to be closer to their maker, and a claw-foot tub was provided for those men who wanted a last-minute baptism. There'd been a shoot-out at the courthouse in 1925 when five thousand people tried to break in to lynch two Black brothers accused of killing a white man and assaulting a white woman. Sheriff's deputies fired back, killing one man and wounding six others. (The prisoners eventually were convicted and executed.) Country singer and cowboy movie star Gene Autry warned of the fifth floor, where the worst prisoners were housed, in his song, the "Dallas County Jail Blues."

"When you get in ol' High Five, no one will go your bail."

Dallas had been so proud of this building that when it opened local officials conducted tours for three days. The building was even said to be haunted by "a tall, dark shadow" dressed in white or perhaps a female ghost.

But faded letters spelling out "white only'" still visible over the water fountains and signs designating different hours to visit Black and white prisoners were stark reminders of the recent past.

Judge Frank Wilson's high-ceilinged, dark and spacious court-room was utilitarian rather than appealing. Spectators were seated in high-backed dark-stained wooden benches. Brass spit-toons were set next to both the prosecution and defense tables in the well; the prosecution table was conveniently right next to the jury box, which might allow jurors to hear a loudly whis-pered word or several. The jurors had been given comfortable reclining chairs, and the Texas flag hung directly over their heads. The judge's high bench sat in an alcove, framed by Vic-torian portraits of plump women representing Freedom and Justice. Portraits of retired judges dating back to 1893 hung on the green-tinted walls. The courtroom was cooled by eleven old-fashioned ceiling fans.

On the morning of February 18, Melvin Belli placed his red velvet briefcase on the defense table, Henry Wade stuck a cigar in his mouth and they went to work trying to find twelve people capable of putting aside what their own eyes might have seen and all the ensuing publicity to reach a fair and just verdict. "They say we can't get an impartial jury here," Judge Brown told a re-porter. "Let's try. The proof is in the pudding."

Tonahill made the defense position clear; they were going to draw out the selection process as long as possible, delve into the beliefs and prejudices of potential jurors to determine "their conscious, subconscious and unconscious thoughts. We want to know if they think Dallas is on trial. We want to know whether they would be prejudice against Ruby because of his religion or his association with strippers."

The court bailiff called nine hundred people for jury duty, the largest number of people ever summoned for a criminal trial in the city. An estimated five hundred people actually showed up. Among them, the defense lamented, there wasn't a single Jew, Catholic or member of a union. Potential jurors could be dismissed for "cause," meaning it was clear they had some conflict, a relationship with participants in the trial, admittedly had formed an opinion, or any other reason that prevented them from reaching a verdict based solely on the evidence. In addition, each side had fifteen peremptory challenges, allowing them to reject a candidate without having to give any reason. The examination of each potential juror began with roughly the same questions: What is your church preference or affiliation? And, do you have any scruples, religious or otherwise, that would prevent you from personally, yourself, assessing the death penalty? The fact that this question was at the forefront afforded prosecutors an early advantage since those who admitted they could not impose death might also have been more defense oriented jurors.

In an odd way, the question of whether an accused person could be fairly judged by people with personal knowledge of the crime had come full circle. The origin of the trial by jury is disputed, but originally, as far back as the eleventh century, a jury was comprised of neighbors of the accused who had that firsthand knowledge. Ideally, they may have even witnessed the event. But as civilization grew and spread, the introduction of evidence replaced that personal involvement. Now thanks to advances in technology, millions of people had witnessed the incident, either as it took place or later in replays that had been captured on film. The defense would use that reality to make a bold claim, that no one who saw the event at any point should be qualified to serve on this jury since "eyewitnesses" could not sit objectively in judgment. The prosecution countered it was possible to witness an event without forming an opinion, particularly when there was no dispute over who pulled the trigger. The voir dire, the preliminary questioning, began with Mr. Hillard Stone.

Asked by Wade if he had any compunction against sending a convicted man to the electric chair, Stone replied evenly, "I would never restrict society so that it could not rid itself of undesirable elements... It's like a surgeon amputating a badly infected toe or gangrenous finger."

Belli watched his hands as he said this. In his thirty-year career he had come to believe he could tell whether or not a juror would vote for the death penalty from his reaction to that question: if his hands remained steady, as Stone's did, he would vote for death; if he twisted or moved his hands, he would vote against it. Stone's hands remained absolutely still.

The prosecution's questioning of the venireman, the potential juror, lasted about fifteen minutes. The defense would keep Stone on the stand for more than three hours, setting the tone for the next two weeks. Stone admitted he had read about the shooting and seen a TV rerun and described it in detail. Belli asked Judge Brown to disqualify him immediately, citing Texas law that barred a witness to an event from serving on a jury that will judge guilt or innocence.

Judge Brown asked Stone if he could disregard that film clip and reach a verdict solely on the evidence. When he agreed he could, the court ruled him qualified. Belli questions filled the morning: How did Stone feel about a plea of mental insanity? Did he watch the popular legal shows on television, *Perry Mason*, *Sam Benedict*, *The Defenders*? Had he heard the rumors that the police had worked with Ruby? Did he believe Dallas was on trial? Throughout the morning and into the afternoon Wade or Alexander objected to almost every question. Belli continued probing, offering hints of the defense to come while seeking to find a reason to excuse the man for cause. When finally he accepted that would not happen, he used one of his fifteen peremptory challenges.

Three other people were questioned that first day, and Belli used up a second challenge with one while the others were dismissed for cause. The day ended with a charismatic and candid librarian. When asked if she could be an impartial juror, she admitted, "It would be hard. I saw it."

I saw it. Those words, and variations of them, would be heard for days. The defense was adamant; no Dallas citizen who had seen the killing could render a fair verdict. They were tainted. At several points the defense tried to put almost every participant in the trial on its witness list, even members of the prosecution, claiming they were eyewitnesses to the crime and therefore should not be allowed to play any role in the proceedings. The defense even obtained a subpoena and attempted to serve it on the tenth possible juror, a move the prosecution called "a legal joke" and a "stunt" and easily prevented that from happening. In this effort the defense cited the 1963 Supreme Court decision in *Rideau v. Louisiana* in which the court had overturned a murder conviction because three jurors had previously seen a television interview in which Walter Rideau had confessed. The Supreme Court had ruled in that case that television could influence jurors and prevent a defendant from being fairly tried on the evidence alone.

Judge Brown essentially ignored the defense strategy. Nothing in the law prevented jurors from knowing about the incident or even the case; they just had to be able to put that aside and render a fair verdict solely based on the evidence presented in court. New technologies were going to impact the legal system in ways no one could anticipate or imagine. The system would be forced to evolve to deal with the changing realities. But without being able to peer into a man's or woman's heart it was difficult to know how much, if at all, they may have been affected by what they saw or read. After the defense motion was rejected,

Belli's team set out to dig as deeply as possible into each veni-reman's life with their questions, but often they were blunted.

No jurors were seated the first or the second day as the two sides maneuvered for position. When a potential juror claimed he had seen or read only portions of the case, Tonahill asked him, "Could you tell us the portions you have not read?"

Bowie leaped to his feet, objecting. "That's like asking J. Edgar Hoover how many Communists are in the United States you don't know about."

Tonahill then objected to the objection, complaining about the "innuendos that we're Communists."

The defense was walking a fine line here as they sought to balance competing interests: selecting fair jurors potentially sympathetic to their client, while continuing to try to convince Judge Brown that this pool of Dallas jurors was hopelessly tainted and unfair. At last on the third day, the twenty-fourth member of the jury pool to be questioned, a cost analyst engineer at the electronics giant LTV named Max Causey, was the first juror seated. Belli approved him after discovering, among other things, that he had a mentally handicapped son, which had given Causey and his wife a deeper understanding of mental illness. Within minutes of his being selected, two national networks had arrived at his house and were setting up cameras in his living room to interview his wife.

Belli had now used seven of his fifteen peremptory challenges in selecting just one juror and clearly realized that he needed to become more judicious with the precious challenges for anything but the most unfavorable of prospective jurors.

Two days later a second juror was accepted. On the seventh day the first woman was seated; although she was a member of a fundamentalist church, Belli was told she liked to drink socially and believed she "was a person of some tolerance." And might even be a liberal.

The defense was searching desperately to find any hint in a

possible juror's background that he or she might be open to accepting the insanity defense or did not approve of the death penalty. They often made assumptions and held tightly to wishes. For example, the next juror was accepted because his company had used lie-detector tests to question its employees, which at least indicated he was acquainted with modern scientific techniques.

The prosecution, conversely, had cast a wide net among supporters and colleagues for information about potential members of the panel. Files from previous cases, which sometimes included how the veniremen voted in a trial, were at their disposal as they were getting the type of background intelligence from members of the community that the defense simply could not match.

It was during voir dire that Tonahill completely let loose with his questioning, establishing himself as the defense attack dog. "Could you find a sick GI guilty of killing a Communist?" he asked one venireman. "Do you believe killing a Communist was no worse than running a stop sign?" he asked another. He asked hypothetical questions like, "If a Secret Service man had shot Oswald, do you think he should be tried for murder," and suggested that a lie detector be used to determine if one candidate "is capable of setting aside his opinion." He wondered of another person, "Would you feel un-Texan if you were on the first jury to send a man to the electric chair for killing a Communist?"

The specter of Communism hung over the courtroom like the cloud of cigarette smoke that pressed against its ceiling. America was fighting a "Cold War" against the Soviet Union whose leader Nikita Khrushchev had promised, "We will bury you." As Tonahill was suggesting, that fear might prove useful in Ruby's defense.

Belli was only slightly more decorous, suggesting to one man, "You want to get on this jury so you can send this defendant to the electric chair, don't you?" And at one point he stopped his questioning midsentence to ask the judge to direct a spectator, a police detective, to stop smirking and smiling.

By statute, only married men and women or property holders were eligible to serve on juries in Texas. (Women were excused if they did not want to serve.) In addition to eliminating many poorer people, who actually could have used the eight dollars a day paid to jurors, it largely ignored the city's African-American population. Belli and Tonahill were infuriated by the way the prosecution curtly dismissed the few Black members of the jury pool, and rather than addressing them as Mr. and Mrs. called them by their first names. In fact, while one Black man was being questioned by the prosecution, Tonahill had become so angry at this patronizing attitude he had thrown his pen on the floor—and once again was fined twenty-five dollars by the judge. Belli was outraged, screaming that Wade was "insulting" African Americans called for jury duty. When reporters questioned the prosecution about it, they changed their tone and began using the more formal titles. In such small ways light was being shined on the long shadows of the city. These episodes, Belli contended, "revealed the true unconscious feeling of Dallas."

The same time as The Beatles returned to London after their "conquest of the American colonies," the "jury wars," as the *Houston Chronicle* described the long process of trying to seat a jury, continued. Belli joked that his six-year-old son, who was present in court, "will be admitted to the bar before this trial is over." By this point the first juror chosen, Max Causey, had been sequestered on the seventh floor of the courthouse, literally living in an unlocked cell for almost two weeks. It was reported he had learned how to play dominoes from a guard to pass the time. But still the selection process continued. A member of the police reserve was dismissed for cause when he admitted he had been assigned to guard duty protecting Lee Harvey Oswald's wife after the assassination. Belli later marveled, "We've got our own Gestapo here and, boy, do we need it." The defense used another challenge when it learned a member of the panel was the son of a guard at the Dallas County jail. In response to a panelist who answered as ambiguously as possible to every question, a frustrated Belli asked if he even had an opinion as to whether or not Oswald was dead. The man hesitated then responded, "I hope he is, because I know he's buried."

A Braniff Airlines mechanic became the fourth juror. The defense may have selected him because he had a cousin with epilepsy. Then the vice president of a tile manufacturing company, then a paper salesman and a mailman who also was a police reservist. By the seventh day, more than one hundred people had been questioned and the number rose over the coming days: one hundred ten, one hundred twenty. There were still some light moments. After being questioned, an attractive blond housewife named Dixie Valetto stopped on her way out of court to shake hands with Ruby. "Can we get any more like her?" Belli asked as the judge eliminated her for cause.

Judge Brown had previously made his appreciation of a woman's physical attributes known, calling Belli to the bench supposedly for a conference but actually to point out a particularly striking spectator; cupping his hand over his mouth he said, "Some doll?"

As the days passed, the prosecution also used its challenges. Wade used the first one on a venireman who said he believed that "a man could be crazy one minute and sane the next." Gone. He used another challenge to dismiss a man who believed "With God's help, I could be fair." Gone.

When Wade asked another female panelist who operated a beauty salon if she had formed an opinion about the case, her answer made it obvious she wanted the celebrity that would come with being a juror. No, she claimed, she hadn't read anything about Ruby. Asked if any women in her shop had discussed the case, the courtroom erupted in laughter when she said solemnly,

"No Sir, I don't allow any gossiping in my beauty shop." Judge Brown excused her.

Another possible juror, a maintenance man, was dismissed after claiming he didn't discuss the case at work because during his break he would usually "eat my lunch then crawl up in a truck and go to sleep," or at home with his wife "because we been married so long [we] know each other's thoughts."

A female oil company secretary was the next juror accepted. Then an electronics engineer who had graduated from the University of Texas. On the eleventh day of jury selection, Belli got into a discussion about people reaching their psychological breaking point with J. Waymon Rose, a handsome former Navy pilot then representing furniture firms. Could someone completely lose control of himself? Belli asked. Here was the core of his defense: Jack Ruby had gone over the emotional edge, committing an act of violence in a state of temporary insanity so severe that he could neither explain it nor recall it.

Rose agreed to the general principle. "I remember a football game in which a tackle came off the bench and tackled the man from the opposing team who was carrying the ball." That famed event had taken place in the 1954 Cotton Bowl, which was played in Dallas, when an Alabama player on the sidelines tackled a Rice player running for a touchdown.

"We accept this juror," Belli told the judge. "We want this juror." The defense later claimed to be surprised that the prosecution had not challenged him.

Ten jurors had been selected when Belli ran out of challenges. He requested the judge grant him an additional fifteen. Judge Brown agreed to just three more to fill the remaining two chairs.

At some point it had become clear to the defense that Judge Brown was not going to move the trial. Belli believed the judge had gone back on his word but now had only one option: to move forward and build the record proving that Ruby could not get a fair trial in Dallas. That continued the next morning.

After the first hour was spent posing pleasantly for photographs with spectators, several more prospective jurors were questioned and dismissed. The defense also used two of its extra three challenges. Before Judge Brown could adjourn for the day, Belli insisted that a copy of a racist, anti-Semitic white supremacist newspaper the *Thunderbolt* be added to the record.

The presence of so many journalists gathered in Dallas had been like a spotlight drawing people wanting publicity. From the beginning of the trial, copies of this newspaper had been widely circulated. Although headquartered in Birmingham, Alabama, Belli suggested copies had been printed locally. Referring to it as "the most scurrilous, filthiest and nastiest" publication he had ever seen, Belli contended its circulation was even more evidence the trial must be moved.

"That isn't a Dallas publication," Wade pointed out. "That comes from California, doesn't it?"

Anger reddening his face, Belli screamed, "We don't have filth like this in California—and we've never had a president assassinated there either." To reinforce his point, Belli began reading from the November issue of the *Thunderbolt*. Judge Brown tried to interrupt him, reminding him that he already had admitted it to the record and asking him to stop this "oratory."

Belli continued reading. Judge Brown called a recess to try to stop him. But Belli kept going, for a total of nine minutes. In the middle of it the judge shrugged, stood up and left the bench. Belli just kept reading as the courtroom emptied and reporters pushed in to fill the empty places.

The most Belli accomplished was focusing more attention on this extremist newspaper than it ever would have received otherwise. While it was not possible to measure the level of anti-Semitism in any American town or city, there was no question it existed and publications like this exacerbated it.

Meanwhile, a man named Maurice A. Melford, director of the National Epileptic League, also arrived in Dallas to take advantage of the press attention. Two weeks earlier the *New York Times* had reported that Dr. Fredrick Gibbs, a national expert on the disease, had concluded that Ruby suffered from a form of it he described as psychomotor epilepsy that can cause a sufferer to have "rage attacks." Once thought to be a God-given punishment or possession, epilepsy's primary symptom is random seizures characterized by uncontrollable muscular shaking. The kind of bizarre physical manifestation that centuries before might have been attributed to witchcraft or even the devil. Researchers still aren't certain what causes epilepsy; potential causes range from a genetic defect to blows to the head. And while in most instances it is treatable it could, in certain cases, also lead to death. It usually isn't known what triggers these episodes, which range in intensity from so mild as to be undetected or violent enough to cause victims to fracture bones.

But no one had ever been known to commit a murder during an epileptic attack.

The myths, the exaggerations, the fears associated with this mostly controllable disease had brought Melford to Dallas to represent those afflicted with it. When court resumed Monday morning, he began handing out thick "educational packages" containing pages of "factual material" to the media and prospective jurors. Belli was questioning a potential juror when he was handed a copy of the material. "Jack Ruby is on trial," it began. "But because of this...the estimated 1,800,000 Americans who are epileptics are also on trial." There is a real danger, it continued, "Because the public knows so little about epilepsy and because so much of what it believes is based on ignorance, superstition and myth" that arguments made during the trial "can further prejudice the public."

Among the many claims was one that quoted expert Dr. Gibbs as saying it was "nonsense" to believe that people suffering from psychomotor epilepsy might commit "murders and criminal activities." Gibbs said flatly, "You don't have to worry too much about a patient in psychomotor seizure."

When Belli read this seemingly factual material, he erupted. This gave him the opportunity to display the courtroom dramatics for which he had become known, and he took full advantage. Recognizing that the material undermined his defense, he waved the packet in the air as he shouted, "I don't know what woodwork these people crawled out of, but this vicious act, perpetrated at the portals of the temple of justice—is the grossest kind of contempt.

"I demand that distribution of this lying hogwash be stopped, as a flagrant attempt to influence justice…"

The prosecution quickly agreed that this material should not be distributed, adding that defense witnesses cease giving "television interviews outside the portals of this temple—in earshot of potential witnesses," but Belli was not going to let the Melford packet go. Allowed to stand unchallenged, or distributed nationally through the media, this information threatened to destroy the foundation of his case, but it also provided a spotlight for him.

Judge Brown summoned the lawyers and Melford into his chambers. Maurice Melford was a small, meek man with rimless glasses, dressed in a tweed jacket and had a pipe stuck solidly in the corner of his mouth. He appeared stunned to discover that he had caused such outrage with what he believed to be a mostly innocuous document that had actually been put together by a local Dallas PR agency (not Sam Bloom's).

Judge Brown recognized the possible damage Melford had done. "Take the first plane out of Dallas and go back to Chicago," he ordered, his words recorded by an industrious reporter who had stuck his tape recorder microphone to the closed door.

That wasn't enough for the defense. Tonahill demanded Melford be publicly cited for contempt, considering the potential damage he had done.

"I was just trying to help the newsmen," Melford explained.

Judge Brown was furious. "You had no right to put this stuff out in court where we're trying a man."

Melford stammered, "I did not... I didn't..."

"You're a no-good citizen," Tonahill boomed. "You're trash. You're dirt. You're not interested in a fair trial by a jury."

Suddenly Melford offered an explanation. "I told the district attorney I was coming."

As that admission sunk in, Belli demanded a mistrial. "This is a conspiracy!" he said, shouting loudly enough that reporters outside the room could hear him without need of a microphone. "That lily-livered district attorney bringing a man down here to stand at the door and pass out this stuff. How the hell can we get a fair trial in Dallas?"

Judge Brown overruled the request for a mistrial, pointing out that the jury panel had not been exposed to the material.

Meeting with reporters later, Wade said smugly, "Ain't no law against passing out literature," calling the motion for a mistrial "a stunt" and "a grandstand play." The defense would, unsuccessfully, raise the issue of contempt several times over the next few days, but Melford would end up having an even larger impact on the trial when he presented prosecutors with a variety of experts who could testify against the defense's claims.

When court convened Tuesday morning, Judge Brown was absent, having gone to the hospital in cold sweats, and he was replaced on the bench by Judge J. Frank Wilson. The defense objected, protesting this wasn't solely jury selection but remained part of the change of venue motion and Judge Brown needed to be present to hear all testimony. Only in Texas, Belli complained, could a judge be replaced in the middle of a case and it continue.

Not just any judge, either. For more than a decade following World War II, Judge Wilson had been one of the most conservative members of the United States Congress. Belli described him as a "gravel-voiced skull cracker" while Judge Brown referred to him as "brusque." In his opening statement, while turning down several defense motions including a request for additional challenges, Judge Wilson said he wouldn't stand for any "nonsense" in his courtroom. He made that point clearly when Belli hesitated after being told to sit down, telling him sternly, "When the court says for you to take your seat, it means for you to take your seat. Now sit down."

Perhaps Wilson's attitude had an effect. The eleventh juror was seated almost immediately, a fifty-eight-year-old divorced woman. Then eleven more veniremen were quickly eliminated, eight of them disqualified for admitting they could not in good conscience vote for the death penalty, two others for saying they already had made up their minds.

The final juror certainly would have been challenged by the defense if it had any challenges remaining. Mrs. Louise Malone's nephew was the public relations officer for the Dallas Police Department. Art Hammett, who hosted a local TV program entitled *Know Your Police Department*, was deeply involved in the effort to relieve the Dallas PD of responsibility for allowing Ruby to slip through security and murder one of the most high profile prisoners in American history. Questioned by Judge Wilson if she really could be fair, she assured him she could. But only minutes later she responded to Tonahill asking her if she was curious about why the shooting had taken place by responding, "Yes, I am." And then adding, "If it happened."

The prosecution accepted her. The defense asked for an additional challenge to keep her off the jury. The judge denied the request, instead saying, "I believe this juror will be perfectly fair."

The twelve-person jury finally was seated. Texas law did not make provisions for additional alternate jurors. The role of an alternate juror isn't enshrined in most statutes. At one time when a juror for whatever reason had to leave a panel, the entire jury was dismissed—and in some jurisdictions the eleven other jurors then were immediately recalled and a replacement juror was added. To prevent that from happening, particularly in high profile trials, additional jurors are selected to sit through the case and be prepared to deliberate should anything happen to a member of the jury. In most cases it is a thoroughly frustrating job; an alternate has to attend every session, sit through every minute and then is not allowed to participate in deliberations in any way.

But not adding an alternate was especially risky in this case. Most trials took at most a full day or two, making it unlikely an alternate juror would be needed, but this trial was expected to last several weeks and should anything happen to one of the "12 men, good and true," as the jury was described in the seventeenth century, the trial would have to be ended and the entire process begun anew.

It had taken fourteen long days, days in which the temperature inside the courtroom at times rose over ninety degrees, to finally seat the jury. To find them, 162 people had taken the stand and been questioned. The jury consisted of eight men and four women, all of them white and of various Protestant denominations. The average age was around forty. Four of them were college graduates. Their professions included two engineers, a bookkeeper and an accountant, a research analyst and a corporate vice president. All of them had been married, one woman had been widowed, another divorced. Six men had served in the military. All but one of them had children. Eleven of them had witnessed all or part of the shooting, either live or repeated on television. Wade described it as the most intelligent jury he had ever had in a courtroom. Belli believed they were intelligent as well, at least by what he viewed as Dallas standards: "I think the intelligence level of our jury is well above what you would expect from a cross section of Dallas residents."

When Mrs. Malone was escorted into the jury room, the

eleven other people stood and applauded. Each of them had been sequestered since being selected. They moved as a group to meals, but had spent most of that time sitting and waiting together. Their most memorable entertainment had been standing on a sidewalk and watching a building being demolished.

That night the now-complete Jack Ruby jury took its first vote and reached a unanimous decision: They would have dinner at Kirby's Steak House.

Finally, the next morning, they were going to work.

CHAPTER FIVE

Many people believed Mel Belli was crazy to pursue this unusual insanity defense.

Among them was Tom Howard, his original co-counsel. Howard intended to argue murder without malice, a crime committed in a moment of insanity or passion—which carried a maximum sentence of five years. Less with good behavior. Howard planned to call several of Ruby's acquaintances to testify he always seemed different, a character, then have one or two local psychiatrists state that he was mentally unstable. Then he would put several more people on the stand to show how torn up Ruby was over the assassination, how irrationally enraged he became over anti-Kennedy rhetoric. In a moment of misguided patriotism, Ruby had decided to protect Jackie from testifying and offer their children the closure they deserved. Howard would call Ruby to the stand to express his profound regret for his actions and show that his client had a good heart. Why, when one of his employees needed twenty-five dollars to pay her rent on that fateful day, he had run right down to the Western Union to wire it to her.

He was ready to play it safe and hope that the jurors, and the country, would understand Ruby's momentary lapse in judgment.

But that wasn't the strategy Belli had chosen. He was prepared to roll the dice on a far more audacious defense, choosing instead to pursue arguably the most difficult case of his legal career. But there was maybe no one better to find the elusive nexus between medical science and the law. His own father, he claimed, had been killed by a pharmacist who had filled a prescription with the wrong dosage, and that had made him determined to apply the law to bring the best medical knowledge into the courtroom and punish those who abused their power. He had studied medical techniques and spent his life winning cases with medical evidence. He had saved his very first client's life with an insanity defense and subsequently had used it, mostly successfully, in several other cases. He took great pride in his knowledge of the latest psychiatric studies, experimental techniques and means of diagnosis. This case, being watched by the world, offered him an incredible opportunity to bring all the wonders of modern psychiatry into the courtroom and change forever the insanity defense.

He claimed to have no doubt about Ruby's mental condition, and that assessment was only bolstered when he learned that Ruby's mother as well as his brother Earl both had been briefly institutionalized for insanity. When his young son asked Belli why he would plead Jack Ruby not guilty when the act was committed on television, he responded, "We didn't see what was going on in his mind. That's the only thing we're going to try."

He was willing to gamble Jack Ruby's life on this belief.

Howard's advice was now marginalized. Several days before the trial began, Howard resigned from the defense team, calling Ruby "One of the finest people I know," and wishing him good luck while pointedly ignoring Belli.

A legal defense is often a balancing act, in which one side of the scale is known, the other piled with speculation and even best guessing. Abraham Lincoln once advised, "In law it is good policy to never plead what you need not, lest you oblige yourself to prove what you cannot." Tom Howard knew the court system in Dallas; he knew and had worked with all the players, the judges, attorneys and jurors. He could have brought that experience to the trial. But he was no longer representing Jack Ruby.

There were many people who didn't understand Belli's rejection of Howard's defense strategy to instead pursue one far more complicated and considerably less likely to succeed. It seemed like he was trying to cut through dense brush in a forest rather than remaining on a clear but winding path out.

The legal definition of insanity had long been debated. The insanity defense has played a role in legal systems dating back to the Greeks and Romans, when it was acknowledged that mental deficiency might mitigate the penalty for murder. Almost all societies throughout recorded history have agreed that mentally ill people should not be held accountable and punished as if they were sane. Figuring out how to measure sanity has always been the problem.

In the fourteenth century, England's King Edward II ruled that a person was not responsible for his actions if his mental state was no greater than that of "a wild beast." Beginning early in the sixteenth century, juries had the right to acquit an accused person for lack of mental capacity, and it required a separate civil hearing to determine if there should be further penalty. The British struggled to find a coherent law applicable to all cases, and finally in 1843 agreed on a broad rule after a high-profile case. A wealthy man named Daniel M'Naghten shot Prime Minister Robert Peel's private secretary in the back at point-blank range, apparently mistaking him for the prime minister. When questioned he readily confessed, claiming he had been driven to the act by Tories, "who persecute me wherever I go, and have entirely destroyed my peace of mind."

At his trial medical witnesses testified that his mental condition had made him unable to exercise "restraint over his actions." M'Naghten was placed in the Broadmoor Asylum, where he died twenty years later. However, the ensuing public outcry, in which his claims of insanity were questioned, caused the House of Lords to assemble a panel of five judges to attempt to find a broadly applicable definition of insanity. The M'Naghten rule, which became the standard that has endured even to this day in many places, decreed that "to establish a defense on the ground of insanity, it must be clearly proved that, at the time of the committing of the act, the party accused was laboring under such a defect of reason, from disease of mind, and not to know the nature and quality of the act he was doing; or if he did know it, that he did not know he was doing what was wrong."

Colonial America failed to employ this standard; for example, as early as 1648 a delusional Massachusetts woman was hanged for murdering her daughter. Eventually though, America adopted the M'Naghten rule as psychiatry became established. In the 1869 New Hampshire case of *State v. Pike*, in which Josiah Pike killed Thomas Brown by striking him with an ax, the jury decided that the killing was "the product" of Pike's insanity, meaning he was not legally responsible for his actions. The definition continued to broaden to include a range of other mental defenses, including "irresistible impulse" and limited crimes of passion.

That law was expanded by the 1954 Durham test. After a disturbed seventeen-year-old man was convicted of breaking into a house, an appellate court ruled that M'Naghten was "an entirely obsolete and misleading conception of the nature of insanity." In their view, the century-old definition didn't go far enough. Overturning the conviction, the court stated, "that an accused is not criminally responsible if his unlawful act was the product of mental disease or mental defect." Meaning that a crime committed by someone living with mental illness is the result of that mental illness.

That, too, proved a questionable standard as it took the ultimate decision of guilt or innocence away from jurors and eventually was disregarded in the states that had adopted it. In 1964, Texas still followed the M'Naghten rule: Did a defendant understand the difference between right and wrong when the crime was committed? Was he capable of understanding the consequences of his actions? There existed no irresistible-impulse exception; instead, the only question was if the accused knew what he or she was doing was wrong when the crime was committed. You either were insane or you weren't. None of that "conveniently crazy" stuff the newspaper railed about. It was the burden of the defense to prove, by a preponderance of evidence, that a defendant was legally insane.

It was a tough standard. But no one had more confidence in Belli's ability than Melvin Belli. Joe Tonahill clearly supported that decision. But then the defense made its own difficult argument even harder to prove. With the permission of the court, Ruby had been given a series of psychiatric tests and had been diagnosed by some with a newly described brain disorder termed psychomotor epilepsy. Little was known about this condition. Like other forms of epilepsy, it was not known what triggered an attack. Its cause might have been present since birth or brought about by disease or even blows to the head. After all, Ruby had a long history of concussions in both teenage street fights and later his union job.

Psychiatrist Walter Bromberg examined Ruby's test results and determined that Ruby had committed the murder while in a so-called "fugue" state, in which crimes might be committed with the perpetrator having absolutely no awareness of what he was doing. It was roughly a form of sleepwalking, except with a murder.

During his first meetings with Ruby, Belli had asked him what he remembered about the killing. "I waved my hand to the guy and walked into Police Headquarters," he'd replied. "Well, there were lights and a crowd… Well, I shot him… Well, they were all on top of me and I kept saying, 'I'm Jack Ruby. You don't need to beat my brains out.' Then they took me inside." In repeated retellings in his cell, he was able to explain in detail what happened right before and after the killing—but nothing about the shooting itself. It was as if he wasn't even there. And Belli would argue that psychologically he wasn't.

Dr. Bromberg presented a similar story when he testified under oath in the bail hearing. Ruby, he reported, "remembers going down the ramp and seeing Oswald, but doesn't remember anything else until he found himself struggling with officers." It was a form of automatism, Dr. Bromberg explained: there was no claim that Ruby did not know the difference between right and wrong—the accepted legal definition of insanity—when he killed Oswald, rather the claim was that he had committed the crime during a seizure and didn't even know he was doing it. He acted without conscious thought, almost robotically.

But even more than that, the tests seemed to indicate that Ruby was suffering from an even more rare form of epilepsy called a "psychomotor variant." It only recently had been described by Dr. Frederick Gibbs, considered the father of encephalography, a method in which the electrical brain impulses are measured and charted. Psychomotor variant was an extremely rare condition, he wrote, but it is a brain abnormality that is real and can be seen and diagnosed by reading encephalographs.

And unlike so many earlier cases in which insanity had been the basis of the defense, most people who knew Jack Ruby did not think he was crazy. They considered him a little different, maybe a little too hot-tempered, but most of the time he got along with people just fine. And he was running a striptease joint, so naturally there were going to be some problems.

The prosecution also had settled on a difficult path. According to the Texas statute, proving "murder with malice" required showing that the crime did not occur "under the immediate influence of a sudden passion arising from an adequate cause, by which is meant such cause as would commonly produce a degree of anger, rage, resentment or terror in a person of ordinary temper, sufficient to render the mind incapable of cool reflection." In other words it required that they prove some element of thought, planning or at least intent on Ruby's part. More than that though, the question was what was the gain for the prosecution in seeking the death penalty? As the *Houston Chronicle* pointed out, "Dallas has a reputation as a hang town among the Texas underworld because of the number of men condemned." Big D's effort to create a sparkling image of itself as a modern American city would not be helped by executing a seemingly distraught nightclub owner, especially as so many Americans shared his hatred of Oswald. Polls taken in the weeks following the shooting showed overwhelmingly that Texans did not support a death penalty verdict; in fact, a significant number were in favor of no penalty at all.

It was partly cloudy with an expected high of a pleasant seventy degrees on the morning of March 4, 1964. On its front page, the *Morning News* reported "Negro Files for School Board Seat." In Washington, Secretary of State Dean Rusk stated flatly his belief that the war in Vietnam, "a mean, frustrating and difficult struggle," could be won without expanding the fighting into the North. In Tennessee, Teamsters Union President James Hoffa was found guilty of trying to fix a 1962 jury, his first conviction after five trials, and faced a decade in prison. And in the heart of Dallas, more than three hundred journalists scrambled for seats in the courtroom to report the trial of Jack Ruby for the murder of the Lee Harvey Oswald.

DONALD UHRBROCK/THE LIFE IMAGES COLLECTION VIA GETTY IMAGES/ GETTY IMAGES

Judge Joe B. Brown had been elected to his position. While he had the highest rate of Appeals court reversals in the state, Texas courts used a rotating system and when he was assigned to this case, assistant prosecutor Bill Alexander pleaded with Brown to step aside, telling him, "You can't handle this case. You don't know your evidence well enough."

Judge Brown had returned to the bench. Perhaps chastised by the accolades Judge Wilson had received for his efficient manner, Brown admitted he had been "rather tolerant" before and warned the media that he intended to maintain strict decorum throughout the remainder of the trial. "There will be no talking, no gesturing, no rushing for the door at any time. With the jury completed and in the box, we're going to tighten up!"

There was legal business to be taken care of before witnesses could be called. The defense offered several motions: Request for a change of venue. Denied. Request for additional challenges to remove the jurors seated while Brown was absent. Denied. Request for a mistrial based on the distribution of "inflammatory literature" by the National Epilepsy League. Denied. Request for a mistrial because the media filled almost all of the spectator seats, denying Ruby his constitutionally guaranteed public trial. Denied. Request that Ruby's two sisters and psychiatrist Manfred Guttmacher be permitted to sit in the courtroom rather than waiting outside. Denied. Request for a pretrial sanity hearing to which the defense was entitled. Texas was one of a few states permitting a separate jury trial to determine a defendant's sanity at the present time and then again for when the crime was committed. "Overruled," the judge said curtly, explaining they had waited too long.

The defense's last request was a bit of legal shenanigans. Joe Tonahill asked that assistant district attorney "Mr. Alexander be sworn as a witness for the defendant." His claim was that Alexander, who had persuaded Ruby to undergo psychiatric testing by a doctor who would become the prosecution's expert, would be able to testify to Ruby's appearance. In fact, if this was permitted, under the ruling made just minutes earlier, Alexander would be barred from the courtroom during witness testimony.

The motion was denied but what the defense really may have wanted to show was that Alexander had subtly snookered Ruby into agreeing to that examination at all. Alexander had known Ruby for over a dozen years. Even though that relationship was often related to minor skirmishes Ruby had with the law, Ruby considered them friends. He had even come to see Alexander the day before Oswald was killed to try to resolve an issue for a pal who had been passing bad checks in town. Ruby trusted Alexander. In the second bail hearing, psychiatrist John Holbrook had testified that he was brought into Ruby's cell by Alexander the day after Oswald was killed. According to Holbrook, Ruby turned to Alexander to ask if he should talk to Holbrook and Alexander responded, "Jack all we want is a fair, square psychiatric examination of you. If you're nuts, you ought to go to the state insane asylum, and if you're alright we are going to have to prosecute you." Ruby then asked Alexander whether this was "some kind of trap." To which Alexander responded, "I've known you too long for that. I wouldn't let any friendship go down the drain just to mess with you." The next day after Holbrook interviewed Ruby, the prosecutors announced they were seeking the death penalty against Ruby.

Finally, Judge Brown asked Ruby to stand. After months of waiting, Jack Ruby had the spotlight. Belli stood with him. The judge asked District Attorney Wade to read the indictment. In a deep, somber voice Wade said, "The State of Texas verse Jack Rubenstein, alias Jack Ruby..."

Belli interrupted. "He answers to the name of Jack Ruby." The point Belli was making seemed obvious; Rubenstein is a Jewish name, Ruby may not be.

Wade ignored him, continuing dramatically, "did unlawfully, voluntarily and with malice aforethought did kill Lee Harvey Oswald by shooting him with a gun." Wade hesitated, like an actor stumbling over his lines, then grimaced. "I can't make out the signature of the Grand Jury foreman."

"Durwood Sutton." Judge Brown helped him, then faced Ruby. "Mr. Ruby, what is your plea to that indictment?"

Dressed that day in a blue suit, Ruby bowed slightly at the waist and in a soft voice replied, "Not guilty, Your Honor."

Belli instantly added, "Not waiving that former plea of not guilty... I ask Mr. Ruby to repeat that 'Not guilty and not guilty by reason of insanity.'"

"All the court is interested in, Counsel, is whether he pleads guilty or not guilty." None of that fancy lawyering was going to be welcome in this courtroom.

Ruby said again the only words he was to utter in his defense, "Not guilty."

In most states a criminal trial begins with opening statements as both the prosecution and the defense introduce themselves to the jury and explain what their case will be and what evidence they will provide to prove that case. It's a first opportunity for lawyers to make a personal connection to the jury and lay out what to expect. But in Texas, prosecutors were not compelled to make an opening statement, and if they chose not to, then the defense didn't get to do so either. Wade, recognizing the advantage of not affording the defense an early opportunity to present its theory, decided not to make an opening statement. Belli asked politely to make his statement, believing he needed to outline his complex defense for the jurors, so they would know what to expect. When Judge Brown turned him down, Tonahill said fruitlessly, "We insist that the District Attorney make one, Your Honor, in the form of the Code of Criminal Procedure." No luck.

The most substantial challenge facing the prosecution was to prove that this murder was committed with malice, making it a death penalty offense, and that it was not an impulsive act but rather had been planned—and literally executed—by Jack Ruby. With no opening statement, Wade began the state's case by calling its first witness, Don Campbell, the advertising salesman for the *Dallas Morning News*.

As the trial began in Dallas, in the state capital of Austin the Texas Supreme Court announced for the second time that it would not hear the defense argument that any person who had witnessed the shooting on television should be disqualified from serving as a juror. That decision was not unexpected. The broader question of how modern technology impacted the legal system was being debated in courtrooms around the country. And this complex issue certainly would figure in any appeal, should that become necessary. But this ruling precluded the defense from relying on this argument that the crime had been seen by those people who were to judge the killer would not be a factor in this trial.

The prosecution ambled casually into the case. It appeared they were going to trace Ruby's movements through the hours leading up to the killing, trying to show that he was carefully tracking Oswald as he waited for an opportunity to strike. That murder was his objective all along.

Campbell, who said he had known Ruby for almost four years, testified that while a parade for President Kennedy was taking place only blocks away Ruby had been busy in the newspaper's second-floor office writing and designing his weekly ads for his two nightclubs. Wade's intention was to challenge Ruby's professed passion for the president, the passion that the defense claimed led him to shoot Oswald, by showing that rather than viewing the parade he had been busy working.

Belli knew exactly what Wade was attempting to accomplish. During his first appearance in front of the jury, he methodically countered every point. His objective wasn't simply to respond to Campbell's testimony; he wanted to demonstrate to the jury that the prosecution was not to be trusted: while questioning Campbell, Alexander had spent considerable time proving that it was possible to see the School Book Depository building from which Oswald had fired his rifle from an office window in the *News* building. He had even shown photographs to emphasize that point. Belli began his cross-examination by asking, "Was [Jack Ruby] anywhere near this office?"

"He wasn't in that office."

And what's more, it turned out, Campbell was not even in the *News* building when Kennedy was assassinated. He had left for lunch and had no idea what Jack Ruby was doing at that fateful moment.

Alexander also had led his witness to testify that there was nothing unusual about Ruby's behavior that day, that he was pretty much the same person he had known for years. Belli picked up that loose thread and pulled it. "When you say he was just Jack Ruby…that was a pretty volatile individual that you knew as Jack Ruby, was it not?"

"Yes."

And as for missing the parade, "You were working at the time…and he was working at the time, and that's the reason he didn't see it." Campbell agreed that was a fair statement. The defense had begun painting the portrait of Ruby it wanted the jury to see.

The prosecution's second witness was equally minor. John Newnam of the *Morning News*'s advertising staff had watched TV reports of the assassination with Ruby, agreeing everyone was "stunned and deeply grieved by the news." Alexander tried to paint his own picture of the defendant. "Was anything unusual about Ruby's behavior over the period of time you knew him? Did he appear to be normal?"

"As far as I know." But then Newnam offered more of an explanation. "I knew him in his business and he appeared normal as far as I was concerned."

Alexander used the witness to demonstrate that Ruby was quite competent to run a business, that he was not the unbalanced character the defense sought to present. But then he almost went a little too far. Most experienced lawyers try to confine witnesses to brief factual answers to which they already know the answer. "I will ask you if he could be characterized as a rather volatile, excitable individual; talked fast, talked loud, perhaps waved his arms sometimes when excited, or just tell us how he appeared to you."

"Well, yes, I think Jack is excitable. Our conversations at times, he would tell me that he was, and sometimes he would be more so than others."

Excitable wasn't insanity and Alexander was trying to bring home that point. "But there never appeared to be anything abnormal about his behavior?"

"No," Newnam agreed. "We got along just fine."

The defense took advantage of the small opening during its cross-examination. Tonahill got Newnam to help him fill in the picture of a troubled man. The witness agreed that, at times, Ruby would get, "what you call hysterical" when reprimanding his employees.

"After these reprimands, when he became hysterical and very excitable, after they were over did then he regain his composure and calmness...and appear as if nothing had taken place at all?"

"As far as I am concerned."

Tonahill asked the witness how Ruby responded to the assassination. "You could tell from his appearance that he was very greatly stunned and shocked and bewildered?"

"Yes." Newnam explained that Ruby responded to the killing by closing his clubs for the next two days.

The defense used this witness to present facts it wanted the jury to know. Tonahill asked Newnam if Ruby had seemed upset about the full-page anti-Kennedy advertisement that had been published in the paper that morning. Newnam agreed. "He was critical of the paper for accepting it, he was concerned about it." The fact that Newnam had nothing at all to do with the ad did not stop Tonahill from making several points about it: The *Dallas Times Herald* had not run that ad. The ad was paid for in cash. And it was signed by the obviously Jewish "Bernard Weissman."

The defense wasn't yet digging a foundation for its case, but it was clearing away the brush. "You have learned and heard of a number of peculiar things Jack has done," Tonahill continued, reinforcing this characterization of his client as a strange man with a bad temper, "when he has these emotional states from time to time, where you describe him as being more excitable at certain times than others... Some of them get very strong, do they not?"

"I would say so, yes."

The prosecution then called Georgia Mayer, described by

the *New York Times* as "a pretty brunette secretary" who also worked in the *Morning News*'s advertising department. There was no obvious reason to call Miss Mayer, other than the fact she might have added a bit of glamour to the courtroom. Alexander asked her only a few perfunctory questions, establishing nothing more than the fact she knew Jack Ruby and saw him in the office that day. The prosecution may have realized by this point that this line of questioning about Ruby's reputation at the paper was not benefiting its case. Then Mel Belli, a friendly smile on his ruggedly handsome face, without raising his voice a whit, showed the courtroom how he had earned his reputation. "You were all upset, Miss Mayer, at that time—we all were in this country, weren't you?"

Oh yes, she answered. And Jack was upset too? He pressed.

"...his eyes were fixed toward the back of the office."

Fixed? Belli inquired.

"Yes, and dazed."

Dazed? Belli had his hook in. This was something the jurors could easily imagine. The witness told Belli she could not estimate how long Ruby had sat there transfixed. "But it was something that was remarkable, was it not?" he asked.

It was, "yes."

More than remarkable, it might be an indication of a deeper emotional problem, Belli suggested, asking, "Have you seen people in states of epilepsy or otherwise, when they have been in this sort of fixed stare?" There was absolutely no reason to believe this witness knew anything at all about behavior in an epileptic state—but Belli was beginning his presentation and hoped the jury would infer that this might well be a symptom or an expression of epilepsy.

"No."

He filled in the image for the jurors. "He wasn't moving any parts of his body when he was in this fixed stare...did he have his hands down...did you notice whether he was perspiring when he was in this fixed stare…did you notice whether he was pallid or his color changed…he wasn't saying anything…did he make any motion to wipe his eyes when he was in this fixed stare?"

No to all of those questions. "I just noticed his stare."

In Alexander's redirect examination, he suggested that Ruby was as disconsolate as everyone else, but before Mayer could respond, Tonahill objected, calling it a "leading question." Judge Brown agreed, sustaining the objection and Alexander quickly excused the witness.

As the prosecution continued its effort to trace Ruby's actions from assassination to murder, it called radio reporter William Duncan, even though it guaranteed an embarrassing situation for Henry Wade. Well after midnight on the day of the Kennedy killing, Duncan had received an unsolicited phone call from Ruby asking "if I would like to talk to the District Attorney Henry Wade," said Duncan. "Then the District Attorney was put on the phone and I talked to him."

Belli interrupted, asking loudly, forcing the witness to repeat that statement. "The District Attorney was what?" He got on the phone, Duncan repeated. Belli made sure the jury understood this somewhat astonishing news. "Wait a second—that is Mr. Wade?"

Ruby and Wade were together the night of the twenty-second? The existence of any relationship between Ruby and Wade was surprising since there was no obvious reason for them to be together. That revelation fed into the rumors that Oswald acted as part of a larger conspiracy, and law enforcement needed to shut him up before he could name names.

Coincidentally, at the same moment Duncan was on the stand, in Washington, DC, the Warren Commission was holding its first public hearing. New York lawyer Mark Lane was repeating under oath a claim he had made weeks earlier that a "secret meeting" between Dallas police officer J. D. Tippit, the officer killed by Oswald, Bernard Weissman, the New Yorker who had placed the anti-Kennedy ad that so enraged Ruby, and an un-identified third man that had taken place in Jack Ruby's Carou-sel Club more than a week before the assassination. He admitted he did not know what was said at that meeting. When Weiss-man was asked about this claim, he completely denied such a meeting took place and challenged Lane's source to confront him "face-to-face."

In Dallas, Duncan's testimony was certain to fuel the rapidly growing number of conspiracy buffs. He testified that Ruby had brought sandwiches and "soda pop, some exotic cola" to the station "and wanted to know if the talks I had with the District Attorney were satisfactory… Jack seemed pleased that he had suggested to Russ (KLIF disc jockey Russ Knight) that he ask the District Attorney whether or not Oswald was sane."

More importantly, Duncan said that Ruby had seen Oswald in city hall. "I am paraphrasing," he said. "'All of a sudden there was a large rush and commotion when Oswald was brought out to meet the press. He said he was caught up in people rushing, and the first thing he knew he was standing in front of Oswald.'…"

A skilled trial lawyer like Belli packs questions with the infor-mation or opinion he or she wants the jury to consider, and does so in a manner that isn't at all dependent on an answer. In this instance he filled in some background in the portrait of Ruby as a troubled person. "Would you say that Jack Ruby…was one of those tolerated characters you find in a community…some-thing like an O. Henry character…that people think are some-times odd but they let them stay if they don't disturb anything?"

Meanwhile, Ruby sat perfectly still, staring straight ahead as his lawyer described him as odd.

Duncan had no answer, explaining he'd never met Ruby be-fore that night.

Belli began asking Duncan about that strange phone call. Then, when the prosecution objected to these questions as hearsay, he pointed out, "Presumably Jack Ruby was there while Mr. Wade came to the phone with his friend Jack Ruby at the time."

"Friend," of course, being emphasized.

When Bill Alexander objected, Belli withdrew the question and asked it again, this time in the proper legal manner. Duncan said there was no way for him to know where Ruby was standing. "What I am interested in," Belli continued, "is that he said he had seen Oswald. Right?" He did. "And he didn't tell you that after having seen Oswald he made up his mind that he was going to shoot him, did he?"

"There was no mention of anything like that," Duncan agreed.

Belli shifted gears, making an important point: "Did you know Jack Ruby had his gun with him and some $1200 at the time he had seen Oswald?....Did he say he was standing on a chair in the back of the assembly room, where he had a clear view of Oswald?"

"Clear view" or clear shot? If Ruby intended to shoot Oswald, his questions suggested, why did he not shoot him at that moment? He supposedly had a gun and a clear shot, and absolutely no way of knowing if he would ever get another opportunity.

As Duncan stepped out of the witness box, it was getting warm in the courtroom. Judge Brown was still not feeling well; he was constantly mopping his brow and an on-call doctor was taking his temperature. But it was noted that even that did not affect his aim at the spittoon. The man just never missed.

While the defense tried to show that Ruby had let opportunities for revenge pass by, the prosecution was setting up its counterclaim that Ruby was stalking Oswald. Dallas detective Richard Sims testified that Ruby had called and offered to bring "a sack of sandwiches" to the Homicide and Robbery Bureau. "At the time of Ruby's telephone call," Alexander asked, "Lee Harvey Oswald was in the Homicide and Robbery Bureau?"

"He was."

During Tonahill's cross-examination, Detective Sims said he'd known Ruby for more than a decade; in fact he'd spent time with him in his office at the nightclub. Ruby also had several times assisted police officers, whether jumping into a brawl to help a cop under attack or raising money for the widow of a slain officer. He was well-known to the police force. But then Tonahill used this witness to show that Ruby was substantially more than just an odd character. "Do you know about Jack and his love for his dogs?" He did. "He called them his children?" He did. "And one his wife, Sheba. You knew that?" He did. "Do you know anyone else that calls their dogs their children, and one their wife?"

"Not offhand, no sir." The fact that Ruby referred to his dogs as his children and one of them as his wife was not mentioned in local newspaper reports of the trial, but its significance would soon become evident.

Next, police lieutenant T. B. Leonard testified he had seen Ruby at Henry Wade's press conference the night of the assassination, holding a notebook and a pencil. Asked what he was doing there Ruby replied, "I brought the sandwiches." They were still in his car, he said, but when asked to get them he said no, "I'm a reporter tonight."

Trying to dispel the ominous impression that Ruby had a sinister reason for being present, Belli asked, "Knowing him as the character that he was…you wouldn't be surprised at anything that he would say; whether he was the reporter for the *Israeli Bugle* or interpreting for the *Paris Match*, would you?"

And, "Did you know at that time that he had his pistol that he regularly carried and this money he was protecting with the pistol?" He did not know that Ruby carried a pistol, Lieutenant Leonard replied, but far more importantly than that, the jury now heard it, and Belli had provided for them a believable explanation for why Ruby was carrying a weapon.

The prosecution next placed Ruby outside the county jail

Saturday afternoon, about an hour before Oswald was initially scheduled to be transferred. A TV reporter named Wes Wise had a conversation with him there and noticed, he said, that when Ruby discussed some gifts that were to be presented to Kennedy he had "tears in his eyes."

The defense pretty much ignored that, instead using the witness to testify about Ruby's mental condition. Wise had known Ruby for several years and seen him often at prizefights. Tonahill asked him if Ruby had told him about a Barney Ross fight in which "he bet against Barney and Barney had won the fight...and he passed out and had a blackout seizure after Barney won?" If the defense could prove that Ruby had episodes during which he had blacked out, that would make it far more believable that it had happened again when he shot Oswald. Wise had heard the story, but he couldn't recall if he'd heard it directly from Ruby or someone else. But he did agree that Ruby was a "highly excitable individual."

Tonahill probed a few other areas without much success, until his final question. A day later, when Oswald was again scheduled to be transferred, Wise had been standing outside the jail with several hundred other people when word spread that Oswald had been shot. Tonahill asked, "Didn't loud cheers go up?"

It made no difference that the state's objection prevented Wise from answering that commentary in the form of a question.

The beginning of a trial is like the opening round of a boxing match; the two sides jab at each other, trying to figure out their strategy, probing for their vulnerable points. The prosecution had spent the morning session establishing a timeline that would be useful later, using the fact that Ruby kept showing up at places Oswald was being held to show his obsession with Oswald and hint at his darker motive. The defense had used those same witnesses to begin its portrayal of Ruby as the odd guy you see around the neighborhood, the one everybody knows is sort of strange, but usually is harmless—until he loses his temper.

Missing from this first session was the rancor and bitterness between the attorneys that had marked the bail and change of venue hearings. Most trials are local, the participants live and work regularly in the area and even get to know their opponents. Not here. Belli was a hired gun who had come to town, and Wade and Alexander had every intention of making him skedaddle with his tail between his legs.

By lunchtime, Wade reportedly considered the entire morning wasted, sarcastically telling Alexander, "This afternoon let's put on some witnesses for the prosecution." To emphasize his unhappiness he decided to take over the questioning. And that placed him in a very unusual situation for a trial lawyer; that afternoon he had to question his first witness about his very own actions.

CHAPTER SIX

Dallas Morning News reporter John Rutledge covered the police department at night. On the night of the Kennedy assassination, he testified, he saw Jack Ruby on the third floor of the police station. He'd heard about Ruby for several years; he knew his reputation. All the people who spent time in Dallas's after-hours world knew about Jack. When Rutledge saw him, Ruby had slipped into the station with "a mass of newspaper and television reporters and cameramen, jammed in like sardines in a can on this floor."

He recalled Ruby identifying ranking law enforcement officers for the out-of-town media. Sometime after midnight Oswald had been brought into the room for a few moments and answered several questions. "When he was gone," Wade asked Rutledge, "the press then started asking me some questions. I was there, was I not?"

The witness agreed with the district attorney; he had been

there. Rutledge also recalled Ruby had been standing directly in front of him while Wade answered questions.

A reporter had asked Wade about rumors Oswald had some involvement in a Cuban exile movement. "I believe I answered something about the Free Cuba movement…didn't I?"

You did, Rutledge agreed, remembering. "That's the time he answered the question before you could answer it… You had it a little bit wrong and he knew it and he straightened you out on it." Ruby had corrected the DA, shouting out the proper name of the organization. "Fair Play for Cuba Committee." A picture of Jack Ruby's movements was beginning to emerge: he had successfully inserted himself at the center of the chaos, confident enough to interrupt the district attorney in front of the media.

Once Wade finished, Belli sat calmly at the defense table as he began his cross-examination. That must have been a really crowded room, he pointed out, and clearly there was tight security. "And yet Mr. Wade and all of these people allowed this man, who was the manager of a strip tease joint, to explain to people from out of town…" He paused, withdrew that question and asked Rutledge how he would characterize Ruby.

"…A loud-mouthed extrovert," the reporter answered quickly, "that just came up there to get right in the middle of that pack…" Belli asked if he meant that derisively. "In a sense I do," he replied, then suggested a reason for his feelings. "He was packed in the midst of a mass of men, who were crowded together so tight you could hardly breathe and, he seemed to me, I recall, he seemed to enjoy being pressed in amongst all those men."

That was the first overt suggestion that Ruby might be…a homosexual. There would be more. The Texas constitution outlawed sodomy; it was a crime to have homosexual relations in the state. The innuendo that Ruby might be gay was a slur in Dallas in that era, and it was meant to be.

Belli carefully peeled back layers from the witness's reserve so that he revealed his own feelings. Ruby was "mean," Rutledge said, although admittedly he had never met him personally. The things he had heard about him "didn't strike me as being anything intelligent." And he did things that "I wouldn't do myself."

"Well," Belli said, helping him, "we characterize you as normal, of course."

"Thank you."

Rutledge saw Ruby several times during that same night. Asked to pinpoint the locations in relation to different offices, he offered to draw a diagram on a blackboard. Belli thought that was reasonable and asked Judge Brown. But the judge was adamant; he wasn't having that kind of prop in his courtroom. "In twenty years, Counsel," he explained, "I have never had a blackboard in my courtroom. Let him describe it."

It had been a hectic night. Rutledge recalled being in the basement of the police building along with Ruby and others when Wade walked in.

Belli asked with genuine-fake wonder, "When Mr. Wade came in, did his friend Jack say hello to him?"

Wade objected, claiming, "I never had seen the man before. He keeps saying 'friend.'"

Belli didn't hesitate. "This man that he had never seen before, being introduced as Mr. Wade…did Mr. Ruby say anything to him?"

"Ruby said… 'Here comes Henry Wade now.' And he turned around and said, 'Henry! Henry. Come over here.'"

Just to make sure the jury heard that, the suddenly hard of hearing Belli asked him, "Would you repeat that. I didn't hear you. What did he say, 'Here comes Mr. Wade now?'"

"No. I think he said, 'Henry! Henry!'"

When Belli was done, the prosecution had no additional questions. But as Rutledge stood Belli stopped him to put more words in Henry Wade's mouth. "When the District Attorney, Mr. Wade, was talking about the Fair Play for Cuba Committee…is that the time that Mr. Wade said that Oswald should be given the electric chair?"

Objection.

Sustained. Yet another of Belli's subtle digs at Wade had landed. During a handful of press conferences before Oswald's death, Wade had said that he couldn't comment on the evidence against Oswald for fear of prejudicing the jury pool, but then proceeded to do just that.

A parking lot attendant, Garnett Claude Hallmark, testified for the prosecution that Jack Ruby had parked a car in his lot on Saturday afternoon about 2:50 p.m. Ruby made a phone call and Hallmark had heard him tell the person he was talking to that Oswald was going to be moved from the city jail to the county jail. He didn't know when that transfer would take place, but "He told whoever he was talking to that he would be there." Since Hallmark could not identify who was on the other end of the line, Ruby informing, or even assuring, someone he would be there for the transfer would provide additional fodder for those who believed in a larger conspiracy.

Hallmark had known Ruby for several years and, once it was his turn with the witness, Tonahill tried without success to ask him whether Ruby was sane or insane. "Do you think Jack may be a little off balance?" he asked. Objection. Opinion. "A little bit mentally off balance?" Objection. Opinion. "A person of sound or unsound mind?" Objection. Opinion.

When Wade got the witness back for redirect examination, he snapped, "You told me you wouldn't testify he was insane, didn't you?"

"I said I could not testify that he was insane."

Now that the prosecution had raised the subject of Ruby's sanity, the defense could try to dig into it. The prosecution continued to object to every approach, but finally Tonahill got his question into the record. "Didn't you tell both Mr. Wade and I, and the investigator, that in light of the subsequent events you sometimes wondered about Jack's sanity?... Particularly having known Jack in the past three years before that?"

"Yes."

Western Union clerk Doyle Lane was scheduled to be a key witness for the defense, but Wade tried to blunt the impact of the testimony by calling him as part of the prosecution case. He would testify that Ruby was in the telegraph office sending a money order only four minutes before he killed Oswald. And since it was impossible for Ruby to have known precisely when the police were going to move Oswald, this was compelling evidence that Ruby had not planned the killing in advance. And if he hadn't plotted it, if he hadn't stalked Oswald, it could be more difficult to prove malice. Without malice there was no death penalty. So rather than allowing the defense to put the clerk on the stand in dramatic fashion, Wade called him late in the afternoon, when the jurors were tired and hot and a sense of malaise lay over the courtroom.

Wade asked Lane a series of perfunctory questions, carefully avoiding establishing a time frame. Ruby was just another customer, Lane said, acting normally. Nothing seemed unusual.

Belli began his cross-examination by cutting right to the salient point: "Mr. Lane, you saw Mr. Ruby about three minutes before he shot Mr. Oswald, fixing it in point of time?"

Wade and Alexander objected simultaneously: "That would be a conclusion," Alexander said. "He should testify of his own knowledge," Wade said.

What mattered was the evidence: A receipt time-stamped four minutes prior to the shooting. There was no way they could keep it out of the record.

"We know the exact time that Mr. Ruby was there because of the stamping on the receipt. Is that correct?" Belli asked again.

"That is correct."

Question by question, detail by detail, Belli prolonged the testimony, giving it the sense of importance the defense needed it to have: Did Ruby come in alone? Did he seem normal? He wanted to send the twenty-five dollars to Karen Bennett in Fort Worth? He wasn't fumbling with money or in a state of agitation? He appeared to be cool, calm and outwardly collected at the time, didn't he? Karen Bennett got the money? You gave him a receipt? Until, "Will you tell the ladies and gentlemen of the jury the date, the month, the day, the hour and the exact minute that you stamped this, and that Jack Ruby was still in the Western Union Station?"

"November 24, 11:17 a.m., 1963."

"...and that could have been as much as 11:17, fifty-nine seconds, one second before 11:18?"

"It could have been."

Tom Howard, who had left the defense team, probably smiled when he heard about this exchange. It provided strong confirmation that Ruby had acted on impulse, but Howard was gone and so was that defense.

Belli continued. Ruby had not left the office in a rush, he'd walked out of there leisurely. He certainly was not a man on a mission. "And there was nothing hurried about his walking...and then, within two and a half to three minutes Oswald was dead."

"Yes, sir."

Next up was Ray Brantley, who owned a sporting goods store and four years earlier had sold Ruby the snub-nosed lightweight Colt Cobra two-inch blue pistol that he had used to shoot Oswald. Brantley's function was to identify the pistol so it could be entered into evidence. In an effort to create drama, Alexander opened a manila envelope and the murder weapon dropped onto the wooden prosecution table with a thud. That got the attention of every spectator in the courtroom.

Tonahill began his cross-examination by once again attempting to highlight the personal involvement of the prosecution, asking, "Have you ever sold any guns to Mr. Alexander, the Assistant District Attorney?"

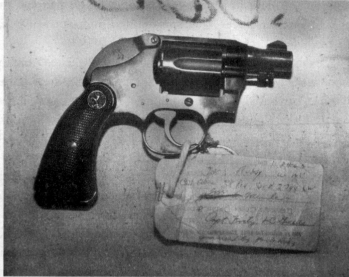

Ruby had purchased the snub-nosed .38-caliber Colt Cobra revolver he used to kill Lee Harvey Oswald for $62.50 in 1960. It was sold at auction in 1991 for $220,000. The new owners fired bullets from the gun, had them mounted on commemorative plaques and sold them.

One or two, Brantley answered.

And then Tonahill created his own drama, asking how the pistol was fired. Brantley pointed at the ceiling and pulled the trigger.

The loud click echoed through the otherwise silent courtroom.

"Do it again, will you?"

Again, the snap of the empty gun being fired: *Click! Click!* It was an ominous, metallic sound. There was little doubt most of the people sitting there were imagining that weapon being fired in the basement of police headquarters.

"Do it several more times," Tonahill requested. That done, the attorney made several more points: Brantley confirmed that Ruby had told him he was buying the gun "because he operated a nightclub and kept large sums of money on his person," and that he may have been accompanied by a police officer when he made the purchase.

Alexander, during his redirect examination, elicited from the witness the precise type of weapon, a hunting rifle, that Alexander had purchased from him, adding, "It was a bargain. I have enjoyed it very much."

Tonahill responded to that, wondering, "You sold him a rifle in addition to a pistol I take it, Mr. Brantley."

"I don't recall any pistol," Brantley responded, but the thought was planted in the jurors' and spectators' minds: that must be true; you can't just make up things like that in a courtroom.

There is an art to presenting a case. It is never a question of simply putting all your witnesses on the stand and letting them tell their story. A case, just like great theater, builds. The prosecution had been diligent in scheduling its witnesses. Just as it tried to bury Doyle Lane in the lethargy of a warm afternoon courtroom, it waited until the end of the day to call a most compelling witness, Detective J. R. Leavelle, who had been handcuffed to Lee Harvey Oswald when he was shot by Jack Ruby. Detective Leavelle has become a part of history as the man seen in the famed photo of the shooting right next to Oswald, wearing a tan suit and a Texas-sized hat. And while his own experience of being part of this murder certainly woke up the courtroom, it was what he had to add about it that startled the defense.

"I handcuffed his right wrist to my left," Detective Leavelle remembered. "...We hesitated just inside the office door until we could ascertain if the security was okay... I could see the area was lit up... I actually had two sets of handcuffs on him... there were a number of floodlights shining directly on us as we proceeded out to where the car was to pick us up...

"...there was a man came from the crowd of reporters and photographers and police officers too...when he first dashed from the crowd I saw that he had a pistol in his right hand, and was raising it... I reached to try to catch the man by the shoulder... [after he fired the gun Oswald] grunted and hollered and said 'Oh,' and slumped to the floor... I had to go down with him... I was watching the gun...the right hand was still contracting on the gun as if he was attempting to fire another shot. I had to swing Lee Harvey Oswald back behind me so that I was between this man and Oswald...soon as I saw that [Detective] Graves did have hold of his gun hand... I turned my attention back to Oswald and with the assistance of another officer picked him up and carried him back inside the jail office..." Alexander showed him a still photo of the moment Oswald had been shot and Leavelle confirmed it. "This is the actual shooting of Lee Harvey Oswald."

Alexander plumbed the witness for his memories, taking him through the historic events. The officer sat straight in the witness chair, occasionally leaning forward as he responded. Detective Leavelle identified Ruby as the man he saw that day, the man who had fired the fatal shot. He had known Ruby, he said, for eight or ten years, since he had a place over on South Ervay.

After carrying Oswald back inside, the officers had examined his wound. The bullet entered on Oswald's left side, about halfway up the rib cage. After that he saw Ruby standing at the elevators under arrest. Alexander asked a simple question that opened up a major issue: "What, if anything, did Jack Ruby say that you heard?"

As the witness began his answer Tonahill objected, loudly, "He was under arrest Your Honor...this is a violation of his constitutional rights."

Belli was furious. "...I do know that once a man has been arrested in Texas the constitutional right is that whatever he says, or whatever is asked of him, is not reportable."

So began a legal argument that was to continue throughout the trial and appeal, a right that had yet to be settled in American jurisprudence: The right against self-incrimination. The Fifth Amendment stated clearly, "No person…shall be compelled in any criminal case to be a witness against himself." It is a fundamental right. But exactly what that meant and how it might be applied had been the subject of debate for almost two centuries.

In colonial America the accused often were compelled to testify against themselves, and the methods to compel these "confessions" at times included torture. An accused person had few rights; he or she was not permitted counsel to represent them or to call witnesses in their defense. British law began recognizing the rights of a defendant at the turn of the eighteenth century. Theodore Barlow wrote in his 1745 *The Justice of Peace: A Treatise containing the Power and Duty of that Magistrate*, "The Law of England is a Law of Mercy and does not use the Rack or Torture to compel criminals to accuse themselves; since these methods are cruel and at the same time uncertain as being rather trials of strength and hardiness of the sufferer than any proof of the truth, by the confession that is extorted from him… The Law has therefore wisely and mercifully laid down this maxim: *Nemo tenetur seipsum prodere.*"

No one is bound to incriminate himself.

Most Americans had become familiar with that Fifth Amendment right against self-incrimination in 1950 and 1951, when Tennessee senator Estes Kefauver held fourteen televised hearings investigating organized crime in America. Those hearings at the time were the most popular events in television history, attracting more viewers than the World Series, and are credited with feeding the explosion of television across the nation. Several of the nation's most fabled gangsters were summoned by the committee, among them Frank Costello, Vito Genovese and Bugsy Seigel. Most of them refused to answer the committee's questions, repeating over and over, "I respectfully decline to answer because I honestly believe my answer might tend to incriminate me." Or, simply, "I'm taking the Fifth." The "Big Tuna," Chicago boss Tony Accardo, took the Fifth more than 170 times during his appearance. By the end of these hearings, Kefauver had become one of the best known politicians in America and "taking the Fifth" became a popular catchphrase and punch line.

The difficulty was that the law remained vague on how broadly that right might be applied. The application of that right had evolved over many decades of American jurisprudence, but it had come to be generally accepted that little an accused person said after being arrested could be used against him. The Texas Code of Criminal Procedure also was clear on the matter: nothing said by a defendant "while he is in the custody of a police officer" is admissible evidence unless a statement was made voluntarily before a judge or written down and signed. It seemed a pretty explicit statute.

But there was an exception to that right known as *res gestae*, or literally "things done." Basically, this meant that statements concurrent with the event, or arising during the passions of the moment, are allowed to be used as evidence against the defendant. This sort of immediate statement therefore would be more implicitly reliable, far less likely to be tainted or coerced, and, in effect, part of the act itself. The concept of res gestae could be traced back 270 years to a 1693 English case, *Thompson and Wife v. Trevanion*. This was a battery case in which Lord Chief Justice Holt ruled that "what the wife said immediately upon the hurt received, and before that she had time to contrive or devise anything for her own advantage, to be given in evidence."

This theory is vaguely comparable to the Texas statute that made homicide justifiable under certain conditions as long as the accused had maintained sight of the victim. But the moment of passion, and the right to kill, ended when visual contact was lost. In the same manner, any statements made while in the heat of the crime could be used, while anything said once it had ended and the accused was in custody was considered protected by the Fifth Amendment.

But here Wade intended to test the limits of the rule. He wanted, maybe even needed, these statements overheard by Leavelle if he was going to demonstrate to the jury that Ruby had premeditated the crime.

Belli objected strenuously, saying that Ruby's comments were inadmissible. Judge Brown did not agree: "I believe it is to be part of the res gestae, and the court will so hold." Glancing at the defense table he concluded, "You may have an exception."

Exception, in this legal usage, means simply that the objecting party wants it noted that they do not agree with the judge's ruling and intend to make that known to the appellate court.

Both Belli and Tonahill continued to object, but Judge Brown remained firm in his decision. Alexander asked the witness once again, "What did you hear Ruby say?"

"He said, 'I hope the son of a bitch dies.'"

Leavelle then told the court he had attempted to converse with the dying Oswald. "His eyes were mostly closed... I asked him if he had anything to say, wanted any particular person notified, or whatever he might have to say...

"...He never did."

Detective Leavelle had accompanied Oswald to Parkland Hospital until, as Alexander asked, "What are the facts as to whether or not Lee Harvey Oswald did die?"

"Yes sir, he did." The defense did not object to that question. This was part of the chain of identification for the bullet that killed Oswald, showing exactly what happened to it, then finally having Leavelle acknowledge that it was the bullet, then entering it into the record as State's Exhibit #10.

Belli began his cross-examination by suggesting Ruby said, "I hope the son of a bitch dies" three or four minutes after the shooting. "I would estimate it would be approximately one minute," the detective corrected him. But then Belli tried to add context, asking, "When Jack said, 'I hope the son of a bitch dies' that could have been followed by someone saying, 'Jack, you son of a bitch, you shot Oswald… Right?"

"You could assume that."

"…and there were other people…that said, 'Oswald is shot, Oswald is shot.' Right?"

"That's what I understand, yes."

"And that was before Jack said, 'I hope the son of a bitch dies'?" Belli was beginning his effort to sow confusion about who said what, and when.

He moved on to another subject, the finger Ruby used to pull the trigger. He was trying to establish the fact that rather than his index finger, Ruby used his middle finger. His purpose, it would later be revealed, was to show Ruby was in a sort of trance when he pulled the trigger, as evidenced by this seemingly unnatural action. More than that, he suggested, even after firing a shot and being dragged down, Ruby continued to try to pull the trigger as if acting automatically, "Ruby then was still trying to shoot, wasn't he…"

"The hand was…"

"Convulsing?"

"The hand was contracting or whatever you want to call it."

"And that hand was pointing at the deck and it was still pulling? Right?"

"It wasn't snapping, no."

"…Ruby then wasn't pointing at Oswald, but he was still trying to pull the trigger, wasn't he?"

"That is the way it appears there."

Belli continued, suggesting Ruby was "in the state of trying still to pull the trigger…" Then he used the witness to estimate the amount of time it took to walk from the Western Union office "down into the ramp, down into the police station," suggesting, "It takes about three minutes." If Ruby was intending to shoot Oswald, his question implied, he sure didn't give himself any extra time. Belli was on his feet as he asked his questions, strolling around the courtroom, creating a rhythm.

Wade interrupted that rhythm. "Judge, I think he can ask questions sitting at that table over here."

Judge Brown agreed. "I think so too."

From his seat, Belli asked the detective, casually, if he knew "who got the dog he had left in his car." It was a statement asked as a question. Previously the defense had established that Ruby so deeply loved his dogs that he spoke of them as his family. Certainly if he had been on a mission to shoot Oswald he never would have left a beloved dog locked in his car, where it might not be discovered for a substantial time. The meaning of that question was obvious: When Ruby parked his car he had no plan to kill a man.

In fact, Belli continued, "The transfer time was ten o'clock you were first told, and then it was changed?" Again, if Ruby had set out to shoot Oswald, he would have been waiting at the police station, not making a Western Union transfer across the street well after eleven o'clock.

"I was informed it would be sometime around ten in the morning."

"And it was on radio and TV too, wasn't it...and then for the benefit of the press it was moved up to eleven something?"

Leavelle had proved a good foil for the defense to make important points. He was there, close enough to see the blankness in the killer's eyes. The expression on Ruby's face when he attacked Oswald "was as calm as if he were sitting in court." His boast, "I hope the son of a bitch dies" was said "in a normal tone of voice." He was "more or less in a blank appearance."

During the prosecution's redirect examination, Alexander also used the witness to counter earlier testimony: It was so noisy people had to scream to be heard. It was not possible to determine which finger was on the trigger from the film or photograph, even using a magnifying glass. Leavelle didn't really notice the expression on Ruby's face because he was focusing on the gun. Then he staged his own demonstration with the murder weapon: "Will you pull the trigger?" Once again the ominous *click!* echoed through the courtroom. Alexander then grasped the gun's revolving cylinder and asked him to fire it again.

Leavelle strained to do so. The silence was telling.

Both sides had used Leavelle to build their case. It was a carefully planned dance the lawyers were performing, meant to appear spontaneous, in which each movement had a meaning and required a response. The immediate audience was the group of twelve sitting in the courtroom occasionally fanning away the heat and at times struggling to stay fully awake; both sides also were playing to the greater public and the defense was dutifully compiling the court record it would need if it became necessary to appeal the decision.

Earl Forrest Rose, the Dallas County medical examiner who officially determined the cause of Oswald's death, then testified that the victim had died of a gunshot wound. As obvious as that was, it was legally necessary to complete the prosecution's case: Ruby bought a gun. Ruby was at the crime scene. Oswald had been killed by a single shot. The bullet that killed him had been fired by Ruby from that gun. Lee Harvey Oswald's corpse was positively identified by his mother and his wife.

Alexander guided his witness through a tour of Oswald's wounds, asking for example, "if the bullet wound was approximately horizontal to the ground if the body had been standing when shot?" The gory details were obviously meant to impress the jurors by showing the brutality of the crime, an important factor when considering whether or not to vote for the death penalty. "Just tell us what organs were involved": the spleen; the stomach; the vena cava; the aorta; the right kidney and the liver.

In other words, Ruby's one shot had killed Lee Harvey Oswald.

Melvin Belli had made his fortune dressing down medical

experts and while there was little to be gained with Dr. Rose, he did not pass up the opportunity to display his knowledge. "The only thing I wanted to ask you about was the air embolus. Wasn't there a cardiac air embolus that you noticed? Even from seeing the massive internal hemorrhage of [the organs] to your knowledge in these cases, it would have been impossible to save this man by any surgery?"

"It would have been impossible. Yes sir."

With that, court was recessed to end the first day. For the participants though, the day was far from over. Just as a Broadway show is the culmination of countless hours of preparation and rehearsal, a trial is the end result of days and weeks and months of preparation, research, investigation and interviewing. That work didn't end with the trial day; after court concluded the attorneys gathered in their "war rooms" to rehash the events and plan strategy for the following day, reviewing information about scheduled witnesses and searching for ways to shore up the vulnerabilities that had been exposed. They worked late into the night, every night.

For the jurors, life was far more dreary. The jury was sequestered, completely removed from normal life. They were housed in open jail cells on the seventh floor of the building. These "bedrooms" were eight feet square and equipped with a bed with a thin mattress, a sink and a toilet. Their access to the outside world was severely limited to prevent them from being influenced by family, friends or the media. For the first people selected, this spartan existence had already been their life for two weeks or more.

For this they were paid eight dollars per day—although they were charged one dollar a meal.

Everything they did was done together. They moved as a group to the dry cleaners, to barbershops and the beauty salon, to restaurants and diners, voting to decide where they would eat. In restaurants they were shielded from other patrons. For

entertainment they played cards, dominoes and a popular combination of both known as "Texas 42." The former naval officer,
Waymon Rose, claimed he learned how to play four different
kinds of solitaire, while Mrs. Mildred McCollum used the time
to get her taxes done.

They were permitted to watch some TV on the one set provided for them, though they were not allowed to view any of
the courtroom dramas, like *Perry Mason* or *The Defenders*, and
the bailiff who lived with them turned off the set when the
news came on. They were not given access to complete newspapers because stories about the trial were spread throughout
the paper, although they were given access to the comics, puz-
zles and classified advertising. Any communications with their
families had to be done through the bailiff, who would be on
the phone passing messages: "He says he loves you very much."
Pause. "She says she loves you more." On several occasions family members of jurors were given seats in the spectator section.
As juror Max Causey remembered, "I got to look at my wife
across the courtroom... I cast a wistful eye in her direction and
without any signal our eyes met... She looked great to me. This
was the first time I had seen her in fifteen days."

The court had taken a substantial risk by not adding any alternate jurors to the panel. The entire trial could be upended
by the absence of any one of the twelve men and women. Early
in the proceedings Judge Brown was informed by the wife of
one of the jurors that her brother, his brother-in-law, had died.
At his wife's request, the juror was not told until after the trial.

Fortunately, the twelve jurors formed a bond and rarely had
any conflicts. One of the few disagreements occurred when juror
Alan McCoy, whose wife had sighed and told reporters when
her husband was selected, "I guess it'll take him another year
to finish our den," had her send him a portable stereo and his
favorite albums. Those albums included mostly classical music.
Meanwhile several of the other jurors got their own favorites,

including Nat King Cole and Ray Charles. Apparently at times when McCoy was outvoted on the music selections, he threatened to get rid of the stereo, claiming that "junk" music might damage it.

The attention of the world was centered on Dallas, and those select people who would decide if Jack Ruby would live or die, serve time or be set free, had no idea the extent of that scrutiny. It is one of the amazing realities of the American judicial system. These twelve people gave up their normal lives, they gave up their families and their jobs, because their number was called. "It's the right thing to do," McCoy's wife had said, "serve when you are called upon."

CHAPTER SEVEN

No trial in American history had attracted this level of world-wide attention. As Radio Prague correspondent Karel Kyncl explained, "People in Czechoslovakia heard the shot that killed Oswald just two hours after it was fired in Dallas."

An estimated four hundred journalists from around the world had been dispatched to Dallas. The corridors of the courthouse building had been transformed into a facsimile of the United Nations. Correspondents from Sweden and France, Germany and Mexico, Canada, Spain, Australia, Switzerland, Italy, Denmark and even Bulgaria, Poland and Czechoslovakia were covering the trial. Reporters from eight British newspapers, in addition to the BBC were competing for news. One of the very few international correspondents missing was a representative from the Russian News Agency TASS, and that was only because government restrictions prevented them from traveling to certain cities, so the national newspaper *Pravda* relied on reporting from other eastern European reporters and the Associated Press and UPI.

Judge Brown later wrote that he had always liked the newspapermen, but oh those cameramen. "They have no respect for public property...the damage they did to the corridors must have run into hundreds of dollars, and they ruined the furniture in...the press room."

Roughly twenty Western Union telegraph operators were transmitting more than one hundred thousand words a day around the world in more than a dozen languages. Western Union's pressroom supervisor boasted his people could transmit an average of sixty words a minute as long as they were written using English language letters. Although, he admitted, they did require significantly more time when words like the Swiss "geschworenenkandidit," meaning a jury candidate, were used.

Through this trial countless people in these countries were being introduced to the mechanisms of the American legal system, as well as the rebranded Dallas, Texas. Big D was doing its best to be accommodating to the world, showing them Texas hospitality. As his deputies escorted Ruby into the courtroom one morning, Sheriff Decker asked photographers if his people were moving too fast. If they were, he offered, "We can slow it down." And Judge Brown gave the press a long leash to enable them to do their work. And he was always happy when not in session to pose for a picture or two. Mostly, for the pictures, he took the cigar out of his mouth.

Mel Belli reveled in the attention and usually was followed wherever he went by a trail of reporters. He was a showman standing in the spotlight, happily answering every question thrown at him—all of it being captured by his own camera crew filming his documentary.

Tonahill followed his lead, taking every opportunity to reinforce the defense claim that Ruby was a sick man who could not get a fair trial in Dallas. Tonahill was too big to be overlooked and during breaks journalists gathered around him like a forest at the base of a mountain. During one brief recess, Judge

Brown stood at the back of the pack trying fruitlessly to get his attention—until in frustration he shouted, "Fire!"

No one responded.

It was obvious the defense was presenting its case not just to the jury but to the assembled media and the millions of people beyond the courtroom as the prosecution began the second day of the trial. The first witness of the day was Detective L. C. Graves, who had been holding tightly to Oswald's left arm when he was shot. The bright lights were in his eyes, so he did not see Ruby come out of the crowd. After the weapon was fired, he had grabbed it out of Ruby's hand. To make certain the jury understood, Henry Wade played the role of Ruby in a courtroom reenactment of the shooting. Using the actual murder weapon, he held it at about the same level as the defense attorneys sitting behind their table, Tonahill asked politely, "Point it a little higher, will you please, Hank?"

Wade responded, "It is not loaded."

With a smile in his voice Tonahill said, "I don't know whether that is loaded or not."

Most of Graves's testimony focused on Ruby's hand. The prosecution had him describe to the jury how Ruby continued trying to squeeze the trigger as he was being taken down. But Belli was far more interested in how he was holding the gun. "You have never seen an ex-GI in his right mind shoot one of these things with a sort of claw hand like that, have you?" Key phrase: in his right mind.

Graves agreed. "I have never seen anybody shoot one like that myself." But as far as anything else, the detective resisted agreeing with Belli that this was an unusually awkward way of firing a pistol. "It's optional with other people" was as far as he would go.

As far as taking down Ruby, the detective explained, "I got ahold of it [the gun] and twisted it down, pulled it down over my leg…"

While that was going on, Belli asked, "He was still trying to pull on it, when it was pointed at your leg, isn't that correct?" Graves agreed, and Belli said, "He wasn't mad at you, was he?"

"I hope not."

Belli was methodical with his questioning and then, as if he just happened to think of it, he wondered, "...All the time that you were there, did you hear Ruby say at any time, 'I hope the son of a bitch dies'?"

"I didn't hear him say it myself."

The witness was firm on that point. "Did you hear Leavelle say to Oswald, 'If someone shoots you, I hope they are as good a shot as you are'?"

He had not heard that either.

Belli used this witness to deal directly with the growing questions about the possible role played by the Dallas PD in this murder. The fact that Ruby had enjoyed such easy access to the police building was startling and caused people to wonder if there was a darker reason for this. It was difficult to accept that the department was simply inept. By permitting his witness to refute the conspiracy theory, he successfully raised it again. "I must ask this to clear something up," he said, while actually doing exactly the opposite. "I think you would want me to ask it. There was no connection whatsoever between the police and Ruby, was there, so that we can wrap this up and dispose of it, and put it in the incinerator—there was no connection between the Dallas Police Force and Ruby on his coming in there that morning?"

The answer should have been a flat no. But Detective Graves was either so committed to not cooperating with the defense or so precise that he said simply, "That I don't know."

"Well, as far as you were concerned, there wasn't?"

The detective refused to answer, even about himself. "I still don't know, Mr. Belli."

Just in case the jury didn't know it, "The whole police force took lie detector tests with reference to that, didn't they?" When the prosecution objected, Belli made his point to Judge Brown while unmaking it: "Is this going to be made an issue or can we stipulate that there was no connection? I would like to have this out of the case, myself, so it's not... I submit then that we have to clear it, Judge, as to whether there was any connection between Ruby coming into the jail with the connivance of the Dallas Police. I don't believe it and I want it out of the case. I want it out of the minds of anybody in the world and that's the reason I would like to get it out," he said firmly, making sure that the thought was deeply and permanently imbedded in the jurors.

Graves still refused to refute the conspiracy theory. "Personally, there was no connection between me and Jack Ruby, as to his getting into the basement... As far as anybody else is concerned, I cannot say." This nonanswer worked perfectly for the defense; Belli played the hero pretending to eliminate the pesky issue from the case and then rather than a firm denial, Detective Graves seemed to be hedging, thereby fueling the rumors.

In his final question to the witness, Belli asked about the arrangements to move Oswald. The armored car waiting at the top of the ramp was to be used as a decoy, while Oswald would be transported in a police squad car. "That was because of so many threats having been made against him, and people around the jail expressing their feelings towards Oswald, right?" Objected and sustained.

In his cross-examination, Henry Wade had the witness verify that one method of quick-draw shooting was to pull the trigger with a middle finger while using the index finger to point to the target. Graves agreed it was an accepted method, at least until Belli pointed out that if "Ruby was pointing with this finger for accuracy, then he was aiming at your leg, Officer, is that right?"

Graves was stuck, and finally said, "If he was aiming at my leg anytime, that I don't know."

During this morning session, the FBI released its annual crime study, showing that Dallas, with a record-setting 113 murders in 1963, including JFK and Oswald, had overtaken Houston as the murder capital of Texas. It was front page news in the *Chronicle*. On that same page Defense Secretary Robert McNamara said there was evidence that North Vietnam was increasing its aid to the Viet Cong guerrilla movement, further endangering the 15,500 American soldiers in South Vietnam. He refused to say whether or not the United States would support retaliation against North Vietnam.

When the afternoon session began, Wade unholstered his bigger guns. The prosecution had shown that Ruby had killed Oswald but had been much less successful proving any premeditation. The timeline presented by the defense seemed to support the argument that the shooting was the result of passion meeting opportunity, rather than having been planned. The prosecution didn't have to convince the jurors that Ruby had planned the shooting to find there was malice, but it could certainly help and they felt the evidence supported it. Wade continued in that effort by putting Detective Don Archer, a balding, somewhat pudgy, round-faced man, on the stand.

His job, Archer said, was "to secure the corridor, allow no one in but the press, and maintain safety in the basement." As a result of being assigned to protect Oswald, he was a witness to the shooting. He began by testifying he heard Ruby shout "Son of a bitch" an instant before firing his weapon. Archer then joined a group of officers that subdued Ruby and carried him into the jail office, where he was put on the floor.

"At that time," Wade asked, "did you hear the defendant, Jack Ruby, say anything…"

Tonahill objected, loudly, "We object to this, Your Honor, he was under arrest."

Judge Brown didn't hesitate. "Overrule your objection to it."

That ruling was hardly surprising based on the judge's previous ruling about the defendant's right not to incriminate himself. While the defense knew it was an argument they probably could not win in Judge Brown's Dallas courtroom, it was essential they established a record for a possible appeal. "That is clearly not admissible," Belli argued. "...Let me make my record, anything that is said after arrest, whatever it is, is not admissible. It could not be part of the res gestae, or verbal act. There is no foundation made here, no showing that it should come in..."

Once again, Brown overruled the objection.

Ironically, as this argument was taking place in Dallas, the United States Supreme Court was hearing arguments about extending all of the federal rights against compelled self-incrimination granted by the Fifth Amendment to all fifty states. While each of the states enforced some version of this protection, in some situations it was not as extensive as the federal law. In the case being argued, a Connecticut court had held a witness in contempt for refusing to answer questions, claiming he had not sufficiently shown that answering those questions would put him in jeopardy.

In Judge Brown's courtroom, Wade had the home field advantage. He knew the law, but he also had known the judge for many years. To satisfy the legal requirement of res gestae he tried to tie closely together the shooting and Ruby's comments. Detective Archer estimated they were made "just ten or twelve seconds from the time the shot was fired." This time it was Tonahill who objected. "For the reason that anything he said would be in violation of his legal and constitutional right since he was under arrest."

Judge Brown had made his decision. Eventually Archer was permitted to respond. "As we got him down on the floor there he said, 'I hope I killed the son-of-a-bitch.'"

And he shouted that, Wade reminded the jurors, "a matter of twelve seconds after the shooting, probably?"

Archer had then accompanied Ruby as he was hustled upstairs in an elevator. In that elevator, according to Archer, Ruby said...

Objection! "It would be a violation of his legal and constitutional rights."

Overruled.

"I said," Archer continued, "'I think you killed him.' He said, 'I intended to shoot him three times.'" There it was, the intent that Wade wanted, that he needed. That was a devastating attack on the defense contention that Ruby had committed the crime in some sort of psychological trance, that he hadn't been aware of his actions. Those words "I intended to shoot him three times" meant that Ruby had a memory of the crime, had no regrets for killing Oswald and had, at least to some degree, planned it.

Wade continued, "The defendant, Jack Ruby that said that… a matter of minutes after the original shooting?"

Five minutes, Archer estimated. An obviously pleased Henry Wade turned to Belli and handed him the witness. Belli began his cross-examination pleasantly, bringing the witness back to the shooting. "The fact that he had just killed a man, his face was still calm and he was still talking in a normal tone of voice, is that right?"

It was.

Belli drew the picture for the jurors. "He was still calm, he wasn't agitated, he wasn't excited, and he talked in a normal tone of voice, and he had just killed a man? Is that right?"

It was. Apparently the witness saw nothing at all unusual about that.

"It was remarkable in that it was such a peaceful looking face under the circumstances, wasn't it?"

Having never before been in such a situation, Archer responded, "I couldn't say." There was a lot of confusion at the time, he testified, but he didn't hear anyone else shouting anything at all. He was adamant; he had not heard the shouts, "Oswald is shot—Oswald is shot!" that others recalled. He did remember that while Ruby was lying on the ground someone had shouted, "'Who is it, who is it?' And the defendant stated 'You all know me. I am Jack Ruby.'"

As Belli's questioning continued, his tone became louder and more accusatory. Archer's testimony had been extremely damaging, and he had to dilute its importance. He had to raise doubt that it ever happened. Finally, he asked, "Have you gone over this with the District Attorney, your testimony." In reality there was nothing sinister about that; every prosecutor interviews their witnesses and discusses their testimony before the trial. But most jurors don't realize that, and Belli used that to suggest that Archer had been coached.

"Yes Sir, I have discussed the case with the District Attorney."

Belli's tone had turned cold. "I didn't ask if you had discussed it. I asked if you had gone over it with him?"

Three times, Archer admitted. Far more importantly, he had given a written statement to the district attorney "about the facts I have outlined here."

The defense wanted to see that statement. The prosecution did not want them to see it. Wade was clear about that. "I have never seen it myself, we don't have it and I don't think it's admissible." But he did offer to "clear this up."

This was another matter on which the law was clear. "Under the rules of evidence of any state, we are entitled to see any statement that a witness has made before he takes the stand and before Mr. Wade's clearing up," Belli said. He had no knowledge of what might be in that statement but he wanted to see it. The prosecution is not entitled to enter a statement into evidence, as it clearly could be self-serving, but the defense may have a right to see it and use it and offer it in evidence if it is inconsistent with testimony.

Judge Brown tried to settle the issue. He clarified that the defense was making a formal request for the statement—and then denied it. Technically this was likely the correct ruling since many Texas cases had determined that defense counsel was not entitled to this type of material.

Belli continued trying to attack Archer's credibility and in so doing asked one too many questions. Archer had testified earlier that he was familiar with Jack Ruby's name. Belli made the mistake of wondering why. "I was familiar with his name since our department had arrested him previously."

Belli jumped on that like he was lassoing a bull; his voice rising again he suggested, "So that won't prejudice this jury, let's tell them what he was arrested for, a misdemeanor, rape, child stealing, kidnapping?"

Archer had to admit he "was just not familiar with what he was handled for."

"You know the rules of evidence," Belli bellowed, now trying to shift blame to the witness for answering the question Belli had asked, "you are not supposed to say that a man was arrested for something else and it's a misdemeanor to prejudice the jury, don't you?"

Wade tried to protect Archer, objecting to Belli "arguing with the witness."

Judge Brown tried to end the discussion, offering to instruct the jury to disregard the comment.

"We don't want them to disregard it," Belli snapped. "You can't unring a bell." Archer was forced to admit he didn't know the nature of Ruby's legal problems, but that it did not involve "moral turpitude." In 1949 Ruby had been arrested eight different times by the Dallas PD for offenses ranging from carrying a concealed weapon to allowing dancing after hours in his clubs. Most of those were dismissed or settled with a small fine. In February 1963 he had been arrested for simple assault for his involvement in a fight at the Carousel Club and had been found not guilty. Belli tried to get back on track walking the witness through the events a step at a time. It had taken between three and five minutes to move Ruby upstairs. An estimated fourteen people had been on the elevator. Archer didn't remember any conversation. That puzzled Belli. "Well, this comes then sort of out of the clear, after they get up there, everybody quiet, and you say the man is dead and he said, 'I intended to shoot him three times.'"

Archer corrected him. "I said, 'Jack, I think you killed him.' He said, 'I intended to shoot him three times.'"

Belli was dramatically curious. Had any other officer said anything? Was it possible he said, "You son-of-a-bitch, if you hadn't grabbed my gun, I would have shot him three times?"

Archer wasn't sure. The details were kind of sketchy. "I don't know whether he did or not, sir."

"Weren't you right there?"

The confidence with which he had told his story for the prosecution had disappeared. "I was right there but I don't know."

Belli closed in. "Did you go over that with the District Attorney, that he might have said that, 'If you hadn't grabbed my gun I would have shot him three times?'"

"No Sir, I did not."

"And which District Attorney did you go over this with, these two or three times?"

"With Mr. Wade and Mr. Alexander."

"At different times?"

"Yes Sir."

"And when did you last go over it and with whom?"

"I talked with Mr. Wade this morning."

"About the subject of your testimony?"

"About the case in general, yes sir."

Archer, Belli discovered, also had been interviewed by FBI agents about the killing. He wondered, "Did you tell the FBI the same thing you told us here this morning?"

"No, Sir, I didn't." He hadn't been asked about Ruby's comments, he said.

Belli had created some doubt about the credibility of Archer's claim: the detective had met with prosecutors three times, including the morning of his testimony, to go over his story. But when interviewed earlier by the FBI he hadn't told them "that Jack Ruby told you, 'I intended to shoot him three times.'"

During a brief recess, the defense had issued a subpoena to Captain J. C. Nichols, compelling him to bring a copy of Archer's statement to court. On his way to the courtroom with the statement, Bill Alexander had stopped him and taken the statement from him.

When the trial resumed Belli was furious. "We brought it here…now this is a rather extraordinary Star Chamber attitude that they're taking…." Star Chamber referring to British Royal Courts that met without juries and ruled mostly by decree.

With the jury out of the courtroom, Belli had threatened to ask for a mistrial if the defense was not allowed to see the statement, not to introduce as evidence but just to read it. "It is in the nature of an instrument that we are entitled to see just as much we would be able to ask him, 'didn't you at another time and place say something that is different, and offer that for the purpose of impeachment'… It doesn't prove what is in that statement or disprove anything. It cancels his statement on the stand."

Judge Brown had remained firm. "I'm not going to let you have it, Mr. Belli… The Court will refuse to listen to it."

The argument became contentious. "We are being denied due process of law under the Texas Constitution and the Constitution of the United States."

"You are not," Judge Brown responded. "I don't want to hear any more about it."

Throughout all this, Jack Ruby sat quietly, occasionally glancing at the floor, nothing more than a spectator. He seemed to have little connection to the Jack Ruby being brought to life on the witness stand. Occasionally Belli or Tonahill would lean over and whisper something to him, as if to acknowledge his presence.

When the jury was brought back in, the prosecution called

Archer's partner, twenty-eight-year-old Thomas McMillon, who looked as if he had been perfectly cast for the role of police detective. He was tall, and his broad shoulders, blue eyes and blond crew cut gave him a young athletic appearance. As he took the stand he smiled at the female juror whose nephew worked for the department, and she acknowledged him with a quick wave.

McMillon was Archer's partner in the Auto Theft Bureau, though on November 24 they had been assigned to provide security as Oswald was being moved. "I saw a man dart from the crowd with a gun in his hand," he remembered. That man was the defendant, Jack Ruby, he said. But then he added an extraordinary detail, one that had not been heard in the courtroom. As Ruby leaped from the crowd, according to McMillon, "He said, 'You rat son of a bitch, you shot the president.' And then a shot rang out."

As he continued to tell his story, Belli interrupted to ask him to describe the scene. "It was very noisy," he responded. "There was TV cameras, reporters, newsmen around the place." Then, he continued, after shooting Oswald, Ruby said...

Objection! Tonahill stood. "We object to anything he said while under arrest as being in violation..."

Overruled.

McMillon continued, "He said, 'I hope I killed the son of a bitch. I hope I killed the son of a bitch.' He said it more than once... He kept hollering, 'You know me, you know me, I'm Jack Ruby.'"

Every time McMillon quoted Ruby in his testimony the defense objected. Every time. And every time they did, they were overruled. And every time they asked for and were granted an exception.

McMillon continued to add details. "Detective Archer had told him, 'Jack, I believe you killed him.' And he said that he meant to kill him, that he meant to shoot him three times, but that we had moved too fast for him and had prevented him from doing so."

Once again, Belli conducted the cross-examination. Each aspect of a trial is governed strictly by rules defining the manner in which questions can be asked. A cross-examination, for example, is limited to subjects raised during the direct questioning. Often, because by nature it is contentious, it is where the fireworks of a case are hidden. As Belli began his cross-examination, McMillon made it clear he had no intention of cooperating; he avoided answering as much as possible and when he did respond his answers were brief, limited in scope. Belli responded with disdain, putting on public display the theatrics that had earned him fame and fortune.

Belli wanted jurors to believe that it was implausible Ruby could have shouted out such a long phrase in such a brief period of time and been heard by only one person. First though, he wanted to use the witness to help clean up the lingering questions hanging over the courtroom about Ruby's criminal history. McMillon had known about Ruby, he testified cool and confidently, "I knew he had some trouble with the police before, had been arrested several times and that he did run some taverns."

When he stated he did not know why he had been arrested, Belli tried to help him. "There were no arrests for robbery, burglary, rape, mayhem, kidnapping, child molesting or sex offenses, or anything that involves moral turpitude. That's correct, isn't it." Belli suggested that Ruby's problems with the law involved liquor licenses at his clubs.

McMillon knew nothing at all about any of that, he said. Nothing. But he had discussed his testimony with prosecutors four different times. That led Belli to wonder, offhandedly, "Who was doing most of the remembering in this conversation, you or the District Attorney?"

It was later revealed that on the first night of the trial Wade had met with his witnesses as a group and discussed their testimony. In addition to urging them to testify about Ruby's statements indicating premeditation, he told them his personal theory of the crime: that Jack Ruby was a man seeking glory, a would-be hero.

McMillon seemed confused by this subtle accusation, so Belli asked him to repeat the words spoken by Ruby. "Jack said, 'Well, I meant to shoot him three times but you all moved too fast and prevented me from doing so.'"

Belli considered that, and following a pregnant pause, then said, "I thought before you said, 'I intended to shoot him three times.' He used the words, 'I meant to shoot him three times.'"

"Well, they mean the same."

Belli played with McMillon's words for the next few minutes, then asked, "This is the thing that you went over with the District Attorney four times before you took the stand. Sort of a rehearsal?"

"Part of the facts that I went over," the detective corrected sternly.

Not surprisingly, Detective McMillon also had provided a written statement to the police department, a statement in which, Belli questioned, "You have exactly what you have testified to on the witness stand, is that right?"

The statement had been written in longhand only a few hours after the shooting "regarding the incident."

The defense again asked to see that statement, and again Judge Brown told them, "The Court will refuse your request."

As the warmth of the afternoon heated up the courtroom, Belli took McMillon through the same steps as he had Archer. At some point as Ruby was being moved—he wasn't certain precisely when or where this took place—the detective testified Dallas PD captain Glen King asked the prisoner, "Of all the low life things, why did you do it?"

Wade interrupted helpfully, "I believe he said 'scum' too."

Then McMillon offered an additional incriminating recollection. "Mr. Ruby replied that somebody had to do it, somebody had to take care of him, that we couldn't do it." The "we," he explained, meant the Dallas Police Department.

Detective McMillon remembered very little else of the conversations that had taken place in those minutes following the killing. Once Belli had established that, he wondered aloud if the witness had heard Ruby asking "what am I doing here?" Meaning Ruby did not remember the event.

Having testified how little he remembered, McMillon had to concede that statements may have been made that he couldn't recall.

Belli was skilled at shaking the confidence of a witness, catching even small misstatements and nuances and turning them inside out, forcing the witness to contradict and correct himself. Once he had McMillon in that state he asked him if he had put Captain King's question in his written statement. He admitted he had not. "When did you recall that, or who helped you remember this...which of the four conversations that you had with the District Attorney, did you finally remember that... Mr. Ruby answered, 'Someone had to do it?' ...Did it take to the fourth conversation before you remembered that?"

"That fact came out the second time I discussed the case."

At that moment the court recessed for lunch. Upon resumption, Belli's first question to McMillon was, "Did you talk with anyone during the noon hour about this case?"

"Mr. Wade, Mr. Alexander, Mr. Bowie of the District Attorney's office." And what did they discuss? "Facts that I could testify to and some that I had already testified to."

As they bantered about the facts, with Belli trying to make the point that the witness had been coached by the prosecution, Bill Alexander actually helped him, telling McMillon, "Go ahead and tell the man."

Belli responded with faux innocence, "I didn't hear what Mr. Alexander said. What are the instructions that Mr. Alexander gave the witness?" As the prosecutors erupted, Belli said calmly to the judge, "Let's do this, let's see what they're trying to bait this man with, so that…"

More and louder objections drowned him out.

McMillon said he had been instructed to tell the truth. Belli asked if that was what he had been told to say if questioned about a lunchtime meeting. Naturally he denied it, but the suggestion hung in the air.

It got worse for the witness. He was shown a photograph in which he was separated from Oswald by several people and yet, Belli wondered, with all that noise how might he have heard Ruby's comments. "The sound would have had to come through all these men in front of you, wouldn't it?"

"Well, I was looking straight at him."

Belli showed him the photograph in which "You're looking the other way."

"I am, according to the picture."

With mock confusion Belli suggested, "Well, according to you. The picture may be wrong."

"I don't know if the picture is wrong or not, but I looked around from this way…" McMillon had become so defensive he refused to acknowledge the picture was taken after Oswald had been shot—even though Oswald was holding his side. Belli continued, demonstrating for the jury that there was always at least one person between the witness and Oswald, making it dubious that in a noisy, crowded corridor that he could have heard Ruby's words.

In fact, later in his questioning he asked specifically, "But you could hear him very plainly, couldn't you? Above all the din and all of the tumult and all of the noise, you could hear him very plainly enunciate these words that you've told us, couldn't you?"

"What I testified here I did hear, yes sir."

McMillon tried to hold his ground against Belli, at one point correcting him by explaining that Ruby had never been thrown on the ground, rather he was thrown on the concrete floor. Belli mocked him, asking, "Was he on the ground, floor, deck or covering that we walk upon at any time…"

When McMillon struggled to avoid answering directly, Belli asked him, "Do you have the question in mind?"

"I think I do," McMillon conceded. "I thought I heard you."

"Could you answer it?"

"I'm trying," the detective said.

Belli returned to the written reports McMillon had filed, confirming that the statements he'd made on the stand were not in them, "not worded exactly as you have put it."

"Are the statements you have given us here, to the ladies and gentlemen of the jury, 'I hope I killed the son of a bitch,' are those in your report?"

"Yes, sir."

"All of them?"

"Everything I've testified to is covered in my report."

Belli was on uncertain ground; having not seen these reports it was dangerous to make them too important. He asked, "And is the statement in there about 'you scum, why did you do this?' in your report?"

"No sir, it isn't… I don't know if that's the only thing [not in there] or not."

The concept that any detective could have left this pertinent information out of one report, much less three different reports, was ideal fodder for Belli. Later he asked him why he had left out this important information, directly attacking the witness's credibility by adding, twice, "if it happened."

"It's one of the things that I didn't recall. There's some more things that I didn't recall, too, so I'm sure they must have happened, but I didn't see them or hear them or didn't know about them."

The exchange got progressively nastier as McMillon repeatedly testified he didn't remember information and Belli continued to challenge him. Asked about Ruby's appearance the detective said, "Parts of his face—including his forehead—was red."

To which Belli suggested, with a dose of sarcasm, "There's only so many parts to a face, so could you tell us which parts were red?"

The abrasion on his forehead, the detective said, "was redder than the rest of his face."

McMillon remained an elusive witness, unsure of when or where the statements he quoted were made or who was present to hear them. Over and over he responded: "What was the question," "I don't understand your question," "I don't recall," "I'm not certain," "I don't remember when." In response to the witness's failure to remember a key moment, Belli suggested, "This is the one thing that isn't just memorized by you, isn't it, Sir?"

In addition to suggesting that this witness had been carefully coached by the prosecution, Belli used McMillon to remind jurors that Ruby had left his beloved dog in the car—a strong indication he intended to be back in that car within minutes rather than under arrest for murder. In addition to puncturing a hole in the premeditation theory, it offered the defense the added benefit of portraying Ruby as an animal lover. "He did tell us that he had a dog parked over in the parking lot somewhere, in the car across the street," McMillon said, but he couldn't recall the dog's name or the details of the conversation.

After a few more "I don't know," "I don't remember," "I don't recall," "I don't understand the question" responses, Belli returned to McMillon's critical "somebody had to do it, you guys couldn't do it" statement. "That wasn't in your original report," Belli noted. "You made two other statements...you talked with the FBI twice... In none of these, until you come to the second conversation with Mr. Alexander, did you mention the subject of low life scum. Fair enough?"

McMillon objected, remembering suddenly that he had included it in his departmental report.

Belli asked if that's what the witness had discussed during lunch with the district attorney. The witness admitted he had discussed that point. Asked what he said about it, he looked at Belli and said, "I don't recall how that conversation went, sir."

This was Belli at his best in a courtroom, using a witness's testimony against him. It was the kind of cross-examination Perry Mason conducted every week on TV. Belli was up and down and at times began walking around the courtroom, only to be reminded by Judge Brown to take his seat. Belli apologized, explaining it was difficult to shake that habit. "I'll help you, Mr. Belli," Judge Brown offered.

"I know you will," Belli agreed, and turned his attention to the witness. "Would you try and recollect back now about an hour and a half, and see if you can't give us the substance of the conversation?" Belli had McMillon cornered and the witness continued to claim he didn't remember, didn't understand the question, didn't recall where and when and who. Belli made it clear for him. "In the departmental investigation did you say what you have told us here, that Captain King said to Ruby, and what Ruby said back to him?"

"No, sir."

"When was the first time that you told anybody about that, that you heard that, allegedly?"

"I don't know when the first time was. I discussed the case some with the officers that were in the jail with me that day."

"Did you discuss that with them in jail that day?"

"I don't recall if I did or not."

He also did not discuss it with the FBI, which Belli found astonishing. "In the department investigation, in the daily press and the FBI, they all wanted to know if there was any connection between Ruby and the police department... Didn't you think that this was important, if it did happen, that Ruby said, 'You guys couldn't do it, I did it for you.' Didn't you think that would be sort of a solution to when they asked you that question, particularly the FBI?"

"Regarding the what, sir?" And then, "That question wasn't asked to me during this investigation word for word like you've asked it."

Belli might just as well have been speaking directly to the jury when he asked, "...if you really knew, and Ruby had said that, wouldn't you have thought that it would have been extremely important to say that he said, 'If you guys couldn't do it, someone had to do it for you?'"

"I didn't remember at the time."

"That's all," Belli said. It had been a tough day for him. He had made a strong effort to cast doubt on the witnesses' claims, but their words hung in the humid late afternoon air. Police officers were respected in Dallas, and if they raised their right hand and swore that they had heard these words it was going to be mighty hard to "unring that bell." But the afternoon was about to get worse.

District Attorney Wade stunned the defense by offering as evidence two statements made by Detective McMillon. Precisely the documents the court had forbidden the defense to see. The reason, Alexander claimed later, was that Belli had threatened to appeal the ruling and "The liberal Supreme Court would probably force us."

Belli was flabbergasted. Irate. That was it, as far as he was concerned. He had been led into the prosecution's trap. This was a legal conundrum: The defense had no idea what was in these reports, and was not given an opportunity to read them before they were entered into evidence, but if they challenged these reports, the jurors would wonder why they had done so after fighting so hard to see them. The obvious inference was that they included some damning information the defense did not want the jurors to know. "We ask for a new trial at this time," Belli said, his lips pursed with anger. "And very sincerely would like to argue this motion for a mistrial… We have not seen this statement, I don't know what's in it…it will be self-serving.

"Now, if I were to stand up and say, after asking to see the statement, that I don't want it in evidence the jury, being unlettered in the law, might think that I am not sincere…"

Not surprisingly, his motion was overruled. Judge Brown then asked if the defense objected to the statement being entered as evidence. After a discussion, the defense did object to it—and only then did Wade decide, sure go ahead, "We have no objection to the defense using it."

This ploy was repeated with Archer's statement. When Tonahill pointed out that this was the same statement that Bill Alexander had taken from Captain Nichols "and refused to permit us to see," Bowie claimed, "There were no such statements made and the record won't reflect any…"

Tonahill politely called Bowie a liar, suggesting they call Nichols to make "this statement he just made, a pure, one-hundred percent falsehood."

The trial was careening out of Judge Brown's control. The court had lost track of which side was entitled to examine Mc-Millon. When the judge ruled that Belli "had passed" the witness, the attorney responded sarcastically, "It's probably my unfamiliarity with Texas law." It was meant as an insult.

Before the prosecution could begin its redirect, Belli asked for the original statements. "These may be as valid as a laundry ticket," he said. "I have no way of knowing whether these are authentic… Are we back in the Middle Ages Judge, that we can't see the original of a document?"

McMillon's memory improved greatly in response to Wade's questions. To dispel any suggestion that the Dallas PD was in cahoots with Ruby, McMillon was asked the question so many had wondered: How was Ruby able to gain access to the fortified police station where Oswald was being held? He testified that Ruby said he had wandered into the station through a door opened to allow a squad car to leave. "He said someone hollered at him," McMillon recalled. "Did he say he kept on walking," Wade asked. "Yes sir." And with that one of the great mysteries of the Oswald killing had been addressed. At least for the time being.

When Belli got the opportunity to question McMillon again, he homed in on his written statement. "And in that report," Belli pointed out, "you don't say anything about what Captain King is supposed to have said to Ruby...secondly, you don't say anything about Ruby saying he intended to shoot him three times either, do you?"

McMillon didn't flinch. "I didn't remember that when I wrote my first one."

Belli was in attack mode, practically bursting out of his seat. Judge Brown had to remind him repeatedly, "Take your seat, counsel."

It was in McMillon's second statement, which he had dictated, that he struck gold. In this statement, Belli continued, "he said, 'Y'all won't believe this, but I didn't have this planned.' Is that right?"

"Yes, sir."

"'I couldn't have planned it so perfect.' Right?"

"Right." McMillon tried to back away from his dictated statement; if it was in the report, he admitted, he'd said it—but he just couldn't remember it at this moment. When Belli pointed out his claim that Ruby had said he intended to fire three shots was not included in his written statement, he explained, "I can't remember every little detail on one report, sir."

Belli exploded, "It's not a little detail! That's the most damning thing that you've said to date."

Alexander interrupted, trying to dismiss the initial report as an investigation into the security breach. McMillon claimed, "I wasn't thinking about what was important and which wasn't when I wrote the report. I wrote a report that covered everything I could remember, the best I could remember, at the time it happened."

"But," Belli said accusingly, "you left out the two main things that you tell us about today..."

At times the detective's testimony resembled a legal comedy routine. Handing McMillon a copy of his statement, for example, Belli asked him when he had last looked at that statement. "A while ago," McMillon responded, "when you handed it to me." And moments later, asked when he had remembered the details included in later statements he claimed, "I guess I remembered it all the time. I just failed to put it in the report. I didn't remember it then. I probably knew it."

Trying to disrupt the defense's rhythm, Wade pointed out to Judge Brown, "I believe you instructed counsel to sit down." Belli was struggling to stay seated. He loved the histrionics of a trial; the dramatic steps toward the witness or the jury box, thrusting out his arms to make a point, sitting on the front of the defense table. All of those movements calculated to reinforce his case. But Judge Brown was practically keeping him hog-tied. It was confining, it was frustrating, as if he were a stage actor forced to say his lines while hidden in the wings.

Belli sat down; the long session finally ended with McMillon telling Wade that at some point during the following few days he had told the FBI about Ruby's incriminating comments.

Even if he hadn't written them down.

To the rest of the world, these first two days had personified Texas, with all the swagger and oversize personalities an outsider might expect. But this was still a confined, relatively regulated courtroom, and to many Texas was the Wild West, a larger-than-life place were men carried six-shooters and wore ten-gallon hats, where Bonnie and Clyde got mean and where someone assassinated the president. People expected big things, extraordinary things in Texas, and the next day, just outside the courtroom, they got exactly that.

CHAPTER EIGHT

The third day of the trial started with the prosecution introducing into evidence two film clips of the killing of Lee Harvey Oswald, one from United Press International, the other from a local Dallas station. Courts had been allowing photographs into evidence for more than a century. The use of "Sun-pictures" in a courtroom was first mentioned by the Supreme Court in 1859, in a land ownership case, *Luco v. US*; "By the employment of the beautiful art of photography," the Court decided, "this tribunal can examine the assailed title, and contrast it with papers of undoubted genuineness, with the same certainty as if all the originals were present, and with even more convenience and satisfaction." Initially photographs were used primarily for identification or in civil negligence cases to illustrate for jurors the scene of the injury; in an 1852 French case, it was noted, "pictures taken upon the spot [of the accident]…explained the whole affair more lucidly than all the oratory of a Cicero or Demosthenes."

Mostly photographs were used to illustrate or support testimony, but rarely as independent evidence. As the journal *Western Jurist* reported about photographic evidence in 1879, "The law of the land is a wary old fox, and scrutinizes a new invention a long time before extending the paw to appropriate it."

As early as 1920, moving pictures were used in civil trials, when an Ohio court allowed an insurance company to show footage of a bricklayer at work—after claiming to have been incapacitated by an injury. But the courts wrestled with the proper use of this relatively new technology. In a 1923 New York case, for example, the court of appeals threw out a $10,000 verdict awarded a vaudevillian who had lost his foot in an auto accident, ruling the lower court had erred in allowing film of his act to be entered as evidence; "The plaintiff's ability as a vaudeville performer was not the issue, and his eccentric dancing, comic songs, and the dialogue and remarks of his fellow performers, had no place in the trial in the Supreme Court of the state of the issues presented by the pleadings. The effect of this radical departure from the rules of evidence is found in the excessive verdict returned by the jury."

By 1935, DeWitt Clinton Blashfield, who published the most respected book on automobiles and the law, acknowledged that film had become an accepted tool in litigation, "Just as the map and engineer's diagram succeeded the rough sketch and as the photograph succeeded the diagram and map, so it appears that the ultimate in legal photography has been reached with the use of moving pictures…"

Any remaining questions about the value and impact of footage in criminal proceedings were answered in 1945 when the surviving Nazi leaders were placed on trial in Nuremburg, Germany. "We will show you their own films," Chief Prosecutor Robert Jackson promised. A week later the world responded with shock when an hour-long film, *The Nazi Concentration*

Camps, was shown. Footage was used extensively throughout the trials, contributing to the conviction of all Nazi leaders.

But there had never been this type of footage, the act itself being shown in an American murder trial. There was no precedent.

It was evidence; the question was what exactly it showed. Mostly it looked like a scramble, people pushing, a man in a hat rushing forward, Oswald being thrust backward, then chaos. The court ran the films without the jury the first time, then brought the jury to watch. Both films were run first in slow motion then in stop-action, frame-by-frame. As they were running, two Dallas PD officers identified those people who were visible. While it might have been a historic moment in legal history, for those in the courtroom it was long and tedious and filled several hours of the morning.

Incredibly, this was the first time Judge Brown and Jack Ruby had seen footage of the incident. Judge Brown later admitted, "No thoughtful person could definitely say from the films that Jack Ruby shot Lee Harvey Oswald... A vague picture of a great deal of violence without being able to tell exactly what was happening. The camera jiggled and jumped. Often it was out of focus..."

Ruby watched with a detached fascination, occasionally leaning to the side and mumbling some indecipherable remark to defense lawyer Phil Burleson. His only comment that Belli remembered was that he "didn't remember the crowd was so big."

Surprisingly, there were people captured on film within several feet of Oswald that the officers did not recognize. In one instance Wade asked his witness, "Who is that?"

Lieutenant Jack Revill admitted, "I don't know this gentleman, Mr. Wade... Captain King doesn't know him either." And yet this stranger had managed to get close to the most notorious accused criminal in the world.

As the footage was shown, the defense was mostly quiet, allowing Revill to identify as many people as possible. But at one point Tonahill asked the lieutenant, "You have McMillon there, do you not?" Revill confirmed it was Detective McMillon. This was about the time McMillon claimed he had seen and heard Ruby making his declaration. Tonahill pointed out that "Mc-Millon continues to look to the rear."

Alexander objected to commentary from the defense. Judge Brown shushed Tonahill.

When testimony resumed, the prosecution put police captain Glen King on the stand. While the other detectives had worn civilian clothes while testifying, Captain King wore his full uniform, highlighted by a glistening gold shield. There was no mistaking his authority. Captain King said he was in the basement when the shooting occurred, but did not witness it. But right afterward he hustled into the jail office; Ruby had been apprehended and was lying on the floor when King heard him say...

Objection! "...he is asking the witness to state something the defendant may have said while he was under arrest, and we ask..."

Overruled.

Exception.

Henry Wade got so distracted that he next asked King how long after the shooting was it before he walked into the office and saw Lee Harvey Oswald on the floor.

It was a silly mistake, the type of slip that might happen to anyone, but as he corrected himself Tonahill loudly pointed out, "He said it was Oswald he saw on the floor."

King was permitted to answer. There was great confusion, he remembered, "People were moving about, they were talking loudly, calling to each other...a lot of noise." And yet he was able to hear Ruby say, "You didn't think I was going to let him get away with it, did you?"

Having learned a lesson the day before, Wade asked if he had included that remark in his official report. "No, sir," he said. "It was not part of what was asked of me."

Captain King then testified that as Ruby was being taken upstairs he had indeed said "something like, 'You dirty scum, you're the scum of the earth.'"

Tonahill handled the cross-examination and he pounced on Wade's mistake, wondering, "How could you have said [that was Oswald lying on the floor] if you had been listening to the question?"

Wade interrupted, pointing out, "I think Lee Harvey Oswald was on the floor too, wasn't he Captain King?"

"That's just the point," Belli shouted out, "who was he guarding?"

Tonahill cut to the quick. "The point is, I am concerned with this man's prepared testimony more than anything else."

Several prosecution witnesses had now testified that Ruby had made self-incriminating comments, all of them allowed into the record by the court. The defense continued its attack on the credibility of those witnesses. Tonahill casually told the witness, "The statement that you heard Jack Ruby make was 'You guys couldn't afford to do it and someone had to do it for you.'" This witness had not said that at all; those were the words Detective Archer testified that he had heard.

"No sir, that's not correct," King objected.

Tonahill feigned surprise. "You *didn't* hear him say that?" He had not. "Well, was Archer standing closer to Ruby than you were?" The witness didn't remember exactly where Archer was standing. Tonahill pressed him, recalling Archer's claim, "...you didn't hear Ruby say, 'Well you fellows couldn't do it, somebody had to do it for you'?"

"I did not hear him say that... I have not heard him say anything else that I recall."

The nastiness between the two sides punctuated all the testimony. During one exchange, Tonahill asked King why he had given two versions of his specific words. Alexander objected to the question, which the court sustained but then Wade said, "Go ahead and answer the question."

Tonahill paused, then told King, "Well, the boss has over-ruled the assistant, so you can answer." The answer itself had little meaning or impact.

The defense used the witness to confirm that none of the officers knew when Oswald was going to be transferred, or who had ordered the transfer. This was a critical issue since if even they did not know the time, how could Ruby have planned to arrive just minutes before Oswald was eventually moved?

On redirect and recross, each side seemingly attempted to leave one far-fetched scenario in jurors' minds. For prosecutors it appeared to be that Ruby might have been planning an escape. King testified that Ruby was found to have $2,015.33 cash in his pocket at the time of his arrest, in addition to $60 in traveler's checks. When Tonahill got the witness back, he seemingly wanted jurors to consider the possibility of another shooter. "You have knowledge that a number of phone calls came into the police station that day, or the night before and that morning that Oswald would never live to get to see the city jail…from the city jail to the county jail." Captain King said he had no personal knowledge of that. In that crowded room where Oswald was shot, the possibility of an escape was almost as implausible as another suspect having shot him, but both sides were well aware that you never know what issue a juror may latch on to.

The captain had been consistent in his testimony, he heard what he heard, he said what he said and had no knowledge in no way about anything else that anyone else claimed that Ruby had said.

The prosecution announced it had one additional witness it wanted to call. A surprise witness. A "time bomb" as Belli described him. Sergeant Patrick Dean. Small and taut and spit polished, everything about him resonated authority. He had been in charge of security in the basement, so if anyone was responsible for the chaos it was him. This public appearance might well be one of the few opportunities he was going to have to rehabilitate his reputation and maybe save his career.

His duties that morning were straightforward, he said, "To secure the basement."

He heard the shot, he saw the commotion and ran toward the "incident."

"About ten minutes" following the shooting he went up to the fifth floor. Ruby was being held there, stripped to his shorts. "Did you ask one or two questions?" Wade asked.

Objection. Belli was on his feet, practically yelling, "…if there is anything clear—or peculiar about the Texas law, it is that questions cannot be asked of a man while he is under arrest, or answers be given while he is under arrest, unless they are in writing… I couldn't waive the privilege if I wanted to. We object to anything that was said after this man was under arrest." Although the defense did not know what Dean would testify he heard, Belli and Tonahill continued to object, raising every possible legal point, calling it "incompetent, irrelative, immaterial, violative of his constitutional right," in addition to being "leading and suggestive."

"I will leave out the leading part of it, Your Honor," Wade agreed.

The outcome of their objections was never in doubt. Judge Brown had shown he liked to let people have their say. And Dean finally got to tell his story. "He [Ruby] said…something to the effect that he had thought about this two nights prior, when he had seen Harvey Oswald on the show-up stand."

That was enough for Belli. That was the evidence of premeditation the prosecution wanted. If the jury believed this testimony, Ruby would be far more likely to receive the death penalty. "We ask for a mistrial, Your Honor, that statement being violative of this man's constitutional rights, whether it is false or whether it is correct."

"Overrule your objection."

After more legal skirmishing, Dean continued, burying Jack Ruby in a matter-of-fact monotone. "He said that he believed in the due process of the law that he was so torn up over this situation, and on the event that had happened...because this man had not only killed the President but had also shot Officer Tippit, and him being so emotionally torn up and he knew that the outcome of a trial, it would be inevitable that he would receive the death penalty that he didn't see any sense for a long and lengthy trial or to subject Mrs. Kennedy to be brought here to Dallas for it."

"Just a minute please," Belli said, standing again, trying again to prevent this testimony, "let's not ride roughshod over statements like this, as long as we have and are still operating under the constitution of the State of Texas. We again ask for a mistrial."

The defense was furious at this perceived trampling of their client's legal rights. When Wade began asking his next question, Belli shouted out, "Leading and suggestive."

Wade turned and looked at him. "I said what are the facts."

"We cite that again as misconduct."

The judge weighed in. "Overrule your objection."

Belli was on a roll. "Prejudicial and error, we ask for a mistrial."

Tonahill chimed in, "He was under arrest. Can we have a ruling, Judge?"

Dean was allowed to continue. "He said that when he noticed that sarcastic sneer on Oswald's face...two nights prior when he was in this show-up room...

"...He said that is when he first thought that if he got the chance he would kill him." The courtroom was absolutely silent. He continued, "And also that he guessed that he wanted the world to know that Jews do have guts."

"Jews," Belli yelled, "J-e-w-s, was it officer?"

Dean answered him, "Yes, sir."

Judge Brown tried to regain control. "Just a minute, Counselor."

Belli was hardly apologetic. "Well, I wanted to be heard, so that word rang out, Judge."

This took place, Dean testified, "some ten to twelve minutes after the shooting."

Sergeant Dean's direct testimony concluded the morning session. As the judge called a recess, journalists raced into the telex room to file their stories. During the lunch break a day earlier, Belli and Tonahill, accompanied by a phalanx of reporters, had visited the sixth floor of the Texas School Book Depository building, staring out of the window from which Oswald had fired the fatal shots. Photographers jostled silently for the best position, and Belli gave them sufficient time to get their pictures. Supposedly they wanted to know if the jury's quarters could be seen from this site. They could not. When asked though, Belli explained, "We just wanted to look at history."

But during this break they retreated to the office they were using. They had been hornswoggled, taken by surprise by Dean. The previous statements made by officers would be problematic, but they were of little consequence compared to his devastating testimony. They had to find a way to attack his claims. They had about an hour to do it.

There was none of Belli's typical courtroom politeness when he began his cross-examination. "Let me ask you first, Ruby told you he was planning to shoot Oswald since Friday night?"

Dean was prepared for Belli's verbal traps. "He didn't use the word 'plan,' no." Asked for his exact words he said, "As I remember it, he said that night that when he saw him on the show-up stand and observed the sarcastic sneer on his face, this was when he decided to do it, or to kill him if he got the chance."

Belli wondered if Dean was aware that a fellow officer had testified that Ruby had said exactly the opposite, "You all won't believe this, but I didn't have this planned," a question asked more to remind the jury of the differing testimony than elicit an answer. To make sure jurors understood how different this testimony was from other prosecution witnesses, he asked if Ruby had told him, "I couldn't have had it planned because I couldn't have timed it so perfectly," or "Just as I happened to get there Oswald was coming out."

Dean had not.

Having made that point, Belli began his attack. Being in charge of security was an important job and after Oswald's killing, "you must have had quite some departmental investigation of your activity."

"I submitted a report."

"How many investigations and interrogations did you have about the breach of security?"

"I submitted one letter."

When Belli asked for a copy of that letter, Dean took two documents out of his jacket pocket. He gave one to Belli and put the other one back in his pocket. Belli took the bait, demanding to know the contents of that other document. Another legal battle took place as Wade offered to enter both documents into evidence—before the defense saw the second document. An offer, Belli described, "As buying a bear in a trap" once again accusing the prosecution of misconduct. It seemed like a small victory for the prosecution; the jurors saw how cooperative Wade wanted to be, while it was Belli, the slick San Francisco attorney, who was causing all this ruckus. Eventually though, the defense was permitted to read it, and Belli was startled at what he read.

He asked Dean, politely, almost as an aside, "What time, Sergeant Dean, did you say you went up with Jack Ruby...you told us this morning that you went up about ten minutes after the shooting?"

"Yes, Sir."

Belli referenced the second document, a statement the officer had given days later. "In here you say 'approximately twelve noon, Chief Curry…instructed me to escort Mr. Forest J. Sorrels, agent in charge of the local secret service, to the fifth floor…'"

Dean hesitated. "Yes sir," he said. "The time element was off there."

Judge Brown was stunned. This testimony was possible cause for a mistrial. He realized he had allowed Dean to testify about Ruby's remarks because they had happened during the res gestae period, roughly ten minutes after the crime. But if this letter was accurate, Ruby had made those incriminating statements at least forty minutes later, long after Ruby had been placed under arrest, long after his Fifth Amendment rights against self-incrimination had kicked in. If this was true, the jury almost certainly should not have been allowed to hear them.

"Which time element is off?" Belli wondered. His probing had found Dean's weak spot.

"The one in the report."

"Did you read the report before you signed it?"

Dean had, and realized it was in error, "after I saw my interview on television. I had no idea at that time as to how long I was interviewed until I saw it on the video tape. This was some three weeks after."

Belli laid out the problem for the jury. "Now, you appreciate this morning you told us you went up to see Jack Ruby about ten minutes after the shooting… You appreciate that that is at complete variance with what you say in this letter…"

The prosecution tried to throw Dean a life raft. "We object to the term, complete variance," Alexander protested. "Approximately twelve noon means within thirty minutes of the time."

Belli withdrew his question, instead asking, "Tell the ladies and gentlemen of the jury why the time element is wrong in this letter."

Alexander objected again, "to the use of the term 'wrong,' for the reason 'approximately twelve o'clock' is within the limits of that time."

Belli wondered, "Within the limits of what time?"

Judge Brown allowed the witness to explain, and Belli focused on the discrepancy as if it were a dent in his Rolls-Royce Silver Cloud. "...ten minutes wouldn't be approximately twelve noon,

"...it was only at that time that Chief Curry contacted you...

"When did you determine that this [time] was off?

"It was after [Oswald was taken to the hospital] that you were interviewed?

"How long was it after Oswald was shot that the ambulance pulled out?"

When prosecutors tried to object, Belli thanked them and asked, "May we cross-examine without suggestions and coaching from the sidelines? I think even in football that's not allowed."

He continued his attack on Dean. "...was the ambulance gone when you were interviewed?"

"You had more than one interview, didn't you?"

"How many interviews did you have...on television, radio, Western Union, cable, anything else?"

"Approximately noon, that doesn't mean eleven-thirty, does it?" He finally brought it all together, asking, "And when you were testifying this morning it was only ten minutes, did you know that you had a written report to your superior in your pocket that said approximately twelve o'clock? You knew that at the time?... When you were testifying under oath?"

"Yes, sir."

Belli had Dean describe his movements until he ended up talking to Ruby. At the time, the officer testified, Ruby "was stripped to his shorts, standing there."

"And there were bars, of course, and he was locked up. To put it more formally, he was under arrest?"

"Yes, sir."

"I beg your pardon?" Belli asked politely, making certain the jurors heard that statement.

"Yes, sir," Dean repeated.

Belli was letting him twist on his own words: The sergeant had not told Ruby he was under arrest. He had not informed Ruby of his constitutional rights. Then Belli asked Dean if had heard any of the comments other officers claimed to have heard. He had not.

Time and again Belli returned to the time frame. It just didn't work the way Dean had testified. "When you use the term approximately twelve noon, what do you mean? Give or take two minutes, five minutes?"

When Dean tried to avoid answering, Belli interrupted him, demanding he answer the question. Alexander yelled out, "He's trying to answer, Your Honor."

Belli smiled at Judge Brown. "If he's trying to answer then Mr. Alexander doesn't have to help him."

Dean finally replied that to him, "approximately" meant "Fifteen on either side...before or after."

Eventually Belli circled back to Ruby's remarks. When he made them, Belli asked, "Was he in full possession of his faculties?" He appeared to be, Dean agreed. "Did he start crying later on?"

"He did have tears in his eyes when he referred to President Kennedy." Dean agreed that anytime Ruby referred to President Kennedy, Jackie or Caroline he became emotional. "He seemed very remorseful and shaken when he talked of the president... He had tears in his eyes."

In response to questions from Secret Service agent Sorrels, Ruby said, "He was shaken and was emotional and said he had been despondent since the assassination of the president...that he knew this would be a long and lengthy trial and the death penalty would inevitably be death, so he could see no sense, even though he believed in the process of law..."

Ruby sat still, his hands clasped on the table, showing no emotion as Belli continued probing, looking for additional problems with the testimony. Apparently Ruby was asked several more questions than Dean initially recalled. "Was he asked by Mr. Sorrels if he knew Oswald and he said, 'No. There's no acquaintance or connection between Oswald and myself of any kind whatsoever?'"

He did. Ruby also talked about his sister being emotionally fragile after Kennedy's assassination. Asked, "Did he say about his sister having a nervous breakdown?" Sergeant Dean replied he had spoken about his sister being in the hospital. Quietly, Belli was laying the groundwork for the defense case, informing jurors that mental illness ran in Ruby's family.

When Belli finally was finished questioning Dean, Tonahill renewed their objection to his testimony asking that it all be stricken from the record and a mistrial be declared "for the reason the defendant was under arrest and this was not res gestae by any legal conception and statements that Ruby made having been made under arrest..."

Belli punctuated that, "Alleged statements."

"...alleged statements is a denial of his Constitutional..."

The defense had no expectation Judge Brown suddenly might strike all of it or start the trial anew, but this was their best legal argument to date and a vitally important point that would be at the center of the appeal if Ruby was convicted. Tonahill was speaking for the record as much as to the court.

"Overrule your objection."

Wade asked a few perfunctory questions of the witness, then announced, "Your Honor, ladies and gentlemen of the jury, the State rests." Putting aside the legal questions, Sergeant Dean had been an effective witness for the prosecution. Belli later called it their most damaging testimony, although he had managed to raise some doubt about it.

The State had taken two and a half days to make its case. It had presented twenty witnesses. But this was not the end of their presentation. Each state has its own unique trial procedure, which had evolved to fit its needs. Texas had a more flexible system than most other states, allowing both sides wide latitude to bring in new information later in the case. Like a cattle rancher rounding up his herd, there always were a few strays that had to be collected. The trial system was the legal version of that, broad enough to allow both sides to bring in information they had neglected to include or forgotten when making their case, in rebuttal, surrebuttals and even sur-surrebuttals.

In fact, Wade had wanted to introduce two additional items found in Ruby's car: a radio program on heroism and another Western Union receipt found in his pocket, but somehow the police had misplaced them. Misplacing items of evidence in this trial with the world watching was yet another stain on the beleaguered Dallas Police Department.

Judge Brown called for a brief recess. It was during this time, shortly after the prosecution rested, that a remarkable event occurred right outside the courtroom, one that might have seemed fantastical, even scripted, had there not been dozens of witnesses.

Seven prisoners being held in a jail cell upstairs at the courthouse staged a daring escape. At 3:30 p.m., just after Sergeant Dean had concluded his testimony, the escapees burst out into a corridor filled with the media and trial participants. The escapees took one hostage and threatened others. Naturally, much of it was captured on camera.

The jailbreak had begun on the sixth floor, four floors above the Ruby trial proceedings. The prisoners were being held in a dayroom awaiting sentencing for armed robbery. One of them had fashioned an extremely realistic looking gun out of soap,

Satisfying the world's image of Texas as the center of the Wild West, seven prisoners being held in the courthouse staged a jailbreak, using a gun carved out of soap to take hostages. As the escape proceeded, a BBC correspondent described it on the phone for his disbelieving London office, "Listen, you bloody fools, this is America, this is Texas... any bloody insane thing is possible here!"

paper, wax, a scrap of metal from a spoon and a tin can lid; the barrel was a pencil stub. It was glued together by sugary syrup then colored with shoe polish and dye. Its cylinder had been carved out of soap and appeared to be fully loaded. A second prisoner had carved a makeshift "knife" out of a toothbrush. Other prisoners carried double-edged razor blades. Then, as a jailer distributed bars of soap he was overwhelmed. The escapees forced him into the visitors' elevators and descended to the second floor. There they encountered a second jailer and took his keys, using them to open the door leading to the second-floor corridor.

The trial corridor was mobbed since the trial was in recess, and the prisoners pushed their way into the crowd. Two escapees took a sixty-year-old clerk, Ruth Thornton, hostage and demanded she show them the way out. As they moved toward the front door, someone started screaming that a man with a gun was coming down the corridor. The woman who would be the defense's first witness, exotic dancer Karen Bennett, was standing with Joy Belli, the lawyer's wife. Bennett, who was almost nine months pregnant, heard the shouted warning and panicked, "My God. He's after me! He's after me!" Then she slumped to the floor. Belli's wife helped her to her feet and pushed her into the safety of a stairwell.

The crowd separated for the escaping prisoners and their hostage, who were trailed by several photographers and television cameramen. Ruth Thornton warned people to get out of their way, telling them "Don't touch me, he's got a gun in my back." As they walked past spectators gathered for the trial, the prisoner reassured her that "I won't hurt you if they stay back." When she tripped going down a few stairs he said, "I'll hold on to you."

The *Morning News* later called it the "best covered jailbreak in history," as the escapees walked through hundreds of journalists. Several correspondents reported it live. A BBC reporter was heard screaming into a phone, "No, damn it, I'm not drunk and I'm not kidding. That's right, a jailbreak."

A twenty-two-year-old CBS News messenger ended up grabbing hold of one fleeing prisoner's arm and held on until deputies tackled the man. The escapee holding the imitation gun was brought down by a young deputy, who came up from behind him. Another one later was found cowering at his home. A fourth man called the sheriff's office to surrender. A fifth man was found at his close friend's house. By the end of the day, two remained on the loose.

While for some this daring attempt might have reinforced Texas's Wild West heritage, for many others it confirmed their image of Dallas as a lawless community. The *New York Times* summed up the bizarre event: "Seven prisoners escaped from the Dallas County jail today...one of them carried a pistol carved from soap. Brandishing it, he terrified a striptease dancer who was waiting to testify in Ruby's defense." While the *New York Daily News*, for example, ran a simple headline: "Oh, Dallas."

There was no mention of the incident in the trial record.

When the defense began its direct case later in the afternoon, Melvin Belli finally got the opportunity to make a brief opening statement. Belli's reputation had created great expectations. It was said nobody went for popcorn when Ted Williams was at bat; and when Belli stood up, he had the complete attention of the courtroom.

Looking directly at the jury, in a friendly voice he explained, "This is what we have to prove on the issue of insanity. We will show you that Jack Ruby has organic brain damage. By that I mean that is damage that is discernible, that can be found... There have been studies made by some of the greatest men in the United States, the evidence will show. They will show that Jack Ruby has the damage that is called psychomotor variant epilepsy."

Belli had made his courtroom reputation by dramatically displaying exhibits to impress juries. But in this case he had little to work with, just a "brain tracing": paper with black lines on a graph representing the electrical activity of the human brain.

Belli told the jurors that the defense was going to prove mental illness was common in the Ruby family, "the evidence is going to be that the brother was in the Veterans Hospital for mental disease, that the mother was incarcerated under a bill of incarceration in Elgin State Hospital."

Finally he got to the facts of the case. He made no claims that his client was innocent; in fact he admitted his client had killed Oswald: "The evidence will show that on this Sunday morning Jack Ruby was home in bed. He got a telephone call about five minutes after ten from little Karen Bennett, who was the strip tease at his club… That was about five minutes after Oswald was to have been moved from the city to the county jail, according to the announcement.

"Mr. Ruby got up and came downtown to the only Western Union office that was open… He left his little dog in the car and he will tell you, if he takes the stand, that he told the dog he was coming back… We also are going to call [the cleaning woman] who he told that morning to come back to his place at two o'clock in the afternoon…that he would be there…

"When he got in the Western Union place he sent the twenty-five dollars over to Karen Bennett. We have the receipt. That was eleven seventeen." As he left the Western Union office "he happened to look down the street…and after spotting a group gathering in front of the jail," Belli said. "Ruby simply walked over, walked down the jail ramp and as he got to the bottom of that jail ramp Mr. Oswald came out. The fates conspired so that Ruby got there at the same time Oswald came out, and Ruby saw him and Ruby went for him and Ruby did shoot him.

"I will have to show what went on in this unusual mind, in this tragic man." Belli would later admit that he had told Jack Ruby, "We're going to do everything to show you in court as the nut you are." His client had agreed to it. And so the tragic man did not display any emotion as his own attorney described him as mentally ill. He simply stared straight ahead.

The first witness called by the defense was Karen Bennett, the "stripteaser" known in Ruby's club as Little Lynn, "the little girl but for whose telephone call this wouldn't have happened." Bennett was a fresh-faced nineteen-year-old, and all the possible variations of "Stripper testifies in Oswald Murder Trial" made enticing headlines for the media. But her background as a stripper made her testimony seem more salacious than the real, nine-months' pregnant woman who appeared in court that day. Her dress was perfect for the role of a reformed sinner, a demure maternity suit with a virginal white collar. While she might not have been Belli's choice to open his case, to the delight of the media he had no choice; Little Lynn was several days overdue and the defense couldn't risk losing her testimony to the maternity ward.

Adding to the sensationalism, Bennett took the stand only moments after collapsing in the middle of that jailbreak. As she testified, dozens of officers were blanketing the city searching for the remaining escapees.

The witness spoke in a soft nervous voice, forcing Belli to remind her to "breathe harder" so she might be heard. She worked in the Carousel Club, she said, as "a strip tease," for slightly more than five months. She had called Ruby Saturday night because the club was shuttered out of respect to Kennedy, and she needed money to get home to Fort Worth and pay her rent. "The amount I needed for the rent was fifteen dollars, so I called Jack and asked him to send me twenty-five dollars... He said he was going downtown and would drop the money off at Western Union so I could get it quicker...he said he would do that for me.

"He sounded as if he had been crying or was about to cry... when I talked to him I had to call him back to the phone three times...because it seemed like he was far away." She had phoned Ruby, person-to-person, she said, when she went to work and found the club closed. "I said, 'Jack, why isn't the club open?' And he said, 'Don't you give a damn about the president? Don't you know the president is dead?' And he said, 'I don't know if I'll ever open the club again.'... he sounded very mad."

Belli was beginning to create the portrait of Ruby he wanted the jury to see. "...you'd never know when he was going to be mad at you. It was just on the spur of the moment, he'd be real mad at you, but then it was over within a few minutes."

Wade began his cross-examination by portraying the witness as something of a wanton woman and yet also a victim of Ruby. "How old were you when you started to work as a stripper for Jack Ruby?" Nineteen. "Had you ever stripped for anyone else?" Yes. And then shifting gears: "You never did think he was crazy, that you ought to carry him to a psychiatrist, did you?"

She did not.

But Wade came back to her reputation. "You're nineteen years old," he said again. "Where did you first strip?"

This objection was sustained.

During Belli's redirect examination, Karen Bennett described how odd it was to hear the sorrow in Ruby's voice, because he "has a high-toned voice, it's a deep voice but it's got laughter in it. He was always laughing, you know, until he gets upset. And then he was quick tempered."

In his recross examination Wade continued using Bennett to attack Ruby's character. "Did he ever go with you?" he asked. As eleven of the twelve jurors were married, most of them with children, Wade's message was obvious: Jack Ruby isn't one of us. He's an older guy preying on young girls. Maybe even a danger to our community. "Did he ever say anything to you about going with him sometime? Did he ever make any statements to you—I believe you're married, aren't you, Karen?"

She was married. And what about Jack? "Jack was a man," she said in her girlish Texas drawl, hinting at far more experience than her years. "I mean, he's going to ask a girl to go out, but after he asked and got the answer no he never did reapproach me."

Wade then wondered if Ruby had "gone with her coworkers, Joy Dale and Tammi True?" This time Judge Brown upheld the defense objection. But the question made the point far greater than any answer.

When Bennett had taken the stand, Belli had hoped the women on the jury might feel some sympathy toward her—she was young and pregnant—and perhaps by extension Ruby, who had gone out of his way to help her. But as she concluded her testimony he walked to the witness box and helped her down, and rather than sympathy, he was astonished to feel "an almost physical antipathy" coming from the jury box.

Wade had done his job.

CHAPTER NINE

Robert Louis Stevenson wrote in his 1886 novel *The Strange Case of Dr. Jekyll and Mr. Hyde* that there exist two sides to each of us, good and evil, and the bounds of society mostly keep evil hidden. When published, it was considered a daring look at mental illness: With a small dose of potion, the evil Hyde, "so long repressed, emerged wild and vengefully savage, and it was in this mood that he beat Carew to death, delighting in the crime. Hyde showed no remorse for the murder, but Jekyll knelt and prayed to God for forgiveness even before his transformation back was complete."

Jack Ruby had a bit of that divided personality, as well. But no one was quite sure how much of it, or what "potion" might spark his transition. He could be violent and compassionate, petty and pious, and he could change in an instant. Belli described him as "a sick man," yet he was able to successfully run several nightclubs, and maintained friendships and personal relationships. Karen Bennett remembered him losing his temper, but she also turned to him when she needed help and he responded. William Howard, another Dallas nightclub owner would testify that Ruby was "unpredictable." "He likes to be well thought of," Howard told reporters, "he's a rough and tumble fighter, a health faddist…and at other times a kind and considerate person."

Until November 24, 1963. Ruby had lived an ordinary, if occasionally shady life; he'd served in the military, lived independently, earned a satisfactory living. Initially, Belli said, he had believed that Ruby killed Oswald as part of a larger plot to keep him from naming other people or that he had been "overcome by some crazy impulse on a weekend when all of us were slightly mad." It was only after becoming involved in Ruby's defense that Belli says he came to believe his client was ill. It became his task to prove to the jury that this extraordinary personality range was the result of a previously undiagnosed, unique mental illness.

What became apparent as the trial continued was that each witness seemed to be describing a different man. William Serur, a thirty-one-year-old sundries and novelty salesman, had known Ruby for about twelve years. "He wasn't like most of the people I've met…it was awful hard for me to figure him out."

One Saturday night, Serur told Joe Tonahill, he had gone to Ruby's Colony Club, which was quiet and nearly empty, after visiting a competitor's club, which was rocking with a standing room only crowd. He made the mistake, he testified, of telling that to Ruby. "…Jack, when he gets mad, he explodes without warning…

"I just kept looking at those eyes, and I got scared. He kept raving like a mad man."

The witness continued talking about his terrifying experience. "…I decided I'd better leave. And I said, 'No, Jack will get mad.' Seven or eight minutes later…when [Jack] walked up to me he was a different person altogether. He laid his hand on my shoulder and said, 'Kid, you want a cup of coffee?' He was just as cool and calm as I ever saw him.

"...He acted as if nothing had happened," the witness continued, "or as if he had said nothing." That outburst was not unusual. "When he explodes and gets mad he does it quicker than any person I ever seen, but he can cool off quicker than any person I ever saw." He added he had been astounded and terrified by these rapid mood changes.

The defense could not have written Serur's response any better. This was precisely the picture of Ruby they wanted to paint. A man acting normally almost all the time and then...boom! He erupted. Perhaps that is what happened that morning in the basement of the police station.

And there was still another aside of him. It turned out Jack was crazy about his dogs. "I don't want you to refer to them as dogs," Serur remembered Ruby telling him, "Those are my children." At one point, Ruby was opening a can of dog food for them and had cut his hand open on the lid. He was bleeding profusely, "and the largest of the dogs was licking the blood off his hand. I said, 'Jack I wouldn't let those dogs lick that blood. I'd be afraid of them.'

"And he said, 'I told you not to call these children of mine dogs anymore,'" Ruby had asked Serur to come over because he needed to repair the seats in his car. The upholstery had been ripped out and scattered on the floor, leaving the springs visible. "What did this?"

"My children did it."

Tonahill's even tone never wavered as he led his witness through this bizarre relationship. Whenever Serur mistakenly referred to them as dogs or criticized them, Ruby became defensive. "He just wanted to take up for his kids, I guess."

The courtroom was silent with fascination. The jury sat impassively, displaying no emotion. Tonahill finally asked the witness if he considered Ruby unstable. "I would say that from the time I first met Jack… I thought he might be suffering from some form of mental disturbance, by the way he acted… I'm positive that it can hit him most any time. That's the way I've got it figured."

"That's all," Tonahill said, sitting down.

Henry Wade sat in his chair, the stump of an unlit cigar rolling around in his mouth. Serur's testimony had made it appear that Ruby was unstable. While that would not be enough legally to support the defense contention that Ruby suffered from a specific mental condition, it certainly demonstrated that there was something wrong with him. Knowing it would be hard for the prosecution to attack Serur's story, the DA had to attack the credibility and perhaps the character of the witness. Wade asked his questions sharply and quickly, often cutting Serur off before he could complete his answer. He established that Serur had known Ruby twelve years. Although Ruby often lost his temper, the salesman continued going back to see him. Serur didn't carry a gun, he said. Wade feigned surprise. "I thought everybody in Dallas carried them?"

Tonahill interrupted, "We'll stipulate [agree] if the District Attorney thinks everybody in Dallas carried a pistol."

Wade continued with his scattershot attack. Serur tried to maintain his composure, shifting uneasily in the witness chair, too often failing to look directly at Wade. In response to potentially embarrassing questions, he responded in a lowered voice, looking down at the courtroom floor. Yes, he said, Ruby always had his dogs with him. Even to the club. Although he had been terrified of Ruby at times, no, he had never called the police.

The defense continued to interrupt Wade after Wade interrupted the witness, trying to slow down the pace, complaining the court stenographer couldn't possibly get every word down. "I want a record…with every word," Belli protested. Tonahill agreed, "That's something the District Attorney doesn't want, a record."

Wade ignored them. He elicited that in the twelve years the witness had known Ruby he had never seen him in a public place with a woman. Apparently he was so "surprised" by that response that he repeated the question several times, just to make certain the jury understood the implications of the answer. Wade long ago had mastered the trial lawyer's skill of leading the jury to his desired conclusion without being blatant about it. A man surrounded by mostly naked young women who was rarely seen with one outside of the workplace? While there was no evidence of it, that did not stop the prosecution from hinting on several occasions that Ruby might have been homosexual. The whispers that Ruby was gay became so loud that in early December the FBI investigated and found no evidence to support those rumors. But in a conservative community like Dallas in 1964, the claim was enough to potentially damage his character. Twelve years without being seen in public with a woman? Wade let the jurors draw their own conclusions.

In addition to not calling the police, Serur also had never taken Ruby to a psychiatrist or a doctor to receive treatment. And finally he made his point. "You kept going back to see him, and see his show there?"

"Every time he had a good headliner," Serur said, speaking firmly, "I made up my mind to go there. I was a free paid patron. I never paid a dime to go in Jack Ruby's place."

"Who was your favorite stripper there?"

Belli objected, telling the witness, "Don't get in an insulting match with the District Attorney, because he can out-insult anyone in the room."

Good friends for that long, Wade emphasized. "You'd do nearly anything to help him, wouldn't you?...you'd testify for him?"

"Testify" being a polite way of questioning whether or not he was telling the truth.

The DA led Serur through his entire history with Ruby,

through all his clubs, the Silver Spur, the Vegas Club… "You went out there often, didn't you?"

"Sir, I was out there practically every other night, or every night."

"Every night." Wade considered that, then made his point. "Are you a married man?"

Yes, he was, he said.

A married man spending almost every night at strip clubs? The decent citizens of Dallas, for example the eleven married members of the jury, would frown upon that type of behavior.

Belli leaped to his feet. Shouting angrily, his face turned red with fury, he screamed, "That's insulting. 'Is he a married man.' And I say this man is a master at insult as any District Attorney I've ever heard, and I've tried them all in this country and abroad…to ask him if he is a married man, what has that got to do with…"

Wade was on his feet too, shouting over Belli, "I think it's important."

"He can outshout me too," Belli shouted ever louder, "but what has that got to do with this man on trial for murder, asking if he's a married man. I submit, Your Honor, that that's incompetent, irrelevant and immaterial. Dirty, salacious, meretricious and insulting."

Bowie was on his feet too. "Your Honor, he's already testified that he's a married man."

Belli turned on him. "Then why does he ask him repeatedly again? To put in a little more prejudice in the case that he's got so full of prejudice here, Judge?"

It would have been the perfect time for Judge Brown to gavel the courtroom quiet, if he had a gavel there and if he had been that type of judge. Instead, he instructed everyone to sit down and Wade continued his cross-examination. Eventually he came around to Ruby's ability to run a business. "Jack Ruby knew what he was doing when everything was going swell," the witness explained, "but Jack was…always upset with the cold drink man and the people who bought him—he was fussing with them all the time."

Wade was attempting to show that Ruby's murderous eruption wasn't an extraordinary and inexplicable outburst, but rather part of who the real Jack Ruby was. Serur described him as "Definitely high tempered, high strung, emotionally upset a lot of times…"

As Wade picked up a rhythm, Belli stopped him with another objection. After a nasty exchange between the two sides, Judge Brown finally had had enough, warning Belli, "One more statement like that, counsel and I'm going to hold you in contempt. I'm not going to put up with this. We've had enough of it… I'm not going to take it anymore!"

Belli apologized, and perhaps meant it for several seconds. Then Wade asked Serur, "Did you go with him to New Orleans at one time to look at some strippers?"

Once again Belli was on his feet objecting.

Overruled.

Just for good measure, Wade wondered if the witness had gone with Ruby "to Cuba, back in '59?" Fidel Castro's Communist Cuba being, of course, anathema to the patriotic Americans of Dallas, Texas. His question served to remind the jurors in case they did not know about or had forgotten the defendant's visit there *after* the Cuban Revolution. "For two or three weeks," he added. That visit would become the subject of great interest to those who believed Ruby was part of a larger plot to kill the president.

During the redirect questioning, Serur described Ruby as a charitable man, a man who took up a collection for the widow of a deceased police officer. Additional attempts to demonstrate "If Jack liked you there wasn't anything in the world he wouldn't do for you," were blocked by prosecution objections, ending Serur's testimony.

The next witness, William Howard, an oil man, also had seen the dark side of Jack Ruby. As he told defense counsel Phil Burleson, "I've seen him in his various clubs getting into fights and brawls and things of that nature…on one particular occasion there was a young fellow who was straddling a chair in one of his places…and Jack commanded him to turn around and face the table, which he did. But when he went by him again he had straddled the chair again and first thing I knew there was a big commotion and Jack went off the handle and kind of beat this fellow up…

"He would get upset and then it would be all over." According to Howard, these outbursts were common and during some of them Ruby's speech would become "disjointed and it would lack continuity…" He was "unpredictable," he continued, why during a dinner "he would get up and leave for no reason whatsoever…" Asked directly his opinion of Ruby's mental state, he frowned, then replied, "Well, with apologies to Jack, I've always considered him…"

Objection! Sustained.

Once the prosecution took over, Wade got the witness to admit that Ruby had a large ego, that he loved to be in the limelight and was a "health faddist," often going "to the YMCA to build his body up… He was pretty tough, wasn't he?"

Tough enough to throw people out of his clubs when they needed throwing, Howard replied. He carried a gun too, although usually he kept it in his money bag. And when going into a restaurant he'd lock it in his car.

When the defense got the witness back for redirect, Burleson began by suggesting the source of Ruby's anger. "You knew that Jack Ruby was in a foster home when he was five years old?"

Objection. Sustained.

After just a little more bickering between the opposing sides, Judge Brown recessed the court for the weekend. The question remained unanswered.

Jack Ruby's Carousel Club was open seven days a week. Its nightly show consisted of four girls, each of whom performed a fifteen-minute striptease. As dancer "Tammi True" once explained, "The fame was exciting, fulfilling a lifelong desire to be in the spotlight and to be adored."

Over the weekend the search continued for the two escaped prisoners. Sheriff Bill Decker warned that they were "desperate and dangerous" men. The more time that passed, the more difficult it might be to capture them.

Heading into the Dallas County jail was twenty-one-year-old Patricia Ann Kohs. She had performed at Ruby's Carousel Club under the stage name Penny Dollar. The "attractive brunette," who was seen smiling broadly while pictured "frolicking in the snow" wearing only a skimpy two-piece costume in a *Morning News* staff photo taken a year earlier, had been arrested in Orange, Texas, on Friday afternoon for possession of harder drugs and marijuana. At the request of the defense, she was flown into Dallas and lodged in the jail and would testify for Ruby the following Monday. The *Morning News* reported, "the defense chief conferred with the stripper in her jail cell shortly after her arrival." The paper also noted that Ruby had a long connection

It was an innocent time. "We were all about looking like Rita Hayworth or Elizabeth Taylor, Hedy Lamarr," explained a dancer known professionally as Angel. "There was no silicon. No facelifts." And no full-frontal nudity. Ruby was known to flirt with his girls but was generally all business.

to her family because "her mother had been a stripper and had worked for Ruby 'about eighteen years ago.'"

Few trial lawyers had mastered the art of using the media better than Belli. He had cultivated relationships with journalists around the world, and that was paying off for him in Dallas. While he couldn't control what the people of Dallas, or even all of Texas thought, he was playing to a national audience. No question, the court of public opinion could have a significant impact at some point. The city was putting Jack Ruby on trial and Belli was putting the city on trial, a risky move considering the jurors were Dallasites. He was accomplishing that with the assistance of some of the best-known reporters and columnists in the country, among them Dorothy Kilgallen and Bob Considine who were covering the trial for the Hearst papers.

Dorothy Kilgallen, a Pulitzer Prize–nominated, nationally syndicated daily columnist for the *New York Journal-American*, was perhaps even more widely known as a permanent panelist on the tremendously popular Sunday night quiz show, *What's My Line*. She was greeted as a celebrity when she walked into the courtroom. Judge Brown shook her hand and agreed to an interview in his chambers. Her lunch with Belli at Vincent's Seafood House was photographed and reported in the local press.

Her relationship with Belli was symbiotic; she on occasion lauded him in her widely read column and in return got "scoops" about his high-profile cases. Her friendship with Belli allowed her access to Ruby, and she was the only reporter to be granted two interviews with him. When she'd met him for the first time, during the change of venue hearing, she wrote, "we shook hands and his hand trembled in mine ever so slightly, like the heartbeat of a bird. 'I'm nervous and worried,' he told me. 'I feel I'm on the verge of something I don't understand—the breaking point maybe.'" Kilgallen told Ruby "I think you're holding up pretty well."

"I'm fooling you Dorothy. I'm really scared," he replied.

While this "exclusive" interview got her readership, it also landed her a permanent spot in the JFK murder conspiracy theories that would emerge. Kilgallen had become convinced that Oswald was part of a much larger conspiracy, wondering in her column "I'd like to know how, in a big, smart town like Dallas, a man like Jack Ruby—owner of a strip tease honky tonk—can stroll in and out of police headquarters as if it was at a health club at a time when a small army of law enforcers is keeping a 'tight security guard' on Oswald." And later telling *Herald* reporter Jim Lehrer, "I don't see why Dallas should feel guilty for what one man, or even three or five in a conspiracy have done."

Eventually she claimed she was going to break the story, calling it "the biggest scoop in history." But before she could do that, in November 1965 her body was found in her New York apartment. Her death initially was attributed to a heart attack, but within days the city's medical examiner announced the cause of her death at the young age of fifty-two was "a combination of moderate quantities of alcohol and barbiturates" which led to her heart stopping. Suspicious people immediately questioned that finding, suggesting she had been murdered to prevent her from breaking the case as she had promised.

Among the claims she had made was that, contrary to Ruby's statements, he may have had a previous relationship with Oswald. In a column published as the trial began she wrote, "Ruby has said repeatedly that he didn't know the alleged assassin of President Kennedy—but then Ruby's plea is temporary insanity and there are a great many things he doesn't remember, and isn't about to.

"To quote one observer, 'the operation of Jack's Carousel Club had its unsavory aspects but if Oswald checked in there a couple of nights a week, he could have made some extra money. That would account for his ability to take trips—like the one to Mexico—on a $50-a-week salary, and it also would account for his lying in a room in the heart of Dallas five nights a week and joining his wife and children in the suburbs only on Fridays and Saturdays.'"

This was speculation, an unverified collection of ifs and therefores from unnamed sources that contributed to the creation of the Kennedy assassination conspiracy industry that would endure for decades. In fact, Oswald and his wife, Marina, were struggling to keep their marriage together, which could have accounted for their living circumstances. But tying disparate facts together or attributing questionable motives to actions fueled various conspiracies.

For example, Bob Considine the renowned reporter, columnist and bestselling author, who had initially gained fame as the coauthor of the stirring wartime story of James Doolittle's bombing raid, *Thirty Seconds Over Tokyo*, also forged links in the conspiracy chain.

Soon after Kennedy had been killed, Dallas used-car dealer Warren Reynolds had come running out of his office when he heard three shots fired, enabling him to positively identify Lee Harvey Oswald as the man who had just murdered Officer Tippit. In January, Considine reported, Reynolds was shot in the head as he was closing his shop just two days after being interviewed by the FBI. He miraculously survived. The main suspect was a man named Darrell Wayne Garner. Garner claimed he had been with his girlfriend, Betty Mooney, at the time of shooting. Mooney supported that story and passed a lie detector test. Perhaps coincidently, Considine revealed, Betty Mooney had worked as a stripper at Jack Ruby's Carousel Club.

Even more curious, a week after taking that polygraph exam, Betty Mooney had been arrested for fighting with a former roommate over a man. And while in custody, she hanged herself with her own toreador trousers. "Call it a series of coincidences, if you will," Considine wrote, clearly indicating he did not.

Jack Ruby's trial, being knotted together with the burgeoning Kennedy conspiracy movement, was the media's dream come true. An audience of millions followed every twist, and at times potentially innocent connections suddenly took on sinister tones. Even Belli, who had admitted his first reaction to Oswald's murder was that it must somehow be part of the conspiracy, certainly was not above using those types of rumors to benefit his client.

Among the spectators lining up to watch the proceedings Monday morning was Oswald's mother, Marguerite. A throng of reporters surrounded her as she pronounced, "I have now decided to attend the trial. I think it will satisfy me as a mother."

In an ordinary case, having the victim's mother present in court could help humanize the victim, engender sympathy for her or anger toward the defendant over the killing. But here, the last thing prosecutors wanted to do was focus additional attention on Oswald. He had assassinated a beloved president. There already was a sizable number of people who applauded Ruby's actions. She had not been on the prosecution's witness list, but they wanted to keep her out of the courtroom so they served her a subpoena right there, claiming they might call her as a witness. She was brought into the courtroom and sworn in, thereby preventing her from watching the proceedings or discussing the case with anyone other than the prosecutors.

She angrily waved the subpoena and told the media, "This is unfair. I came as a spectator to see if I could pick up scraps of information to help prove my son's innocence." Wade defended that action suggesting facetiously Mrs. Oswald "might be used on rebuttal." She did not look at Ruby while in the courtroom.

The defense's next witness was Dr. Fred Bieberdorf, a fourth-year medical student who had examined Jack Ruby twice the day of the killing. Belli and Tonahill were well aware that the testimony about Ruby's self-incriminating statements was potentially devastating; but they also believed Judge Brown should never have allowed the jury to hear them. The key to their admissibility was the timing. Should Ruby be convicted there was no doubt the defense would base part of its appeal on the expansive use of res gestae. So if the timeline could be stretched by prosecutors to make them part of the emotional outburst connected to the crime, an appeals court might allow them, but if it could be proved they were made (assuming Ruby actually made those statements) long after the criminal act ended their inclusion may have fatally infected the jury's deliberations.

As part of his medical training, Dr. Bieberdorf was serving as the first aid attendant at the jail on November 24. In that capacity he had examined Jack Ruby; "I saw him on two occasions," he told Belli. "One time at 2 o'clock in the afternoon and then later on in the afternoon about 6 o'clock... 2:05 to be exact."

And when the young doctor examined Ruby at precisely 2:05, what was he wearing? "He had on his coat and shirt, and a pair of slacks, which were all street clothes…"

"But he had his suit coat on?… And his suit pants?… And he had his shirt on?"

"That's correct." The doctor had brought with him his record to confirm the details.

His answer was in complete conflict with previous testimony. On Friday, Sergeant Dean had testified Ruby had been stripped to his underwear when he made his self-incriminating statements. If he was still wearing street clothes two hours later, it destroyed the prosecution's timeline and could eliminate any possibility of those statements being admissible.

Later, Bieberdorf continued, when he examined him a second time, he was wearing "the type of clothes that the cooks in the City Jail wear."

Wade's cross-examination strayed from the timeline, questioning Ruby's physical and mental condition. But when he asked if Ruby had "assured him…that the officers had done what their jobs called for…" Belli was on his feet, bringing back the essential point, "This is two hours after he was under arrest and he hadn't had his clothes taken off, and it wasn't ten minutes as the officers testified the other day."

Alexander and Bowie both objected to the objection, playing into Belli's hands by claiming that "was exactly opposite from what the record will show."

Judge Brown sustained Belli's objection, but that still didn't stop him from adding, "They said he was stripped and he wasn't stripped."

The defense then called the trial's celebrity witness, legendary boxer Barney Ross, to the stand. Born Dov Rosofsky, he was a Jewish kid who had grown up with Ruby on the tough streeets in Chicago and had even worked for Al Capone as a kid. When he became a professional fighter, he Americanized his name. He won championships in three divisions and in eighty-one fights was never knocked out. While the Nazis were conquering Europe and worldwide anti-Semitism was prevalent, Ross became a symbol for the Jewish community; a man of great strength, tremendous fortitude and courage, a man who simply refused to go down. In the final fight of his career, against Henry Armstrong, he was battered and beaten but refused his trainer's pleas to stop the fight. He just wasn't backing down.

After enlisting in the Marines in 1942, he refused to accept a ceremonial job helping morale and selling war bonds, instead serving in combat. He earned a Silver Star for heroism on Guadalcanal, single-handedly killing two dozen enemy soldiers. During recovery from his wounds, he became addicted first to painkilling morphine and then to heroin and his public fight against addiction enhanced his reputation. Ross was mostly there as a "character witness," testifying that even as a young man Ruby was a strange character, a good person with mental issues. Ross had come to Dallas from New York to "keep the jury interested," Belli admitted, and to help the defense "show sympathy for Ruby from a cross-section of society, always an effective technique with a jury."

"You are the Barney Ross who was the World's Champion welterweight?" Belli began, before taking the boxer through his testimony. Ross wore a trim suit and dark glasses, even in the subdued light of the courtroom, to protect an eye he had damaged in the ring. He told the story of his childhood on the West Side of Chicago. "It wasn't the easiest place to be raised in, but it turned out to be nice enough as we got a little older—and got smarter."

Ross and Ruby had been close friends from teenagers into adulthood. And just like the heroic Ross, Ruby was "as patriotic as all of us." As a kid, Ross recalled, Ruby was known as "the authority on handicapping." When his friends refused to take his betting advice he would have a "tantrum," screaming at them until he "almost turn[ed] purple." He would walk away, "disappear...sometimes for a day or two and we would miss him."

While the two men once had been close friends, time and distance had come between them. But obviously it had not destroyed the affection they had for each other. Ruby was far more animated during this testimony than at any previous time, leaning forward to make certain he heard every word, occasionally turning to Tonahill and whispering a few words.

Belli stood at his desk as he asked these questions—until once again Wade interrupted to request he sit down. That had become a recurring theme in this trial. The courtroom was subdued as Ross testified, knowing they were watching an American icon. "Sparky," as Ruby was known to his friends, was "a good hustler" who had carried Ross's equipment in his early fights. Ross remembered one fight in particular, a 1935 bout with Ceferino Garcia in San Francisco. "I was knocked down in the first round, which I found out later, but with my conditioning and the instinct I had...the bell rang and my manager jumped into the ring with a sponge soaked in ice water, and threw it in my face...he asked me what his name was and I said, 'Your name is Art Lynch.' He said, 'I must have been asking you for five rounds and this is the first time you were able to answer me.'" Ross had blanked out for five rounds, but came back to win the decision. He recalled seeing Ruby after the fight. "That's when I found out he had blacked out (too)."

Objection! Sustained! But Belli made sure the jury knew that Ruby had suffered blackouts.

Assistant prosecutor Bill Alexander had the difficult job of attacking Ross's testimony without attacking the popular athlete himself. After establishing that Jack Ruby also had fought several amateur bouts, Alexander challenged Ross's memory, claiming he had given different answers to the same questions Belli had asked to the FBI because "You just didn't want to be connected with him, Mr. Ross?"

Ross objected loudly, "I wanted to be connected with him, I was on his side at all times."

As the trial continued through the morning, the United States Supreme Court was making history in Washington. The nine justices reversed a lower court ruling in Montgomery, Alabama's police chief, L. B. Sullivan's historic libel suit against the *New York Times* (and four civil rights leaders). A unanimous court found that a public official cannot be defamed for comments made about his performance in that position—unless it can be proved there was "actual malice." This ruling, Justice William Brennan wrote for the Court, "prohibits a public official from recovering damages for a defamatory falsehood relating to his official conduct unless he proves that statement was made with 'actual malice,' that is, with knowledge that it was false or with reckless disregard for whether it was false or not."

Also that day, the block of Southerners in the United States Senate began a filibuster against President Johnson's civil rights bill. Georgia Democrat Richard Russell told reporters he saw "no room for compromise" and promised to "fight to the last ditch."

Barney Ross told the court that Ruby had gone with him to "at least 50 fights" and, contrary to the prosecution's claim, he had never told anyone that he didn't want to have anything to do with Ruby or be connected with him. Yet he also said his group of friends didn't think Ruby was emotionally capable of holding a job, and "I think he understood his own trouble, and that's why I believe he was on his own all the time."

But Ross made a point of describing Ruby as "a well-behaved, quiet individual," saying specifically that after Ruby had one of his tantrums, "He wouldn't step on a fly or a caterpillar, that's how quiet he would become." And Ruby rarely cursed either; he was adamant about it, which the defense obviously hoped would cause jurors to question the prosecution's claim that Ruby had continually referred to Oswald as "a son of a bitch."

Unlike most trials, Judge Brown's rules of engagement remained casual, with each side asking a question or two then handing the witness to the other side to rebut or repeat earlier answers. It was as if they were having a catch with Ross.

When Ross finally stepped down from the stand, he made a show of stopping at the defense table and warmly shaking hands with his old friend, in case anyone doubted his sincerity. The two men exchanged whispered words and the champ left the courtroom.

The defense put these early witnesses on the stand to establish that Ruby was and always had been a strange guy. He was quick-tempered, sometimes violent, subject to blackouts, could not work easily with others but was at heart a good and decent man. After laying down Ruby's behavior patterns, the defense intended to show there were diagnosable mental reasons for it.

Ruby's roommate, fifty-year-old George Senator, took the stand. Questioned by Tonahill, the stocky, gray-haired Senator provided much the same testimony as he had given during the bail hearing. He had known Jack Ruby for eight years and described his temperament as "highly emotional." Just as Ross had said, "He would flare up and go into sort of a rage...when certain people got out of line and would make a lot of noise or try to touch any of the girls or girl or disturb the MC he would go up to them and tell them to keep quiet...

"...sometimes it could be a battle."

While Tonahill was questioning the witness, Belli wandered over to the jury box and leaned on the rail, friendly-like, until Alexander interrupted to tattle, "Mr. Belli is at it again, he is away from his seat..."

The court paused while he took his seat. Senator recalled seeing Ruby for the first time after the assassination the following morning and "He had a look on him which I had never seen before..."

Loudly, Belli asked Senator to "Repeat it, I am not getting that."

"...He was deeply upset and he said to me, 'Why did this thing have to happen to his wife and children?'" Senator said Ruby was especially disturbed by that full-page anti-Kennedy ad that had appeared in the *Morning News* the morning of the twenty-second, which "he connected with the Communist Party and with the John Birch Society, a combination of both of them." He also was deeply disturbed about a billboard on the expressway demanding "Impeach Earl Warren," the chief Justice of the Supreme Court, who was a target of the Birchers. In fact, at 3:00 a.m. in the morning on the twenty-fourth Ruby had awakened Senator and demanded he drive him downtown so he could take Polaroid pictures of it.

The billboard upset him? Tonahill asked.

"Yes, very much so...he was sort of looking out into space, in other words it was a starry look."

From there they went to the post office to see if he could discover who had placed the anti-Kennedy ad, because Senator said, "He thought there was a connection between both of them." Senator agreed with Tonahill's claim that Ruby was acting "nutty," but went along with him, he said, because "I would always go along with him."

Senator described the apartment they shared as having two bedrooms, a living room and a kitchen in preparation for the smear that the defense suspected was coming from the prosecution. He had moved into the apartment because he was unemployed "and through the good graciousness of his heart he said, 'George, you can move in with me and I'll take care of you.'"

On Sunday morning Ruby and Senator had watched JFK's funeral procession. Throughout the weekend Ruby's emotional condition "was getting worse." He was mumbling, Senator remembered, "he sure had a moody look and a very far away look to me. It was a look that I had never seen before on him, like I had known in the past... I was worried about him."

After Ruby had left the apartment with his dog, telling Senator he was going to the Carousel Club, he saw him next two or three days later, in jail.

Bill Alexander began the cross-examination by asking the witness if he had ever used a slightly different name: he had not. Alexander then asked an odd series of questions, suggesting Ruby was going to send his dog to a man in Los Angeles, the inference being he was planning to send his beloved animal away because he knew he would not be able to care for it. Senator said he'd never heard of the guy, knew nothing about that plan and Ruby had never told him he was getting rid of the dog.

Most of the prosecution questions were intended to simply plant thoughts in the minds of the jurors. For example, "Did Ruby say...the people who had placed that ad in the *Dallas Morning News*...should be put in jail, shipped out of the country and be sent to Russia, executed or anything like that?"

"No."

When asked by Alexander how Ruby looked that Sunday morning, Senator replied, "He looked pretty bad."

"Well," the prosecutor asked, indicating the defendant, "Does he look bad now?"

The witness glanced at Ruby. "Yes," he said.

The prosecution then went after Ruby's character. Senator said he had seen Ruby throw drunks out of his club as many as ten times, sometimes resulting in a fight. But "You never saw him have a fight with a man as big as he was, that was sober, did you?"

"Size made no difference to him."

"He picked on drunks and women, didn't he?" Ruby, sitting only a few feet away from Alexander, did not show any response to this provocation. Senator simply disagreed.

Alexander's attack on Ruby continued, "When he is thinking, looking into his eyes it's just like looking into a crawfish's eyes, isn't it… Take a look at him and see if you don't agree."

"I don't know."

Belli countered that by asking if Senator knew "whether Jack rescued Officer Blankenship who was about to be murdered by a couple…"

Objection. Sustained.

Senator's testimony had something for each side; prosecutors could argue that Ruby's emotional response to the shooting showed the evolution of a premeditated decision to kill Oswald, while the defense hoped it added to the mental illness mosaic being carefully pieced together. It would, however, serve as an obstacle for those who would claim Ruby was part of a larger conspiracy because if Senator's depiction of Ruby's despondent reaction was accurate, it would mean that Ruby wasn't just a conspirator but also a polished actor fooling even those who knew him best.

As Senator stepped down he was greeted publicly, reported the *Chronicle,* by two "friendly IRS agents who wanted to talk to him about returns of recent years." Perhaps just a reminder exactly the type of people with whom Ruby hung around.

Jack Ruby's world fascinated the still conservative Dallas community at large. The cast of witnesses brought this nighttime world, and the people who lived and worked in it, onto the front page. The next witness was Patricia Ann Kohs, who had briefly danced in Ruby's strip club, mostly on amateur nights, under her stage name, Penny Dollar. Perfectly in character, according to the *New York Times,* "She was demurely clad in a plaid jumper and a powder-blue blouse with long sleeves," and a floppy little-girl bow pinned at her throat. Although that paper's Homer Bigart added, "She is currently under arrest on charges of possessing dangerous drugs."

No one was surprised that Belli, given his reputation as a man who enjoyed talking to attractive women, did the questioning. He asked her specifically about one incident in which Ruby had fought with a taxi driver. "It was closing time at the club," she remembered. "The cab driver had come to get someone and evidently that person had left and Jack knocked him down the stairs. I didn't hear exactly what started it. He knocked him down the stairs and out the door...and when I got there Jack was beating his head on the sidewalk.

"...and then he stopped all of a sudden, and he said, 'Did I do this? Did I do this?' He acted like he didn't know that he had done it."

"What was the cab driver doing?"

"Nothing. He was groaning."

And what happened after that? "I don't know. It was confusing and I was upset. It just struck in my mind the way he could do that, and didn't even realize...he acted like he didn't realize he had done this." This was arguably the most relevant witness for the defense thus far. She wasn't just saying that Ruby was volatile and odd, but that he seemed to not recall a violent incident immediately after it happened. Precisely what the defense was arguing here.

Once again, Bill Alexander asked the questions for the prosecution. And once again he attacked Ruby's character, claiming the witness had told the FBI she had seen Ruby "shove a woman down those stairs and struck her escort, who was a much smaller person than him."

"No," she insisted. He repeated the question several times, and always got the same response: No.

When that failed, he went after Ruby's vanity. "He was proud of his physical build, wasn't he?" He was. "He used to come back in the girls dressing room and show off his muscles...he liked to take off his shirt to show his chest?" Yes.

Belli's first question on his redirect picked up Alexander's theme: "Did you think he was mentally sick, Penny?"

"Well, I'm not a doctor," she said in a slight, breathless Marilyn Monroe–like voice, "but in my personal opinion I think there was something wrong with him, yes." As she was getting ready to leave the stand, Belli asked Judge Brown, knowing she was housed in the jail upstairs, "Could she call her mother. Her mother called me and asked if she would call."

Objection.

The defense followed with a series of witnesses who would create a fuller picture of Ruby. Roy Pryor, a printer at the *Times Herald* who had worked at the Carousel Club as a musician and MC, had gone with Ruby when he distributed Christmas gifts to children at a Catholic orphanage. He also recalled Ruby the hustler, who had gotten the franchise rights to a square plywood device he referred to as a twist board, which supposedly helped people lose weight, and was looking for ways to promote it. He had seen Ruby after the assassination, and testified that Ruby believed he had "scooped" his competitors by getting an ad in the paper, with a black border, announcing his clubs would be closed that weekend "as a memorial to the late president."

Throughout the day sheriff's deputies continued searching for the two escaped prisoners who had still not been found. The first defense witness after the midday break was WNEW radio reporter Ike Pappas who had been standing next to Oswald when he was shot. Pappas was all New York, a chunky, feisty, self-assured man. "You are the man who was standing closest to Jack Ruby…" Belli began. He was five or six feet away from him. Pappas was using a state-of-the-art Nagra tape recorder made in Switzerland, considered the best machine currently available "for broadcasting quality."

His broadcast was replayed: "There's Oswald. That's the prisoner, wearing the light sweater. He has changed from his T-shirt. Being moved out toward an armored car…" Pappas could be heard shouting, "'Do you have anything to say in defense?'" But before he could respond the shot was heard.

The courtroom was calm. The jurors looked up and straight ahead, listening.

"'There's a shot. Oswald has been shot. Oswald has been shot. A shot rang out. Mass confusion here...'

"'He appears dead.'"

What was vital to the defense was what was not heard on the tape: "Did you hear Jack Ruby say anything from your position?"

"I heard nothing before the shot went off... I heard two moans after the shot..."

Specifically what he did not hear is what Detectives Archer and McMillon testified to, that Ruby had shouted at Oswald, "Take that, you son of a bitch," as he fired.

During his cross-examination, Wade tried to mitigate the damage, sitting at the prosecution table about ten feet away from the witness and biting down hard on his cigar as he suggested, "That thing [the mike] won't pick up a voice plain, for instance where I'm sitting, or things where you could understand. You might hear a noise but to hear everything they said, you couldn't hear it, could you?"

Pappas corrected him. "No sir, I say it would pick it up quite clearly."

Wade was in a combative mood. "You mean nobody said anything in the basement in all of that?" He waved his cigar in his hand. "I heard you ask Captain Fritz something, did he say anything?"

"You heard me talk to Captain Fritz on the tape?"

"Yes."

"No, I didn't talk to Captain Fritz on the tape."

It got worse for Wade as he attempted to correct the witness. "You asked him do you have anything to say, Captain?"

"No, that was to Oswald, I was talking sir... He just looked at me."

Following Pappas, the news director of the local TV station WFAA, Robert Walker, testified that his station had been informed that Oswald was scheduled to be moved at 10:00 a.m. Sunday morning and had broadcast that repeatedly Saturday morning, reinforcing the defense contention that Ruby was in the basement by chance rather than by plan. Walker verified that a brief WFAA film clip showed the killing. Those men in the clip were identified, including Pappas, who was standing so close to Oswald that his microphone surely would have recorded Ruby's shouting. Tonahill also focused on a clock in the city hall office, asking "What time does the clock say there?"

The answer was 11:20.

Two more witnesses rounded out the preliminary portion of the defense case, including ambulance driver Michael Hardin who had been called to the scene and recalled, "We picked him [Oswald] up and put him on the stretcher…at eleven twenty-four."

The defense had done a credible job making its case that Jack Ruby was a strange guy, subject to violent outbursts and perhaps even blackouts, who had inadvertently been at the scene when Oswald was moved. They had at least raised questions about prosecution witnesses who claimed to have heard Ruby screaming as he shot Oswald and later expressing satisfaction with his success. In an ordinary murder trial this might have proved sufficient to show Ruby had not acted with malice and therefore should not be convicted of a death-penalty crime. At the least there appeared to be significant reasonable doubt about the most serious charge.

But this was hardly an ordinary trial.

It was still up to Belli to justify his curious defense. He had to prove Jack Ruby was insane.

CHAPTER TEN

On a cold February day in 1859, Congressman Daniel Sickles caught US Attorney Barton Key, known as "the handsomest man in Washington," signaling Sickles's wife to arrange a romantic rendezvous. The enraged congressman approached Key and screamed, "You scoundrel, you have dishonored my home. You must die," then shot him several times with his derringer. The wounded man pleaded for his life, but Sickles killed him with one final shot.

Congressman Sickles was charged with murder. But public sentiment strongly supported him, his wife confessed her infidelities, and even President James Buchanan sent a warm, public letter. His legal defenders, including future Secretary of War Edwin Stanton proposed a unique defense that had never before been used in an American courtroom: not guilty due to temporary insanity.

According to his lead attorney, John Graham, Sickles had acted "under the influence of a frenzy..." During the trial, as

Sickles sobbed loudly, one witness testified the defendant was suffering, "an agony of despair, the most terrible thing I ever saw in my life.... I feared if it continued he would become permanently insane." While insanity had been a defense, there was no precedent for the concept of temporary insanity, acting in a fit of passion. In his charge to the jury, the judge told the twelve men that they must consider the state of Sickles's mind at the moment he committed the murder. To the cheers of the courtroom he was acquitted, and the concept of temporary insanity became an accepted defense.

In America's first sensational crime of the twentieth century, Harry K. Thaw, the heir to a coal and railway fortune, shot and killed famed architect Stanford White. White had designed several of New York's iconic structures, including the original Penn Station and the Washington Square Arch. Thaw's defense lawyers contended their client suffered a "brain storm," a temporary loss of reason, after being told by his new wife, a beautiful young chorus girl named Evelyn Nesbit, that White had raped her several years earlier, taking her virginity.

The trial mesmerized the nation; for the first time in American legal history a jury was sequestered. Famed defense attorney Delphin Delmas claimed Thaw was a perfectly sane young man—except for that one night, when his love for his beautiful wife drove him temporarily insane. In this case Delmas put the emerging field of psychiatry on trial. "If Thaw is insane," he railed to the jury, "it is with a species of insanity known from the Canadian border to the Gulf... I suggest that you label it Dementias Americana...that species of insanity that persuades an American that whoever violates the sanctity of his home or the purity of his wife or daughter—has forfeited the protections of the laws..."

After a trial lasting several months, the jury was deadlocked. A new team of defense lawyers in a second trial changed the plea to not guilty by reason of insanity. After listening to the testimony of several psychiatrists, the jury found Thaw not guilty; he was committed for life to the Matteawan State Hospital for the Criminally Insane in Beacon, New York. He and Nesbit divorced and she became a sensation on the vaudeville circuit. After several years, and one escape attempt, he was released.

In 1924, legendary trial lawyer Clarence Darrow's defended teenaged "thrill killers" Nathan Leopold and Richard Loeb, who murdered fourteen-year-old Bobby Franks in an attempt to commit "the perfect crime." Darrow had pled his clients guilty to murder in order to avoid a jury but then proceeded to try to persuade the presiding judge that Leopold and Loeb were mentally ill and should not be sentenced to death. "We have sought to show you…the condition of these boys' minds," he told the judge. "Of course it is not an easy task to find out the condition of another person's mind…" As several psychiatrists testified, he continued, "brains are not the chief essential in human conduct… The emotions are the urge that make us live… They are instinctive things… Whatever our action is, it comes from emotions and nobody is balanced without them…

"The old indictments used to read that a man being possessed by the devil did so-and-so. But why was he possessed by the devil?… Very few half-civilized people believe that doctrine anymore. Science has been at work…and intelligent people now know that every human being is the product of endless heredity back of him and the infinite environment around him. He is made as he is…and under the same stress and storm you would act one way and I act another…"

Both the prosecution and defense called eminent psychiatrists and neurologists who supported their contrasting positions, causing the *New York Times* to complain these men "of equal authority as alienists and psychiatrists…" provided "opinions exactly opposite and contradictory…supporting a predetermined purpose…" The two young men avoided the death penalty and were sentenced to ninety-nine-years in prison. Loeb was killed in prison; Leopold was paroled after serving thirty-three years.

By the time of the Ruby trial, what had been known as temporary insanity or "heat of passion" was increasingly treated as a defense that could lead to a lesser charge and reduce the sentence rather than leading to an all-out acquittal. But Belli had decided to follow a different path. He was going to show that Ruby had not been temporarily insane but rather suffered from a rare mental illness that only recently had been discovered. Belli intended to use the relatively new art of encephalograms, the charting of the electrical brain waves, to prove Ruby had been in a "trance-like state" when he acted and therefore could not be guilty of murder.

Doing so required putting a long line of medical experts on the stand and dragging jurors through a morass of often dense and complicated medical testimony. Making it even more difficult was the reality that the prosecution likely would counter with its own expert medical witnesses who would offer very different opinions. As *Scientific American* had complained as early as 1872 "As now presented to juries, the testimony of the both competent and incompetent witnesses, only serves to muddle their intellects, and to complicate rather than make plain the facts."

The first of Belli's expert witnesses was Yale University clinical psychologist Dr. Roy Schafer, a tall, slender man dressed in the Ivy League requisite tweed jacket and horn-rimmed glasses. Dr. Schafer had testified as an expert in only one other case, and that took place almost two decades earlier in Joplin, Missouri, where a minister's son had killed and dismembered a church caretaker. Schafer testified that the young man was schizophrenic and the jury agreed, finding him not guilty by reason of insanity. He was also an author or coauthor of three widely used books on psychological testing, had lectured extensively and served on important boards.

Belli began by using Schafer to educate the jury. Clinical psychology, Schafer explained, could be defined as "the attempt to study the behavior of man in scientific ways," while "psychiatry concentrates specifically on mental disorders, and the causes and management and treatment and diagnosis of mental disorders." Electroencephalograms and electrocardiograms, he continued, were important tools. "The function of various parts of the body...involve electrical activity...and these can be recorded and analyzed. They are used extensively for purposes of medical diagnosis and research." And finally, he explained, a *clinical* psychologist deals with the nonmedical aspects of mental disorders.

He had spent a total of eleven and a half hours examining Ruby. Based on that he had made a diagnosis that he believed would be borne out on electroencephalograms. Belli asked, "Have you come to an opinion as to whether Jack Ruby does or does not have organic brain damage?"

Schafer had. He replied in a slow professional monotone, "I have come to the conclusion that he did have organic brain damage, and that the most likely specific nature of it was psychomotor epilepsy." To reach that conclusion he had administered about ten different standard psychological tests, including the most widely used intelligence tests and even a Rorschach test.

Dr. Schafer continued to build a foundation for the defense case until prosecutor Jim Bowie objected, "The question before the court, Your Honor, is sanity or insanity...and if he has no opinion about that then we haven't laid a proper predicate for this testimony." In other words, was Ruby legally insane or not? If this witness wasn't qualified to state his opinion, the prosecution contended, then he should not be permitted to testify. Judge Brown let Belli's examination continue, but warned him to hurry up and make his point.

He said the Rorschach test was especially revealing. "He showed the signs of confusion, fluidity of thinking, tendencies toward incoherence and misuse of words, breakdown of sentence structure..." He continued, explaining the test has shown an array of deep psychological problems ranging from "emotional instability" to an "irrational, explosive temper."

Judge Brown called a brief recess at that point. When Belli's questioning resumed, Bowie again objected to Dr. Schafer's testimony. "The only relevancy of this, Your Honor, is on which [test] he might have based an opinion. We have never heard from this witness that he has such an opinion…we think we should first find out if he has an opinion and then these things might be admissible…"

As innocuous as it sounded, this was a direct attack on the heart of the defense case. What Bowie was asking the judge to do was apply the basic test of legal sanity: Did Dr. Schafer believe Ruby was aware he was committing a crime when he killed Oswald? Was he legally sane under the M'Naghten rule of understanding right from wrong?

That was not the reason this witness was called, Belli explained. "I've got to put on a psychologist, just like I have to put on an X-ray technician, a nurse to test the urine and protein of spinal fluid and then give this all to the internist or the diagnostician and ask him what do you make of all this…"

The judge sustained the objection, finally forcing Belli to ask the question he had been artfully avoiding. "What is your opinion with reference to his [Jack Ruby's] mental state?"

Before the witness could respond, Alexander was on his feet again, drawling out, "Now, Your Honor, we object to that. That's not a proper question. It should be as to whether he knows the difference between right and wrong and understands the nature and consequences of his act." The prosecution had laid a legal trap and Belli was ensnared. He had argued his way out of similar situations numerous times. His problem was that those other cases were different in so many ways including that Judge Joe B. Brown Sr. wasn't on the bench.

Judge Brown agreed with Alexander. "Let's get down to the

meat of the question, Mr. Belli; the legal test of insanity. Let's get on that."

Belli was on his feet too. "This man's not a doctor, Judge," he thundered. "He can't answer the legal test... This man can testify only to what they found in the laboratory..."

Jim Bowie stood. "Your Honor, if he had no opinion as to the sanity or insanity of Jack Ruby on or about the 24th day of November, 1963, and to the extent that he didn't know the difference between right and wrong and the consequences of his act, all of this is irrelevant and immaterial."

"The Court's going to sustain you in that, counsel."

Belli was irate! "Sustain him in what?" This testimony was the foundation for his entire defense. It laid the groundwork for the psychiatric testimony that was to be presented. If it wasn't allowed, the defense could collapse.

The M'Naghten rule, Judge Brown said, leaning forward and speaking in a derisive tone that suggested the answer to that question should be obvious, "Whether or not the man knew right from wrong and if he has an opinion as to his ability to determine the nature and consequences of his act."

"This man hasn't even taken a case history from him," Belli fumed. He was fighting for his case with all of the legal skills acquired throughout his long career. "You can't ask the nurse who has taken a temperature, or a bowel specimen, whether she thinks the man has smallpox...if he answered a question like that he'd be infringing the medical domain. He is a PhD and a psychologist in a particular field... I'm not going to ask him questions beyond his own field."

Judge Brown did not waver. He placed the palms of his hands firmly on his desk and leaned forward. His normally casual demeanor had been replaced by a stern, slightly threatening attitude. "The Court has sustained the State's objection. You may have an exception, sir, to the sustaining of the objection."

"I don't want an exception. I want what this man has done

laboriously over a hundred hours…" He asked the court reporter to reread his question to Schafer about his opinion, in which the doctor stated Ruby was suffering from psychomotor epilepsy. He was trying to find a path around the objection. "I ask you next, what is psychomotor epilepsy?"

Objection.

Belli appealed to the judge. "I make an offer of proof to show that psychomotor epilepsy does give these blackout states. Now, he was not there at the time of the shooting."

"That's not what you asked."

Belli did not back off. "If he were dishonest and I were dishonest we'd pop right out and say this is the M'Naghten Rule case, but I want your honor to hear what this man has to say."

"Mr. Belli," Judge Brown said, perhaps revealing more than he intended, "the Court is not interested in what he has to say, except from the legal standpoint, an admissible standpoint."

Belli tried again to talk common sense. "Judge, he's not a lawyer… I make an offer of proof to show that the particular clinical character and course of [psychomotor epilepsy] is that they do automatic acts under stress. This man will say that is the most likely course of conduct from him [Ruby] that day."

"To which we object…"

"Mr. Belli, I've sustained the State's objection to it."

"I don't even know what they're objecting to," Belli continued, his loud voice filling the courtroom. "I mean, if you want to shut us off here and close our briefcases and say we can't show the most modern in medicine as to what is in a man's mind, that's one thing. But if we're going to be given part of a defense here and then shut off, then I just don't know, under the law of Texas or any other law where I can go."

As the argument continued, Dr. Schafer sat back in the witness chair, a puzzled look on his face. He looked as if he might stick a pipe in his mouth at any moment. Belli had little ammunition left, other than threats of an appeal. He suggested the judge remove the jury, warning, "...so help me, I'm going to make a record on this for some court, Your Honor," adding, "and I say that respectfully."

After the jury had been removed, Judge Brown told Belli, "I'm going to hold him to testimony concerning the law of insanity in Texas... If Dr. Schafer has an opinion as to whether the man was sane or insane on the day of this occurrence, I have no objection to his testifying."

Belli then launched into what would have been his long and detailed opening address, explaining the fundamentals of his case. His psychiatric experts were there to testify "that this man did not know the difference between right and wrong, the nature and consequences of his act, or what he was doing at the time he shot Mr. Oswald." The purpose of putting Dr. Schafer on the stand was to show where they got the tools that enabled them to reach that conclusion. "This is the lab work they need in order to corroborate their opinion. If he is stricken from the case these [experts] can still testify, just like in the middle ages they would know that a leg was broken by seeing it askew. But with the X-ray they are better able to tell which is broken; the tibia, the fibula, the femur or what...

"I am not permitted to ask him under Texas law his opinion with reference to M'Naghten's Rule because he is not the doctor... I cannot press him...into the field of psychiatry because if I did, Your Honor, the Supreme Court would wonder why they are allowing a psychologist to testify in psychiatry."

Clearly Judge Brown did not miss Belli's reference to the Supreme Court. Almost all of the cases he adjudicated ended forever in his courtroom, but whatever the verdict this case clearly was going beyond that and would take with it his reputation.

Belli continued his impassioned argument. "If you cut him off then you may as well throw out the X-rays...and just call in psychiatrists and say, 'Just from talking to a man, from that you should be able to tell, looking in a crystal ball, whether he knows the difference between right and wrong at a time you weren't there."

Based on his testing, he explained, Dr. Schafer was able to correctly predict the electroencephalograms would show psychomotor variant epilepsy. Belli went beyond that in his argument, asking Judge Brown to appoint an impartial examiner. He finally concluded, "If you deny us his testimony then you deny us the stepping stone and the foundation of all modern psychiatry and psychology..."

Alexander had heard enough, interrupting to repeat the prosecution's insistence that basic legal question be answered. Essentially, they argued, "if he is testifying as an expert we're entitled to hear his opinion."

Belli faced Alexander and explained, "If I were to ask this man, 'How do you take out tonsils?' and he were to answer me, I think he'd be guilty of malpractice..."

Judge Brown repeated his decision. "I'm going to exclude his testimony. The Court's going to sustain the State's objection to it, Mr. Belli."

Suddenly Belli saw a small opening, and he raced to it. "Being that we can't put any of this testimony in?... Your Honor is going to tell this jury in 1964 not to take the testimony of this great man from Yale University..." And then he stuck in the knife, "...in Dallas."

"Yes."

At some point during Belli's seemingly hopeless plea, the prosecutors suddenly realized what they had done: based on their objection it appeared the judge was ruling that all medical testimony that might be offered to explain how a doctor reached an opinion also was barred. Every lawyer in that courtroom recognized the danger of that decision; it almost certainly would cause any guilty verdict to be thrown out on appeal.

The prosecution began backtracking, trying to cover its footprints, asking Belli for an assurance that defense experts were going to testify that they used Schafer's report as the basis of their conclusion. Belli knew he had them. "I'm not telling anything," he said, now back in control. "I'm going to play by Texas law. I'm not telling anybody nothing."

Judge Brown was ready to move on. Decision made. Let's go. But Jim Bowie started looking for an escape route. He suddenly became conciliatory, asking the defense to assure them this testimony would eventually be connected to expert testimony. That was precisely the point Belli had been making, but he wasn't about to let the prosecution off so easily.

"I'm not assuring anyone of anything at this stage of the game, Your Honor... I believe my brother is very concerned with the error that he has again led Your Honor into in striking this testimony."

As if he had been hit on the head with his own nonexistent gavel, Judge Brown finally got it. Recognizing the danger, he started looking for a legal path out of it, asking Belli the obvious question, did his psychiatric experts rely on this material to reach their conclusions? A yes would give him the excuse he needed to allow it.

Belli savored his rare victory, refusing to help the court resolve its own error. "They can do this without it," he said. "As I said, in the middle ages we could tell whether a leg was broken by looking at the configuration of the limb." He picked up the thread, explaining the value of Schafer's testimony. The defense, he explained, must show what was happening in Ruby's mind when he killed Oswald. And yes, this testimony was vital to accomplishing that.

By this point the prosecution was in full retreat. "If they want to assure us—some doctor has used his results in forming an opinion...that may be somewhat legal. We would have no objection to going into it."

"Mr. Belli?" asked Judge Brown, "are you going to connect it up?"

"Certainly… This is the basis of all of it."

"I don't want to preclude you…"

"I know Your Honor doesn't."

For the first time in this argument, Wade spoke up, surrendering. "Judge, let's let him go on. I think we could have finished by now. So let's go on and let him testify."

With a verbal smirk, Belli agreed, "I think they see the magnitude of their error…"

Seemingly having been guided by the prosecution, Judge Brown quickly changed his decision, snapping, "Let's hear some testimony." Having won that skirmish, the defense continued to methodically lay the medical groundwork for later psychiatric experts. Epilepsy, Dr. Schafer explained, "is a group of conditions that vary a great deal in their clinical signs…

"Probably the most familiar type of epilepsy is what's called grand mal epilepsy, frequently known as the falling sickness, where there's a loss of consciousness and large jerks of the body and frothing at the mouth… Petit mal has to do with brief periods of apparent blanking out, interruption of activity, then picking up when the person comes to." Dr. Schafer continued as if teaching an introductory course. "The psychomotor epilepsy is another variant in this group…and it's defined chiefly by an alteration in a state of consciousness." That altered state, he continued, would result in "confusion, disorientation as to where they are or what they are doing. They may afterwards have amnesia of the attack…they may go on carrying out organized types of actions, but without being aware of what they're doing or the connection of it with what they have done before. Very frequently the attacks involve expressions of rage of some sort, but not always…

"…Some patients with psychomotor epilepsy act very bizarrely during their attack and frequently are thought to be schizophrenic until neurological examinations are conducted on them and they may be capable of more or less organized action during attacks." These seizures, which also were known as "fugues," might last anywhere from a few seconds to a day or even two.

While medical science could not identify either a cause for this condition or a trigger for the attacks, Dr. Schafer thought it might be connected to the several head injuries Ruby had suffered earlier in his life, or perhaps encephalitis, an inflammation of the brain perhaps caused by a virus, or a bacterial infection.

Without interruption now, Belli led his witness through an explanation of the various tests he had given Ruby, some of them familiar to jurors. Like the well-known Rorschach test, for example, which requires an individual to describe inkblots, there was no right or wrong answers, just results that then could be compared with those of people with known mental issues. These tests were varied, including concepts from word association to story recall. Dr. Schafer told the jury that he had spent about one hundred hours working on this case. And as a result of all this testing he concluded, "I was certain there was some kind of brain damage present." Among the general observations of Ruby he had found "a very great preoccupation on his part with being moral, doing the right thing, making a contribution to society, taking belief in God seriously."

Hearing that, Belli asked the obvious question. "Did you know that he ran a strip tease joint at this time, when you were taking a history?"

"Yes." Dr. Schafer continued, "It was impressive to me...how preoccupied with himself in every respect he was. What he believed, what he felt, what he worried about, what in the outside world agitated him. Himself as the center of all the thoughts was a quite striking feature of the results...

"...his attitudes were consistent...which was the enormous importance of being liked, appreciated, esteemed, even to take on the glory of other people, of the status of other people, by associating with them."

This was Belli in his element, questioning an expert to educate the jury, making complex information simple enough to be understood, informing them how the conclusions were reached and trying to answer the questions they don't yet know they had. As for Jack Ruby, he often seemed more of a slightly bored spectator than a man fighting for his life. He listened as this respected psychologist said things about him to the world that might have led Ruby to fight the man had they been uttered at his club.

Belli began wrapping up this testimony, asking if Dr. Schafer had an opinion if "Jack Ruby would be subject to rage states in which he would not know what he was doing?"

"That is the case with him."

Then, "Based upon your opinion of Jack Ruby, as stated in your report and as stated to the ladies and gentlemen of the jury, do you have another opinion as to what sort of stimulus…would set him into these episodic states?"

"Well, such things as a very strong emotional stimulation… such as his readiness to take offense, sensitivity about how accepted or esteemed, or how disparaged he is… States of fatigue often seem to…precipitate seizures…"

It was already early evening, after six o'clock, as Belli's direct testimony eased to an end. Several of the jurors were beginning to show their irritation and impatience, particularly those chosen early who had now been sequestered for weeks. In an attempt to speed the pace of the trial, Judge Brown decided to continue into the night. When he announced that, Belli sighed. "I hope justice doesn't depend on an endurance test."

The judge looked at him and said evenly, "You started it."

Henry Wade began his cross-examination by asking the question Belli had refused to ask: "Did you form an opinion as to whether or not Jack Ruby knew right from wrong?"

"No."

How about whether he knew right from wrong at the time he shot Oswald?

"Not as a definite conclusion."

Wade continued his questioning in a derisive, mocking tone, as if Schafer was a big-city professor trying to fool these working-class jurors with psychobabble. At one point he showed his own confusion, misstating Schafer's testimony then becoming angry when Schafer would not defend that error. Without losing his own temper, Schafer pointed out politely, "You asked me about something I said before which I didn't say."

Wade probed Schafer's testimony, looking for loopholes. He was loud, contentious and contemptuous, at times shouting at the witness. "What do you mean when you said they were confused and you said they were disoriented and had amnesia where they didn't remember anything?"

"That's not inconsistent with their carrying out a purposeful act."

"Well, if they carry out a purposeful act then they know what they're doing, don't they?"

The witness considered that. "Well, that would depend a great deal on how you define the word purposeful."

Wade tried to explain, "…The word purpose is when you have—in common language, it means when you have a purpose you do it. So purposeful would mean with a purpose, wouldn't it?"

"Someone in a seizure state would not necessarily be purposeful in that sense."

Wade then tried to bring it back to primary issue at hand. "Let's get down to killing somebody. When he gets down to killing somebody, when he takes a gun and shoots him in the stomach, isn't that purposeful activity?"

Calmly, Dr. Schafer responded, "Anything that's an organized, efficiently carried through act could be called purposeful, but it involves a person having a clear idea of what he's doing and why…"

Wade's tone made it clear he didn't believe that. "Could a

man in a fugue state pick a target out of a crowd of two hundred people and would that be a purposeful act?"

In that same professorial monotone, Dr. Schafer repeated, "A person in a fugue state can commit murder, according to what the neurological experts say."

Wade was getting increasingly frustrated. "Anybody in any state can commit murder... I asked you if he could pick a target out of two hundred people, if he had no purpose for it? If he did, wouldn't that indicate a purposeful conduct?"

Perhaps reminiscent of the way the prosecution's law enforcement witnesses had refused to directly answer during cross-examination, the defense witness refused to be cowed. "Well, I think it's again a question of what you mean by purpose."

Frustration dripping from his increasingly raspy voice, his face reddening, Wade said, "A man with a purpose, with a gun in his hand."

"I don't consider that a clear enough statement of what you mean by purpose."

After increasingly unproductive questions and answers, Wade shouted at Schafer, "Under the theory you have expounded any person that wanted to, with intent, malicious intent and purposeful activity, pick a man out of a crowd and shoot him, remember all of it and you'd turn him loose on society again, wouldn't you, from what you're testifying to on psychomotor variant, or something."

In that same monotone, the witness replied, "I don't believe I said anything like that."

Belli and Tonahill objected. Belli suggested Wade ask where the witness might place Ruby. "In a state institution?"

Tonahill pointed out Wade was doing a lot more arguing than questioning.

Wade persevered. "If his conduct was purposeful, he had the intent, he remembered what happened, not confused, would you still stay he was in a fugue state?"

"He might have been."

"Oh, he might have been," Wade taunted.

Wade finally gave up on this line of questioning and turned to the proven way of discrediting testimony, suggesting Dr. Schafer had been rehearsed by the opposing side, or that the doctor was being well paid for his helpful testimony (Wade: "I assume Mr. Belli will pay you…") and finally trying to show him up. Pointing out that Dr. Schafer had conducted hundreds of memory tests by asking the patient to repeat a story, he asked the doctor to repeat the story from the test from memory.

"The American liner, *New York*, struck a mine near Liverpool on Monday evening. In spite of a blistering snow storm and heavy seas…" the doctor recited.

Wade interrupted. Holding a sheet of paper he said, "This says darkness here."

"Darkness. Yes." Then he continued, getting four words wrong and forcing Wade to give him a passing grade.

When asked if he was able to determine that Ruby had organic brain damage from what he left out or what he put in on the same test, Schafer asked permission to refer to his notes.

"Don't you remember it?" Wade asked sarcastically.

"There's no need for me to memorize his response." Ruby had scored a dismal 7 of a possible 23 on that test, he added.

Wade finally returned to his original point, after all that testing, after one hundred hours. "You have no opinion as to whether he knew the difference between right and wrong when he shot Lee Harvey Oswald?"

"No, sir."

Belli started his redirect exam by citing Wade's threat that Ruby was going to be "turned loose on society" and asking the witness what other forms of treatment might be applicable. Wade objected. At times the two lead lawyers seemed to enjoy insulting each other. When Wade complained, "Your Honor, that's leading," Tonahill pointed out, "It's a quarter of seven too, Judge," and Belli smiled at Wade and told him, "That's all right, I'm just warming up."

Then, at that late hour, Belli brought up another word that few people understood. "What is confabulation?"

"It's a term," Dr. Schafer responded, "...that has been used for organic brain damaged patients who fill in gaps in their memory." Rather than admitting they have no memory of their actions, "...they draw material from everywhere, from outside, from imagination, but anything to give the appearance of continuity and coherence."

It means "filling the vacuum of the mind," Belli suggested, with "things they pick up from other people?"

It was common among brain-damaged people, Schafer agreed, people who find it "very difficult to recognize any sign of having a defect... It's an attempt to gloss over or blot out any sign of it."

Belli proceeded to tie up the rest of the threads Wade had pulled: the defense did not influence his testimony; Ruby did not "try to malinger or mislead." And in his entire career, Schafer had testified only once before.

He never raised his voice. With a dismissive wave of his hand, Wade declined to ask any additional questions. Perhaps Wade was aware of the result in that other case where Schafer had testified.

It seemed Belli's strategy was, at the least, being taken seriously.

Court was adjourned for the night.

CHAPTER ELEVEN

At one point during the psychiatric testimony, Bob Considine had excused himself from the courtroom for a period of time. When he returned, he asked *Kansas City Star* reporter Bob Sanford, "What happened?"

"I don't know," Sanford admitted, "I was asleep."

The difficulty with much expert testimony, especially involving medical issues, is that it can be too difficult or technical for the average juror (or reporter) to understand. The world of medicine has its own language and most lay people don't speak it. As a result, while the testimony proceeds, jurors zone out. They lose interest. Throughout his career Belli had managed to overcome this tendency by using visual aids, for example unwrapping an artificial leg or displaying a human brain. The kind of unusual exhibits that fascinate people. As he had demonstrated in his past cases, it was not nearly as important for jurors to understand the complicated medical testimony as it was for them to feel his clients' pain.

The question of how jurors finally reach a verdict is complicated; often it's a brew of facts and feelings. No one would deny the role that emotions play. If a juror sympathizes with a plaintiff in a civil trial or a defendant in a criminal trial, the chances of finding for that person increase significantly.

Trial lawyers approach the presentation of complicated medical testimony in several different ways. They might try to keep it brief and confined to easily grasped concepts or they might try to overwhelm the jury with information, believing that while the jurors may not understand much of it, the sheer weight of expert testimony might be enough to believe there must be something to it, otherwise all these experts wouldn't be testifying.

Jurors could look at an X-ray of a bone and see it was broken but could not so easily look inside a man's brain. In addition, for many people particularly at the time, the whole field of psychiatry was suspect. A lot of it seemed like mumbo jumbo. The next day, as the participants arrived at the courthouse to resume defense testimony, they were met by protestors questioning the value of psychiatry: One of them accosted Belli, shouting loudly enough to be heard by reporters a widely held belief. "All you have to do if you don't like someone is kill them, hire a psychiatrist and get off." Another picketer carried a sign reading, "America would not need psychiatry if we all would get right with God and our fellow man." Television cameras dutifully broadcast other signs reading, "A person who does wrong is not insane" and "Psychiatry is not the hope of killers."

Belli was visibly perturbed by the demonstration, telling reporters he intended to take it up with Judge Brown—while knowing there was really nothing that could be done about it.

The defense began the day's presentation by calling to the stand Dr. Martin Towler, a specialist in neurology and psychiatry, but equally important, a Texan. A real bona fide Texan, with the requisite local drawl. Towler was a short man, with neatly combed red hair and a florid complexion. As Belli established, Towler was on the staff at the University of Texas branch hospital in Galveston, Texas. He had been trained at the University of Texas in Austin. During World War II, he had been Chief of Neuropsychiatric Service at Fort Sam Houston, located in San Antonio.

Towler had initially been brought into the case as a court-appointed consultant but after submitting his initial report, which did not support the prosecution, he became a defense witness. Dr. Towler was an expert in reading and interpreting electroencephalographs, having studied and written about EEGs for decades. "I read approximately four thousand a year," he explained to the court, "and I have over quite a few years."

Dr. Towler had examined Ruby; in addition to EEGs there also had been "X-ray studies of the head and skull." While the X-rays showed nothing at all unusual, he had found "abnormalities" in those EEG charts, which he described as "slow wave activity." In addition to taking Ruby's neurologic history, Towler interviewed his brother Sam and sister Eva Grant about the family's mental history. Grant told the doctor that Ruby was "a very over-active child." During that interview, Towler continued, "The sister repeatedly injected statements relative to the state of destitution in their family, alcoholic excesses and threatening and abusive behavior on the part of the father...[Jack Ruby] had dropped out of school in the ninth grade at the age of 15 because of his lack of funds and adequate clothing and the need to work and try to help support the family."

Throughout his life Ruby had suffered a series of head injuries, many of them in fights and brawls. He had been beaten by men and pistol-whipped by police officers, injured in an auto accident and fallen from a pile of lumber and on an ice-skating rink. The tip of his left pinkie had to be amputated after he was badly bitten in a 1954 fight. As a result of it all, Towler continued, Ruby claimed to have suffered attacks lasting thirty or forty seconds during which he felt "like my head was cracking up... I

LAWRENCE SCHILLER/POLARIS COMMUNICATIONS/ GETTY IMAGES

Ruby was the fifth of ten children of Polish immigrants Joseph Rubenstein and Fannie Turek Rutkowski. At various times he worked as a salesman for his brother Earl and then got into the nightlife business managing his sister Eva Grant's Singapore Club. Earl and Eva, seen leaving the trial, actively participated in his defense.

did not feel like I was there" and that he was going to blackout. Initially, Ruby told Dr. Towler these "spells" had begun fifteen or twenty years earlier, but then said they had started eight or nine years earlier; a day later he claimed they had started three or four years earlier and finally admitted he didn't know when they had begun.

There was more; Eva Grant had told Towler about her brother's persistent memory problems, giving "examples of the subject having given her funds to deposit in the bank and later insisting he had not done so. She cited other examples...when confronted with this the subject would become extremely fractious and irritable and a squabble would ensue."

The only way to determine the validity, or perhaps the cause of these sudden attacks, Towler explained in his slow and methodical drawl, was to take EEGs. Belli finally got to the key question: "In your opinion, first you have an opinion that he has an abnormal mental condition, is that right?"

"An abnormal electroencephalographic pattern and a seizure disorder...this type of seizure disorder most accurately falls into the category of psychomotor variant. This type of seizure phenomenon has recently been described by Dr. Frederick A. Gibbs in the December 1963 issue of *Neurology*."

While it elicited no unusual response, this comment was incredible: Belli was staking his entire defense, his client's life, on a rare condition that had first been described in the official journal of the American Academy of Neurology only three months earlier.

Minutes later he tried to question the witness about his collaboration with Gibbs on that recent report. The prosecution objected because "Dr. Gibbs is beyond the jurisdiction of the Court," meaning he could not be questioned about any claims Towler made on his behalf. Judge Brown sustained it, but now the shadow of Dr. Gibbs hung over the trial.

To make sure the jury accepted this testimony as unbiased, Belli established that Dr. Towler was not being paid a fee. The reason he had decided to work without payment, the doctor explained, was that, "I felt there was a real need here for someone to look at the neurology aspects of this question...that it should be done as objectively and in as totally unbiased a manner as could be. If I allied myself with either the Prosecution or the Defense..."

Objection. Self-serving. Sustained. But it was too late; the jury could not unhear that testimony.

Belli did a little catching up. The jury was now familiar with the concept of a "psychomotor seizure" but didn't really understand what it meant. Towler explained "psychomotor seizures manifest themselves in a multiplicity of things...an unusual detachment from reality...strange feelings of familiarity, during which time there may be some impairment, conscious awareness, total loss of conscious awareness...overwhelming feelings of anxiety or apprehension, feeling of impending catastrophe... moodiness, despondency or despair...

"...and unpredictable behavior."

Unpredictable behavior. During a psychomotor seizure Towler continued, people "can perform ordinary everyday routine with a high degree of precision... One case that is most outstanding in my memory is that of an enlisted man, who proceeded to get into an automobile belonging to the Commanding General and to drive it several blocks down the street and wrecked it."

"During the time of the seizure or spell from the automatic behavior, does the man know what he is doing?"

"No," Towler said softly. "He is behaving as an automaton. He may have smattering bits of memory. Most patients will be amnesic for the entire episode..."

The type of behavior the doctor was describing was eerily similar to that portrayed by author Richard Condon in his 1959 bestselling novel, and the subsequent movie *The Manchurian Candidate*, starring Frank Sinatra and Angela Lansbury. In that story an American soldier who was captured and brainwashed by the North Koreans during the Korean War had been programmed to commit a political assassination while in a sort of hypnotic trance. While in that state he was able to take actions and perform tasks but would have no memory of doing so. He would not be able to describe what he did, how he did it or who else was involved.

While few people were suggesting Ruby actually had been brainwashed, the possibility that a human being could perform horrendous acts without being aware of it, as Dr. Towler was testifying, had been debated in newspapers since the release of the movie only two years earlier without reaching any conclusion.

The possibility that Communists were involved in both the Kennedy assassination and the subsequent—and some claimed "convenient"—murder of the assassin was one of the pillars of the growing conspiracy theories. Oswald *had* lived in Russia and *was* married to a woman he met while living there. Ruby *had* visited Communist Cuba and some people had claimed to have seen Oswald in his club. At the height of the Cold War, the battle between western democracy and eastern bloc Communism, this speculation hardly seemed far-fetched. For many people, it was terrifyingly possible.

Ruby's own explanations of the killing might well be "confabulation," Towler continued. "Confabulation is a description of something that did not happen," he continued in that same pleasant Texas manner. "The individual is trying to cover up his memory gap..."

Finally Belli got to his exhibit, the "wow" factor that jurors could see with their own eyes. In this case, the evidence consisted of six hundred feet of multifolded chart paper with black spidery lines stretching the entire length. These were two EEGs, two studies of the electrical activity in Jack Ruby's brain.

Belli began with a brief history of the electroencephalogram: EEGs had been in wide use since 1934. There was little a subject could do to alter or influence these recordings; any attempts to influence the tracings would be reflected and easily interpreted on the charts. Schizophrenia or paranoia would not show up on these charts as they are not caused by organic brain damage. None of the abnormalities that can be interpreted from an EEG would be visible to the casual observer. A person could be having an episode without it being outwardly detectable.

Belli and Tonahill unfolded the charts right in front of the jury box. Each of them held an end. Wade and Alexander stood behind them, peering over their shoulders. The jurors clearly were fascinated by the display, as Belli had hoped. The jurors in the back row stood. Max Causey sat back and continued chewing gum while Waymon Rose held his cigar in his hand and leaned forward.

Using a red grease pencil, Belli circled those places on the chart where, Dr. Towler explained, "We recorded abnormal discharges." These "sudden and complete changes in the pattern and frequency of the voltage" were the visual evidence of mental impairment, and after some explanation it was simple for the jury to pick them out.

The testimony began to get overly technical, and at one point Tonahill glanced at Judge Brown and was shocked to see him on the bench reading a bright yellow comic book. Later, in his own defense, Judge Brown would point out it wasn't a comic book, "It was a lurid account in text and drawings of the assassination" that had been given to him by Joe Tonahill himself. "Almost any judge can follow testimony automatically when there are no legal snarls to engage his attention. In fact," he added, somewhat perplexingly, "if I had indicated an unusual interest in the EEG tracings it might have been construed as improper interest."

Page by page, chart by chart, impulse by impulse Towler explained what was taking place in Ruby's brain: "Most of the abnormal discharges here were recorded in a state of drowsiness."

"Was there any significance in it picking up the drowsiness?"

"I don't know if it is significant. I know it is a fact."

Great trial lawyers can "read" juries. Belli liked to tell people he was expert at understanding body language. But as the morning light flowed across the courtroom he continued droning on, making the same point over and over and over: there were abnormalities in Jack Ruby's EEGs. There was something mentally wrong with him. Gradually the jurors sat down and settled back into their seats. Even Jack Ruby began yawning. At last, Belli finished.

Henry Wade began his cross-examination by asking the obvious question. "You found nothing abnormal other than the few seconds that you mentioned, on the encephalogram?"

"All of the studies were normal, with the exception of the

electroencephalographic recordings… The neurologic exam was all normal."

But Wade went a step too far when he suggested that this EEG was common, that "a lot of people have abnormal discharges that are not epileptic?"

Towler corrected him. "A very small percent of normal people, in fact less than one percent of normal people, might have this type of abnormality and not have seizure manifestation."

Wade just plowed through, moving quickly past those answers that did not square with his argument. Finally he got to his most important questions: Would a person in this fugue state "know the difference between right and wrong, and the consequences of their acts?"

"In most instances, no…"

But Wade persisted, almost as if he hadn't heard the previous testimony. "As a matter of fact, they wouldn't perform any purposeful behavior while in a fugue state, would they?"

"They could perform what seemed to be purposeful behavior."

Wade never wavered. His tone made his disdain for these claims obvious. "…Driving a car is a lot different from taking a gun in your hand… Now, do you think a man in one of these fugue states could find his way into the basement of the Dallas city jail, slip past a policeman with as gun in his hand, two hundred people in the basement;…fight his way through all of them and kill one person, and while killing him say, 'You son of a bitch.' Do you think that sounds like a person who didn't know what he was doing?"

Towler never raised his voice. Admitting he could not know if the subject was in a fugue state, he explained again, "The behavior of an individual during a psychomotor seizure, or in a fugue state is unpredictable."

With his voice rising until he was shouting at the witness, Wade asked with incredulity, "You have no opinion on whether he knew the difference between right or wrong or the nature and consequences of his act?"

The witness responded evenly, "I have not attempted to establish that."

Unable to shake him, Wade finally tried to disparage his testimony. "That's just your opinion," he said. "Do opinions of experts vary on what this means?"

"There can be differences of opinion," Towler admitted. The readings might be interpreted differently. When asked to name some of the outstanding EEG men in the field he, replied instantly, "Of course, Dr. Frederick Gibbs is considered to be the father of encephalography, having done, I think, more basic research." Dr. Gibbs had been asked to testify by the defense and refused, telling Tonahill he would not testify unless summoned by the court as an expert witness not by one of the parties.

Dr. Gibbs's article in *Neurology*, "Psychomotor Variant Type of Seizure Discharge," reported that he had discovered this condition in 253 of 50,000 consecutive encephalographic studies he had done. It was quite rare, he wrote, "We believe it is an abnormality for we have found it in only 2 of 1700 control subjects…"

During his redirect examination, Belli pointed out that Towler had sent his findings to Dr. Gibbs for…

Objection. Sustained.

When the afternoon session began, the defense called Dr. Manfred S. Guttmacher. During the lunch break, Belli had told reporters, "We either make it or break it this afternoon."

Dr. Guttmacher actually was a strange choice to be the key defense witness; in his book *Psychiatry and the Law* he had essentially dismissed the concept of temporary insanity. "A supposed form of disorder," he'd written, "frequently encountered in the courtroom, though not elsewhere is temporary insanity." It existed "solely in the minds of lawyers seeking a defense for their clients." Insanity doesn't come and go, he believed; a person does not go crazy in sudden bursts of insanity, therefore there is nothing temporary about it.

Asked about those comments by journalists, he replied that a mental condition could not suddenly develop then just as quickly disappear. That's not the way mental illness works. Putting him on the stand to make or break this case was a dicey matter, and Belli had chosen to roll those dice.

Long before the trial had begun, the defense had to consider a critical question: Would they put Jack Ruby on the witness stand? Until the late 1860s an accused person was prohibited from testifying in his or her own behalf, based on the assumption that their testimony could not be trusted. Prior to that, several states permitted a defendant to make an unsworn statement to the jury, allowing those twelve people to reach their own decision about its validity. Whether to have a client testify can be the most difficult decision a criminal lawyer has to make. In reality, most quickly decide that the risk is too great, particularly in murder cases. But in his opening statement, Belli had suggested to the jurors that they would hear from Ruby. Behind the scenes, however, it was far from certain.

Belli later claimed that he had struggled to reach a decision. He had stayed up late at night weighing the pros and cons. He had made lists. He had discussed it with Tonahill. There just was no way of knowing how Ruby would react under the prosecution's harsh questioning. If Ruby remained composed and responded lucidly—if he appeared completely normal—it might make it more difficult for jurors to believe he was mentally ill. It would be hard to look at a respectful, well-dressed man answering questions and visualize him in a trancelike state in which he had been able to cold-bloodedly kill a man. In other words, the defense was in the unlikely situation of worrying that their client would appear to be too sane.

While Belli admittedly had been reluctant to allow Ruby to

testify, he said the final decision was made for him in a small washroom of the courthouse. On occasion during breaks in the proceedings, Belli and Ruby would meet in a small restroom in the judge's chambers, knowing their conversation would not be overheard or recorded. In one of these discussions Ruby stood there, "white-faced and quivering...in tears, his eyes wide and staring, his hands shaking" as Belli remembered, and said, "Mel, I can't do it. Don't make me testify. I'll go all to pieces."

"Look Jack," Belli recalled responding, "this isn't some high school debate. You've got to get it through your head that you're on trial for your life."

"I can't do it," Ruby insisted. "I can't do it."

But Belli may have been even more concerned about the substance of what Ruby's testimony might be. He later recounted another conversation in which Ruby said: "What are we doing Mel, kidding ourselves? We know what happened. We know I did it for Jackie and the kids. I just went in and shot him. They've got us anyway. Maybe I ought to forget this silly story that I'm telling and get on the stand and tell the truth."

While Belli may have doubted this was true, he recognized that if Ruby said anything like that on the stand, the jury might well believe him. That was potentially deadly for Ruby. Literally. It demonstrated premeditation and malice, elements that could justify the death penalty. But there was another option presented by Dr. Guttmacher; he offered the defense a unique opportunity to put Ruby on the witness stand, virtually. Ruby had told his entire story to Guttmacher during their sessions together. Under questioning, Ruby's words could be presented to the jury without having to put him on the stand.

But there was one additional factor known only to the defense that made putting the doctor on the stand even more risky than perceived. In a memo sent to Belli after Guttmacher had examined Ruby, he stated that he could not support the main defense claim that Ruby had killed Oswald while in a psychomotor seizure. "It is my belief that it is scientifically unsound and legally imprudent," he had written, "to assert with absolute assurance that Oswald's murder took place while Ruby was in an epileptic attack of some sort. That this could have been the case can be maintained, but that it is actually so cannot be substantiated by the data..."

His testimony, as Belli had told reporters, might "make or break" the defense case.

Dr. Guttmacher was a big man who bore an uncanny resemblance to French president Charles de Gaulle. He was tall and heavy-set, with white hair, spoke in a deep, resonant voice and moved with an air of great confidence and professionalism. He was comfortable on the witness stand, having testified in hundreds of previous cases—including numerous murder trials—earning a reputation as the nation's leading expert on the criminally insane. The defense had intentionally avoided calling him during the bail hearing because they did not want to give the prosecution an early chance to question him.

As he took the stand, the defense casually placed two of the textbooks he had authored about criminal minds on their table, in full view of the jury. Unlike when questioning his previous witnesses, Belli began by asking Guttmacher the qualifying question: Having interviewed Ruby, "Do you have an opinion as to whether he knew the nature and consequences of his act, the difference between right and wrong, and knew what he was doing at the time he shot Lee Harvey Oswald."

The courtroom remained absolutely silent. Dr. Towler's often boring, repetitive explanation of each rise and fall of the EEGs was forgotten. In his clear, slightly accented voice Dr. Guttmacher pronounced, "I don't think he was capable of distinguishing right from wrong and realizing the nature and consequences of his act at the time of the alleged homicide."

The nation's leading forensic psychiatrist had declared Jack

Ruby legally insane when he committed the crime. Those were the words the defense had been waiting to hear.

Belli began going through Guttmacher's impressive background: A graduate of Johns Hopkins and Harvard Medical School, he had been a forensic psychiatrist since 1929, while presently serving as director of a psychiatric clinic attached to Baltimore's court system as well as a professor of psychiatry at Johns Hopkins Medical School. During the war, he had supervised psychiatric clinics on thirty-five military bases; he had published four books, more than forty articles, served on the editorial board of two prestigious journals and consulted on an average of five hundred criminal cases a year. During the Korean War, the Surgeon General of the Army had sent him to Korea—to inspect psychiatry in that country.

As he had asked Towler to define psychology, Belli asked Guttmacher to introduce the jurors to psychiatry. "Psychiatry comes from two words," he began, "meaning 'mind' and 'treatment.' He is a person who treats minds, while a psychologist is a person involved with the scientific study of the mind…the psychiatrist is a trained medical man who is involved primarily in treatment, while the psychologist is more involved in theoretical learning problems, in personality testing…very few psychologists treat patients."

The world had long been intrigued by the complexities of the human mind, trying without much success to understand what causes people to take the sometimes bizarre actions that they do. Four centuries earlier Shakespeare's *Macbeth* asked, "Canst thou not minister to a mind diseased,/ pluck from the memory a rooted sorrow,/ raze out the written troubles of the brain,/ and with some sweet oblivious antidote/ cleanse the stuffed bosom of that perilous stuff/ which weighs upon the heart."

Hollywood had mined a rich vein of increasingly insane killers, and Alfred Hitchcock's *Psycho* had been released a few years earlier, in 1960. That film was in part inspired by the case of

Edward Gein of Wisconsin. Gein was a grave robber and murderer who was creating "a woman suit" so he could literally crawl inside and "become his mother." The court found him incompetent to stand trial and he was ordered to be incarcerated in a hospital for the criminally insane. Such stories of deranged behavior were mesmerizing for readers and viewers. Now here was the austere Dr. Guttmacher, a man who dealt with these people every day, introducing his profession to millions of fascinated people. Belli wondered, "Do you have any opinion that all or most murderers are insane?"

Casually he responded, "Most murderers are sane." Surprisingly, when questioned about epileptics he cited a study in England that suggested, "Homicide is more frequent among epileptics than the general population," although he did point out that even that number is very low.

In his clinic Dr. Guttmacher had treated several epileptics, including a few with psychomotor epilepsy, which he described as a form "in which the activity is both in the psychic area and the motor area." It was a strange condition, he continued, "It isn't always discernible… He may be carrying on quite complicated activities and until one gets a better understanding…one wouldn't know this was a psychomotor attack."

Dr. Guttmacher started to give examples of this behavior, remembering the case of a man who "worked at an A&P store, and he followed a little girl who was a customer, a nine or ten year old child who…"

Objection. "Specific on Jack Ruby, your Honor," Alexander insisted.

Sustained.

Belli wondered if the unconscious state of sleepwalking, during which people had been known to commit antisocial acts, might be compared to the fugue state. While Guttmacher did not state unequivocally there was a similarity, he did explain "The idea of people never hurting themselves while in a somnambulistic state I'm sure is wrong. I had a patient, a man who put his arm through a window…"

Objection. "That's what we object to," Wade complained. "Are we going to have to listen to all the patients he ever treated."

Belli appealed to Judge Brown, his frustration apparent. "In order to make an opinion on an individual, it calls for a whole background of medical knowledge… This man doesn't spring afresh, like someone born out of a nurse's head. He has his whole background…"

The prosecution as well as the defense understood the importance of this witness. The trial might well turn on his ability to convince the jury that Ruby was suffering from a serious mental disorder. Wade needed to derail that effort. Guttmacher began tracing the history of epilepsy, which was first described in the 1920s. "They were generally people who were very aggressive, very hostile, given to explosive outburst, very stubborn…there are a great many people who have epileptic patients who don't answer any of these criteria and…"

It appeared he was about to paint a far more realistic portrait of the condition as understood by modern medical science when Wade objected in his homespun manner, "Judge, we object to this rambling on."

Belli leaped to his feet, shouting, "I resent this cornball talk, 'rambling on' Judge! Now this man is a learned scientist, and to say he is 'rambling on' is insulting to him, from a sophisticated town like Dallas… We had it yesterday, Judge. Are we going to put up with it again?"

"Well, I object to it," Wade leaped to his feet. Pointing directly at Belli he asked Judge Brown, "I think he's rambling on something that has nothing…"

Belli faced him. "That's because you don't understand! And for one person who doesn't understand to say something is rambling, I think is the height of ignorance!"

Prosecutor Jim Bowie joined the shouting, suggesting that

Belli "learn something" about Texas law: "He has given an opinion. He is now entitled to use those facts upon which he bases his opinion as they concern this defendant, and not someone back in 1920. That merely happens to be the law..."

When the courtroom quieted, Guttmacher did elaborate on his opinion. Jack Ruby, he said essentially, was a victim of his own life: "This patient has an abnormal background that is highly significant from the standpoint of psychopathology. His father was a drunken immigrant carpenter who tyrannized his family... The family was so disorganized that a Chicago social agency had to scatter the children into various homes. Jack Ruby...was in half a dozen foster homes...

"The mother was apparently well-meaning but an ineffectual individual. She suffered a paranoid psychosis, necessitating hospitalization in a state psychiatric institution. The younger brother had a brief period of psychiatric hospitalization...a sister recently had psychiatric care..." Heredity, Dr. Guttmacher explained, might be the most important factor in a person's mental condition.

When the defense tried to put a record of the institutionalization of Ruby's mother, Fanny Rubenstein, into evidence, the prosecution asked to question the witness about that before agreeing to its admission. It probably was as much a strategy to disrupt the defense presentation as a need to learn more about the documents. When Wade questioned the impact of heredity on a person's mental stability, Guttmacher explained, "...the more psychic morbidity you have in your family background, the more likely you are to have in your next generation..."

Wade did manage to get the witness to agree that the fact that Ruby's mother was a paranoid schizophrenic probably would not have been the cause of his psychomotor epilepsy. Having established that, the prosecution objected to the admission of the document into evidence.

Belli simply had Guttmacher reiterate his opinion that Fanny

Rubenstein's paranoia and schizophrenia impacted the personality of her son. "Yes, definitely." The result, the doctor continued, was that "We're dealing with a very abnormal individual, who has a very abnormal personality structure." His fragile mental condition collapsed under the emotional stress of Kennedy's assassination, he continued. "I think he was struggling to keep his sanity during this period… I think there was a temporary, very short lived, psychotic episode… All his defenses crumbled and the deep, heavy, hostile, aggressive part of his makeup, which is very strong, became focused on this one individual, and the homicide was the result of it."

Despite that, Judge Brown sustained the objection to the report, refusing to allow it to be entered into the record.

But Belli persisted in bringing Ruby's whole family into the testimony. They were troubled people, Guttmacher said, and with one exception "have always exhibited an abnormal degree of instability. They are a quarrelsome, inflammable group, at one time feuding, at another time making sacrifices for each other."

Summing it up, Guttmacher said, Jack Ruby was "a suicidal risk…[who] has all of his life exhibited extreme emotional instability and episodic outbursts of aggression…

"He's an extremely impulsive individual. He acts and he thinks, rather than thinking and acting, to a very large degree."

His paranoia was so pronounced, Guttmacher said, "When I would see him in the room up in the jail he would look under the table, look in the ceiling to make sure it wasn't wired… There's a very paranoid flavor to his thinking…to an unusual degree."

Guttmacher was teaching a course in the complex, confused psyche of Jack Ruby. Like all people, the defendant was the sum total of all his experiences, his needs and desires—all of it filtered through his unique, troubled mind. Ruby was unusually narcissistic, the witness explained, desperate for approval; he worked out incessantly, he was known to flex his muscles to show off and while he currently had no girlfriend he previously had contracted gonorrhea "four or five times," which was treated successful with penicillin; he regularly took a variety of self-prescribed patent medicines and drugs, adhered to food fads and was overly concerned about his weight and his baldness. "He stopped one of the medicines he was taking because he felt his hair was falling out more rapidly than it had before..."

Belli tried to cover as much ground as possible, responding to the prosecution's arguments before they could be made. Sure Ruby got along okay in the world; yeah, people sort of liked him and he was able to run a business, but it was "a façade...a mask that he wears. Despite an outwardly friendly and ingratiating manner, this patient seethes with hostility...incapable of establishing deep and meaningful relationships with other people."

The entire courtroom was paying rapt attention; undoubtedly some people were listening to this testimony and wondering, as is normal, how much, if any, might also apply to themselves.

In most criminal trials motive is a key factor: Why did the defendant commit the crime? Greed? Jealousy? Hatred? In those trials the motive can be identified. But when the defendant's mental state is the issue, normal motives don't necessarily apply. The motive isn't what actually is happening, but rather how what is happening is perceived by a troubled mind. Rather than a motive it is more of a trigger. It was Dr. Guttmacher's opinion that Jack Ruby was infatuated with President Kennedy. At one point he had said, "I feel for him." For Ruby, the doctor explained, JFK was "not merely the idealized and idolized father figure as head of the State, but he was in addition seen as the leading member of the perfect family group. The patient, in all probability, because of his own wretched early life became, in a sense, a vicarious participating member of that group."

In addition, Guttmacher recalled that Ruby had told him that as a Jew he was aware that he was "a member of a minority group" and he admired and appreciated Kennedy's progressive stance on civil rights issues.

With the horror of the assassination still reverberating throughout the country, it was easy to understand and maybe even appreciate that attachment. Americans had spent three years living with Jack and Jacqueline and their children. Beautiful photographs of the handsome president and his beautiful, stylish wife had graced every possible magazine as often as possible. Adorable pictures of the baby son and daughter playing in the White House had captured the hearts of Americans—and for an unstable person, Jack Ruby for instance, the killing broke his heart. More than most people, Guttmacher emphasized, "because of his own wretched early life," Ruby had idealized Kennedy as "the leading member of a perfect family group."

Most of the nation, even those who disagreed with the president politically, had cried through the long weekend of his death and funeral. Almost everyone in the courtroom, including the jurors, could identify with that.

Having heard from Guttmacher that Ruby's mind was fragmented, sort of a jumble of jigsaw pieces rather than a finished puzzle, Belli asked if it would be healthy for Ruby to testify in his own behalf? While every jury is instructed not to construe the fact that a defendant did not testify as an indication of guilt, human nature forces people to wonder, if he's innocent, why didn't he tell us himself? Perhaps even more so when there is no question that the person committed the act. Jurors like to hear from those people with the most at stake. But mentally unstable people can unintentionally destroy their own case. As Jack Ruby sat only a few feet away, hands clasped in front of him on the table, leaning slightly forward, Guttmacher refused to predict how Ruby might react on the stand. "I think he could crack up, actually...on the other hand he might present a more normal picture than I would anticipate... I think this man could become flagrantly psychotic."

Having established that it was potentially dangerous to Ruby to put him on the stand, Belli then did exactly what he intended to do, he let the witness speak for the defendant. Guttmacher said that Ruby had told him that he had been "very upset" about the anti-Kennedy ad in the *Dallas Morning News* especially because it was signed with a Jewish name. He had been devastated by the assassination. "He said he would have to leave Dallas... 'I felt like a nothing person, like the world ended. I didn't want to go on living anymore.'... He twice made the comment. 'He needed the job like he needed a hole in the head,'... he kept thinking, 'he was such a beautiful man,' Friday evening he went to synagogue... He drove around Dallas... He thought of the hard-pressed police force, which was working extra hours, and had sandwiches made for them...' It took away the tragic feeling. I was in complete change of the mental reaction.'

"Oswald appeared. The police took Oswald to the assembly room. 'I'm standing on the table above everybody.' I think this was important. He had a very prominent position. He's above everybody. History is being made..." Guttmacher took the jury through the entire weekend; the moments at the police station, waking his roommate and taking pictures of the Impeach Earl Warren billboard. Going to the post office to try to discover the owner of the mailbox referred to in the anti-Kennedy ad. Searching for the man who had signed the ad, "Bernard Weissman." Grieving with his sister. Receiving the phone call from one of his performers. Being unable to sleep. Until finally "he left his apartment around ten thirty...going to send the telegram and go to the club and walk the dogs...

"Suddenly, much to his astonishment, Oswald appeared between two guards. 'He had a very smirky expression. He looked cunning and vicious, like an animal, like a Communist. I felt like I was looking at a rat. I don't recall if I said, you killed my president, or if I said anything at all'...

"The patient professes a hazy memory of the actual events. He doesn't know why he didn't shoot more than once, nor whether he was wrestled to the floor in the elevator or in the area… I don't get a very clear picture from him as to what he did or did not remember…"

Guttmacher continued, practically channeling Ruby. "…he hates the vacuum, he hates to feel there's a period in his life when he was awake and yet he doesn't know really, what was going on… He said, 'It flashed in my mind why are all these guys jumping on me, I'm a very known person to the police. I'm not somebody who's a screwball. After I was brought up-stairs in the elevator I felt relieved.'"

Belli used this witness to clear up a lot of questions he would have asked Ruby, for example why he carried a gun. "He told me he always carried a loaded pistol in his right hip pocket," Guttmacher replied, "and that all night club owners…in Dallas carried such weapons. He states that on that Sunday morning he had about fifteen hundred dollars on him. He insisted…the shooting was due to a sudden, momentary impulse. The thought of killing Oswald had not occurred to him previously."

As for feelings of guilt, Guttmacher shook his head as he said, "I don't think he has any guilt feelings about having taken the life of another human being… I don't mean to say if you asked him, whether that was right, whether he would say no…

"I think what he said illustrates this. He said, 'If I had only been kept in that telegraph office longer'…" Recognizing that his actions were wrong after the fact was very different from whether he understood it was wrong at that moment.

Belli asked the doctor what had finally happened, what was it that caused him to act? Guttmacher had been on the stand for more than two hours; it was 4:30 in the afternoon, but he still had the full attention of the courtroom. "I think he was struggling hard to maintain his equilibrium, and his sanity re-ally. And then this situation arose where there was a great deal of excitement and the lights, and the man suddenly coming out and I think he just decomposed. I think the lid came off and this violent act took place."

Belli was reaching the end of this direct testimony. To make certain the jurors understood the depth of Ruby's psychiatric problems, he asked for Guttmacher's "full, detailed opinion."

"I've concluded we are dealing with a person with a damaged brain...who has persistently demonstrated a very poor control of aggression by episodic and explosive outbursts... It's my opinion that his weak ego, for a day and a half, was constantly assaulted by strong emotional stresses and was suddenly overwhelmed, permitting unconscious, hostile aggressive impulses to gain ascendency and to rob him of the realization of the wrongness of his action and an inability to control his destructive impulses."

The guided tour of Jack Ruby's mind was done. Belli turned to the prosecution table and with a smile and a bow said, "You may cross-examine." Belli's much maligned strategy had finally come to life.

CHAPTER TWELVE

The renowned legal scholar and teacher John Henry Wigmore claimed that cross-examination was the most significant contribution made by the Anglo-American legal system to trial procedure. It is, he wrote, "the greatest legal engine ever invented for the discovery of truth. You can do anything with a bayonet except sit on it. A lawyer can do anything with cross-examination if he is skillful enough not to impale his own cause upon it."

The concept of cross-examination, the questioning of witnesses by the opposing side, is biblical. The Book of Daniel recounts the story of Susanna, who was accused of adultery by two lecherous elderly men who claimed to have witnessed the assignation, then sentenced to death. Daniel saved her life by cross-examining the two men, who told conflicting stories.

A cross-examination often is the dramatic highlight of a trial. It is where Perry Mason tripped up the accusing witness, shattered their credibility, exposed their motive and destroyed their integrity, thus saving his client. Among the memorable cross-examinations in American legal history was the questioning of Charles Guiteau by retired Judge John K. Porter in 1881. Guiteau had shot President James Garfield, who eventually died from an infection caused by the gunshot wound. In a defense somewhat similar to that of Jack Ruby, Guiteau claimed he was legally insane when he had shot the president, saying God had taken away his free will and forced him to act.

"You intended to kill him?" Porter asked.

Guiteau responded, "I thought the Deity and I had done it, sir. I want it distinctly understood that I did not do that act in my own personality. I unite myself with the Deity, and I want you gentlemen to so understand it. I never should have shot the President on my own personal account. I want that distinctly understood."

"Who bought the pistol, the Deity or you?"

The assassin answered excitedly, "I say the Deity inspired the act, and the Deity will take care of it."

"Who bought the pistol, the Deity or you?"

"The Deity furnished the money by which I bought it. I was the agent of the Deity...the Deity inspired me to remove the President, and I had to use my ordinary judgment as to ways and means to accomplish the Deity's will."

Porter wrote that this extraordinary cross-examination, "made apparent to everybody that Guiteau's vanity was inordinate, his spirit of selfishness, jealousy, and hatred absolutely unbounded. He was cleverly led to picture himself to the civilized world as a moral monstrosity." The jury did not buy the idea that he was divinely inspired, or insane. Guiteau was convicted and hanged.

Now in Dallas, Bill Alexander began the cross-examination for the prosecution. The first rule of a good trial lawyer, as Harper Lee had reminded readers in her Pulitzer Prize–winning novel, *To Kill a Mockingbird*, was "Never, never, never, on cross-examination ask a witness a question you don't already know the answer to..." That principle made the task of questioning a medical expert like Dr. Guttmacher far more difficult. Alexander had prepared for it by obtaining transcripts of the doctor's testimony in other trials.

Alexander began by probing for any contradictions from previous testimony, but then he ignored that primary rule of cross-examination. "In your opinion," he wondered, "when did this fugue state begin?"

The witness didn't hesitate. "I think at the very moment he saw Oswald."

"Allright, now let's talk about fugue state just a little bit. By fugue state, don't you mean a period of unconsciousness or blackout?"

"No."

Alexander might have deftly changed the subject; instead he plowed forward, asking, "What do you mean by fugue state?"

"Confused or diminished consciousness or unconsciousness. It doesn't have to be unconscious."

"Would a person in a fugue state, in your opinion, know what he was doing?"

"No."

Alexander dug his hole a little deeper, repeating the question incredulously, "You feel he didn't know what he was doing in a fugue state?"

"I think he became an automatic, that he no longer had—"

Alexander tried to stop him. "You mean you don't know, or just don't care?"

Guttmacher repeated, firmly, "I think it became an automatic thing, very much like a sleepwalker."

Alexander searched for an escape, perhaps speaking more to the jury than the witness. "Do you feel a sleepwalker could pick a moving target out of two hundred people, move in on it and hit it dead center?"

"Sleepwalkers have done some quite remarkable things," Guttmacher responded.

"Yes, sir, but how about picking a man out…"

Guttmacher was too experienced a witness to remain passive. Quite firmly he said, "I don't know whether they would do that or not."

Alexander wouldn't quit. "Don't you think it would be rather remarkable for a man in a fugue state who has diminished consciousness or perhaps in a blackout state to pick one man, a moving man, a moving target if you please, and hit it dead center with a pistol?"

"Of course I didn't say this man was in a sleepwalking state. I said it's comparable to that. He wasn't fully conscious. I think he had some degree of confused consciousness."

Raising his voice, Alexander once again asked a question for which he did not know the answer: "Then, Doctor, in that degree of confused consciousness he knew what he was doing enough to zero in on his target?"

Boom. "I don't think he knew right from wrong at this time. I think this is the test, not whether he knew who his target was."

The jury watched without expression as this exchange continued. "Don't you think he knew it was against the law to kill?"

"No, sir."

Alexander did get Guttmacher to repeat his admission that it was impossible to tell if Ruby was in a state of psychomotor epilepsy when he committed the crime, although the doctor reiterated that he did believe Ruby suffered from that condition and it was possible. Instead, he attributed Ruby's actions to "a rupture of the ego and a period of episodic dyscontrol…"

Guttmacher said, "My best diagnosis is that this man is a mental cripple and was carrying on his shoulders an insufferable emotional load and, to use the vernacular, he cracked under it momentarily…"

Appealing subtly to the jurors, who might have their own doubts about psychiatry, Alexander tried to dismiss psychomotor epilepsy in his down-home way as some sort "of wastebasket you psychiatrists throw things into when you can't figure them out otherwise?"

Guttmacher kept his cool, explaining once again, this time as if responding to a student's question, that there were many types of clinical evidence of the disease, then ran through them. But throughout the cross, often his answers were cut short or interrupted, finally causing Belli to shout, "Let him finish, Mr. Alexander."

Sarcastically, Alexander responded, "I'm just so anxious for his answers, Mr. Belli, I get eager."

Judge Brown tried to calm things down, suggesting, "Let's don't get eager."

The prosecution continued to explore the uncertainty that the public in general, and perhaps several of these jurors, held about claims that mental illness caused criminal behavior. Alexander asked, for example, "If I knew when I pulled the trigger it would discharge a weapon and hurt the person it was pointed at, would that not be awareness of the consequences?"

It certainly seemed logical. Probably every kid in Texas had learned this fact early: You fire a gun at someone, that person is likely to get hurt. But it wasn't quite that simple, Guttmacher responded. The human mind does not always work logically. "Not the consequences to you," Guttmacher explained. "Or the consequences to society."

A common strategy when cross-examining an expert witness is to diminish their experience. If they haven't testified very often, then they are neophytes who don't understand legal procedures; if they have testified often, then their opinion is for sale. And when dealing with a rare condition, as Alexander suggested, no one really is an expert. Guttmacher admitted he had personally examined no more than five or six patients suffering from psychomotor epilepsy. "That's out of approximately what," Alexander asked, "three thousand patients?"

Once again, Alexander had committed the mistake of asking

a question without knowing the answer. "Well, four of these would be murder cases, out of some three hundred some murder cases," Guttmacher answered. He had testified in several of those cases. Asked if those defendants had been found insane or sane, he replied, "My memory is that two were found insane and one was found sane. We had no electroencephalographic evidence to support the diagnosis, but unfortunately for the man and fortunately for my diagnostic skill, which certainly isn't always that good, he died in an epileptic seizure. So the diagnosis was later pretty well established."

That patient, the doctor remembered, had been in court twice. "The second time...because he had picked up a large cement block and dropped it on the head of a man (a stranger) who happened to be passing... He didn't kill the man." When the victim regained consciousness, his assailant was still standing nearby. "He didn't run, he was there..." Guttmacher's point was that the brief fugue state had ended and the defendant could not recall what he had done while in it.

Guttmacher was firm; he had no doubt about his diagnosis in Ruby's case. In fact, he said, Jack Ruby had been affected by this condition for much of his life. "There are periods that his sister spoke of his going into rages, jumping over the bar, knocking people down for very little reason. There was some story about his taking a taxi driver and banging his head against the pavement. He has had rages and assaultive outbreaks before. He had never shot anybody before. I think he had never been under the same degree of emotional pressure sustained over a day and a half..."

Alexander was put into the odd position of contending this was somewhat normal behavior. "You recognize that hitting first is one way to keep down trouble in a night club, do you not?"

The doctor replied wryly, "I'm afraid I have very little experience with night clubs."

Later in his testimony he would add, "According to his sister and his brother he lost his first job at seventeen because he knocked down the manager of the store in a fight... And this was, according to them, a really uncalled for type of reaction. So it's been going on for a long time."

Forced to listen to himself being dissected, Ruby continued to sit calmly, looking straight ahead, showing no overt emotion as his life was being ripped apart in front of him. He gave no hint how the diagnosis that he was mentally ill, that he had been mentally ill for much of his life, impacted him.

Alexander was like an enemy outside the walls of the fort, probing lightly at the defenses, trying to find a weak spot without taking casualties. Earlier Guttmacher had told Belli that Ruby simply wanted to be loved and admired, causing Alexander to once again state the seemingly obvious. "Don't you think most people want to be loved and admired?"

"It's a question of degree," he answered, then put it in somewhat graphic terms; "It's normal to want to love, but if you love to the point of starving yourself it's no longer normal."

Alexander couldn't resist making a nasty comment. "There is, of course, no indication Jack Ruby ever starved himself."

Guttmacher replied coldly, "I was trying to make it clear to you what I mean...from day-to-day it was a strange, unstable, emotional kind of personality, but he would not have been out of contact with reality.

"...It's the syndrome, the picture that you take together as a whole that is the indication. I think if you break it up into this thing and the other thing, I think there are very few things alone that are indicative of an unsound mind."

When it became obvious to Alexander that he was not going to be able to shake Guttmacher, he began playing to the jury, offering alternative motives for why Ruby might have committed the crime for them to consider. Perhaps Ruby wasn't mentally ill at all, he suggested. "Doctor, if you felt that the real motive for the shooting of Oswald was the desire to gain fame and for-

DAN ABRAMS AND DAVID FISHER

tune, and Ruby had misjudged public temperament and public feeling, would that make any difference in your evaluation?"

The answer didn't matter; the point was made. Guttmacher replied that he would think Ruby had "sick judgment" if he had believed that.

Alexander pursued his theory, pointing out that Ruby had already sold his story to the media, then wondering, "Would the fact that he looked forward to making money out of the act of killing Oswald make any difference in your opinion?"

Ironically, while Belli, Judge Brown and even one juror would eventually publish books about the trial, Ruby would not profit from it at all. Any money he had made went right back to his lawyers and associated legal costs.

Finally the prosecution got around to Guttmacher's previous publications in which he dismissed the concept of temporary insanity. Published materials, speeches, comments, previous testimony all offer a potential gold mine for attorneys to attack the credibility of an expert witness. Guttmacher and the defense obviously knew this was coming and had prepared for it. So when Alexander quoted the doctor's past comment from his book *Psychiatry and the Law* that "temporary insanity is found more often in the courtroom than in the mental institutions," Guttmacher responded, "I think my coauthor, the law professor, Weihofen, wrote that but I could be wrong. It's in the book. And I think if you look in my *Mind of the Murderer* you'll find it is treated somewhat differently, which is a later book."

Alexander then read from *Psychiatry and the Law* at great length; perhaps though he included too much detail when he read the passage, "The temporary insanity dear to the hearts of defense lawyers is wholly a thing of the moment; a man without any history of mental abnormality prior to the act, and exhibiting no symptoms upon examination afterward..."

That did not apply to Ruby, Guttmacher reminded the court. That passage referred specifically to defendants who came into court without any history of mental disruptions in their life who suddenly claimed they were somehow temporarily insane. But as Dr. Schafer, "a man of great ability and great conscientious" had testified that his tests showed conclusively "the difficulty this man has in his...thinking and emotional areas..."

Alexander interrupted. Again. As he had been doing throughout Guttmacher's testimony. When Belli complained that Alexander refused to let Guttmacher finish his answers, Wade jumped in to defend his assistant, followed quickly by Bowie. The frustrated Belli said, "Now we've got all three of them. I don't think there's one of them that hasn't objected here." Then he muttered something indistinguishable to spectators—but obviously loudly enough to be heard by the prosecutors.

Wade jumped up and shouted with indignation, "Judge, are you going to let that lawyer keep referring to us as ignorant and all that?"

Belli didn't back down. "They've asked for it each and every time..."

"He's referred to my assistants here as being ignorant ignoramuses."

Pointing at Wade, Belli retorted, "You were a cornball a long time ago." He then pointed at Alexander. "This man calls the people of Dallas peasants..."

Judge Brown tried once again to keep order. "All right, take your seat."

Sweeping his arm around, Belli then pointed at Ruby, "...and he called him a Jew boy too!" At the second bail hearing, while cross-examining a defense psychiatrist, Alexander referred to Ruby as "Jewish boy," when asking how Ruby's upbringing might have impacted him, but with his Southern drawl it sounded to many like he had said "Jew boy." Throughout the trial, Belli accused Alexander of using that slur.

"Sit down, Mr. Belli."

Tonahill stood, not about to be left out. "And he took the Lord's name in vain too, and I resent that."

The entire courtroom broke out in laughter. When order finally was restored, Alexander resumed attacking the psychiatric testing, wondering if a person might try to "throw the test" or even "be coached."

Guttmacher shook his head. "Most of these tests you can't throw, unless you have had a very extensive experience in psychological techniques. I don't think Ruby has that kind of graduate training."

For the first time in the entire trial, prosecutors seemed to acknowledge Jack Ruby's presence, asking, "Would the fact that Ruby is watching this proceeding with a great deal of interest and assisting his attorneys make any difference to you in your opinion?"

"Wait a second." Belli was on his feet again. "That's assuming facts not in evidence, that he's assisting his attorneys. I represent he is not able to assist his attorneys... And," he reminded the court, "we have entered a plea of insanity."

Ruby sat silently.

There were some moments of humor as the afternoon began reaching into the early evening. Prosecutors continued hammering on the concept that people could perform common tasks while in a fugue state without conscious knowledge of their actions. Driving a car, for example, Alexander pointed out, is an automatic reflex, deeply ingrained in people from a young age, like combing your hair or brushing your teeth. Guttmacher disagreed. "I don't think it's that simple."

"You don't?"

Guttmacher shook his head and once again the courtroom burst into laughter as he said, ruefully, "Not in Baltimore driving. No, sir!"

A good cross-exam will successfully create an alternative narrative, a plausible what-could-have-happened in contrast to the main testimony. If Ruby wasn't mentally incompetent when he killed Oswald, what could have caused him to do something he had never done before? Drugs, Alexander proposed, in particular that weight reducing drug Ruby was taking called Preludin. "It has some stimulant, it's something like amphetamine or one of those stimulating drugs, I believe... I remember he gave it powers that very few people have been able to experience with it. I mean, it's not nearly as potent a drug, I think, as he felt it to be..." Combined with liquor, Ruby told Guttmacher, it made him "Nasty and argumentative."

Ironically, this German diet pill chemically known as phenmetrazine would later be rumored to have also been used by President Kennedy, as well as Marilyn Monroe. It became known as the first drug taken by The Beatles. In 1965, a year later, it was taken off the market.

Alexander asked, "Do you remember him telling you...that when he combined it with liquor, 'I am very sadistic when I am handling people who want to tear my head off. If somebody cuts at me, I cut back at them. This is a homicidal town.'"

Guttmacher responded that he had not realized that statement was in connection to Preludin, but that statement "goes with the personality make-up of the psychomotor epileptic. They are very violent in their reactions as a group."

Alexander used those words to make what seemed like a direct plea to the jury. "You wouldn't want to encourage them by turning them loose onto society, would you?"

"No," the doctor agreed, then added, "I think he should be treated."

Until this point Alexander had done a credible job keeping the testimony at a level that might easily be understood by the jurors. He had mostly stayed away from the scientific jargon that might have put the jurors to sleep. But as he began winding up his examination, he asked if Ruby might be psychotic, if he was suffering from "functional mental psychosis?"

"Functional, not organic," the witness agreed.

"Well...do you mean a psychotic condition for which there is no known organic cause?..."

"I don't think my answer was quite accurate. People with damaged brains are much more liable to develop a psychosis or psychotic episode than people who don't have a damaged brain... there's not very much doubt about that."

Belli already had been criticized for settling on this rather obscure condition as the center of his defense strategy. Now Alexander suggested the real cause of Ruby's mental problems might be more typical conditions. Schizophrenia? "No." Manic depression? "I don't think so."

Psychotic depression? Well, maybe. Ruby had a history of serious depression. In fact, during their interviews, he'd confessed to Guttmacher that at times he had been suicidal. A decade earlier he had suffered a serious financial setback and contemplated suicide. Guttmacher quoted him, "'Everything went bust. Our name [his and his partner's] was on the place [the Silver Spur nightclub] and we owed taxes. I felt I was dead in Dallas. I had given the Silver Spur away to some friends to run the Ranch House. I wanted to commit suicide and to kill this guy [his partner] who screwed me... It was just a thought. I laid in this Cotton Bowl Hotel for a while, then finally returned to Chicago...' He said he wished he had guts to do it. It's pretty typical of a depressed state."

"With you psychiatrists," Alexander said disdainfully, "anytime a patient mentions anything about suicide, that raises the hair up on the back of your neck and puts your teeth on edge, doesn't it?"

"Well," Guttmacher conceded, "it's one of the things we have to be aware of."

The assistant prosecutor shook his head. "All a man has to do is mention suicide and, 'Wham!' here you go."

Guttmacher simply pointed out, "Well, that does make him committable in Maryland. I imagine it would here."

And finally the usual question of expert witness: What are they paying you to testify? Alexander sweetened it. "I would like to inquire…what financial arrangements have been made to procure your attendance here, which is just a nice way of saying what are they paying you to testify?"

"No definite arrangement has been made…the fee was set by Mr. Belli…" he glanced at the defense bench, "and I have confidence in him… I'm sure I'll be compensated. I have been here now for, I think eight days."

Eight days. Several of the jurors must have smiled to themselves when they heard that, as they were now in their third week of sequestration.

As the prosecution finished its cross-exam, Alexander offered into evidence a two-page underlined portion of *Psychiatry and the Law*. Belli half rose from his seat and made his own offer. "We offer into evidence the whole book—and stipulate the jury may read it! Okay?"

"No, not okay," Alexander responded.

"Why not?" Tonahill asked, clearly facetiously.

Alexander did not appreciate the humor. "If you think a jury is going to sit there and read a four-hundred page book after they have been empaneled this long…"

There was a verbal sneer in Belli's reply. "If you think they are going to read four lines out of an eight-hundred-page book without an objection, that'll be the day. We object to that part out of context. If they want to put the whole book in, we have no objection."

"They don't *have* to read the whole book," Tonahill offered helpfully, suggesting, "they can if they want to."

Belli agreed, "That's what I mean, respectfully."

The court overruled the objection, and Dr. Guttmacher's cross-examination was done.

Belli began his redirect examination by asking about another murder case in which Dr. Guttmacher had testified. "Was that a psychomotor state?"

It was. "This was a man who had stabbed his wife thirty or forty times," the psychiatrist explained, "and he told the police where the knife was, so he had some fragments of memory connected with it...

"Later the man, interesting enough, had blotted out the whole—denied the whole thing. He was a man that was very devoted to his wife. And he had blotted out the whole episode and wanted to know later on why his wife hadn't come to see him." That was a defense mechanism, he continued, like fainting or amnesia. That killer "was never fit to be tried," instead he was institutionalized.

After Belli finished, in the prosecution's brief recross Alexander asked for a more complete diagnosis of that killer. He was suffering from various forms of epilepsy, Guttmacher replied, "But he also had schizophrenia... He was in bad shape, I think that's fair to say." Point made: In that case the killer's mental problems were far more extreme than Ruby's.

Before Guttmacher stepped down, Tonahill asked Judge Brown if the jury would be entitled to look at his book. Guttmacher asked hopefully, "How about putting my other book in?"

Dr. Guttmacher had been a solid, if not spectacular witness for the defense. He had taken the jurors deeper into the world of mental illness, mostly without complicated explanations. His salient points were that mental illness can cause people to perform antisocial acts and that Jack Ruby was out of his conscious mind when he killed Lee Harvey Oswald. While he did not confirm the defense's narrow path, that Ruby committed the crime while in a psychomotor state, he did agree it was possible. There was no way to tell, he had concluded.

It was a thoroughly professional and at times compelling testimony, as the defense had hoped. Or, as the prosecution contended, exactly what he was being paid for.

The defense, through its three professional witnesses, had presented a range of possibilities buttressed by expert witnesses. There was a lot of information for the jury to consider, but it all fit into their theory of the crime: Jack Ruby had simply stumbled upon the scene while doing a favor for an employee and his outrage had triggered his condition, leading him to act.

After Guttmacher had left the stand, the defense tried to enter a recording of the sights and sounds of, as Tonahill described them, "the four days that shocked the world," into evidence. His purpose, he explained, was to remind the jury how intense the emotions of the four days between the Kennedy assassination and his funeral had been. As it had taken place only five months earlier and the nation was still reeling from the horror, it probably wasn't necessary. The twelve jurors had lived through every minute of that long weekend; no American had forgotten it.

Also, if a reminder was necessary, the Warren Commission was meeting to assess if there could have been a greater conspiracy to murder the president. As Guttmacher was testifying in Dallas, members of the Commission interviewed four witnesses who claimed to have seen a rifle protruding from a window at the School Book building. One of them, an unemployed twenty-year-old James Richard Worrell, was adamant he had heard four shots fired "right in succession" rather than the Commission's eventual conclusion that Oswald had fired three times. After Judge Brown adjourned the trial for the day, the jurors were taken as a group to a suburban restaurant where a surprise awaited them. The jurors dined in a different restaurant every night. The location was never revealed to ensure their privacy. But when they arrived, they learned that their families had been informed of the location and several of them were eating in another section of the restaurant. The jurors were not permitted to greet or speak to their family members, but they waved and smiled at each other.

It was a welcome break in a difficult routine. Privately, Judge Brown was worried that he could not hold the jury together too much longer. In addition to being housed above a jail, every aspect of their lives was monitored. They continued to have limited access to television and could read newspapers and magazines only after Weldon "Bo" Mabra, the deputy sheriff assigned to the jurors, cut out any material that could be remotely related to the case. Juror Waymon Rose recalled how right outside their windows, they could see marriages performed on a stairway to an adjacent building. As it turns out, a retired minister had positioned himself at the marriage license office looking for couples in need of a quick ceremony, and maybe willing to offer a gratuity for his services. "As we caught the couple's attention after the embrace," Rose recalled, "we all smiled and cheered. They smiled as if happy they had some company."

But most of the time outside the courtroom, and sometimes inside it, they were just bored. The sacrifice they had already made was enormous, and Judge Brown sensed that several of them were close to rebelling. They had asked him several times to keep the trial in session later into the night so it might be done sooner, though he was uncomfortable forcing the attorneys to do that. But he was reaching his own limits too.

Since joining Ruby's defense team, Mel Belli had spent a considerable amount of time in Dallas but had yet to feel comfortable there. It just wasn't his kind of city. Very few lawyers ever achieve the kind of renown that allows them to try cases in the distant corners of the nation. Most trial lawyers work almost exclusively in their home city, a majority of the time in the same building. They get to know the people who work there: the guards, the bailiffs, the judges. But Belli had a stylish briefcase and he did travel. He went where the action was, living out of a suitcase, trying to adapt to local customs and traditions. The nation was changing rapidly; for example the classic jet airliner, Boeing's 727, had been put into commercial service a month earlier, making cross-country travel even easier. But in Dallas Belli was still an outsider, a carpetbagger. It remained a bad fit.

A night earlier, for example, he had taken his three psychiatric witnesses to dinner in the so-called "Court club" of the Dallas Hilton. In actuality it wasn't a club; membership was granted to anyone registered at the hotel, but treating it as a private club allowed management to bypass local laws prohibiting anything other than beer and wine being served in public places. While Dallas was growing larger every day, it still had not shed its conservative nature. For a man like Belli, who had lived in several of the great cities of the world, this parochial atmosphere was alien and disconcerting.

It was about to get worse. Belli claimed he had tried to find the rhythm of the city. He had attended church services most Sunday mornings, made himself available to the local media, spent his money at local stores and whatever he was feeling privately he did not intentionally criticize the city in public. But that ended the next morning when he went to get a haircut before going to court. Years later he still would be telling this story as it encapsulated his feelings about the city. He walked into a local barbershop, he remembered. Although his picture had been on the front page of the newspapers almost every day, the people inside that shop didn't recognize him.

They were discussing the trial as he settled into the chair. The barber snapped a cover sheet over Belli's tailored suit and he leaned back. As he did, he heard the man in the next chair complain, "...and they got those Jew psychiatrists out from Maryland."

Behind him, someone agreed, "Yeah, those slick Jew psychiatrists with their slick Jew lawyers..."

According to his story, he angrily ripped off the cover sheet and got out of the chair. Looking directly at the startled barber, he thrust his right arm high into the air. "Ach-tung" he yelled mockingly. "Achtung! Heil Hitler." And then he goose-stepped out of the barbershop.

No one had ever accused Melvin Belli of being shy or reticent.

There is no record that his hair was unkempt or that he was unshaven as court began later that morning. Each court session begins with doing legal business, clearing up issues or confusion in the record, entering items into evidence, laying groundwork for what is to be presented. The defense began the proceedings of March 11 by attempting to enter the Ruby family history of mental disorders into evidence. Specifically the fact that Ruby's mother, brother and sister had each been diagnosed with psychiatric issues. The prosecution objected to that on technical grounds and, to no one's surprise, Judge Brown ruled, "The Court feels they are inadmissible."

When that was settled Belli surprised the court with his next words, "The defense rests, Your Honor."

The quick conclusion was completely unexpected. But the defense believed its case had been successfully laid out by the testimony of the three doctors. The actual decision to rest had been made the previous evening in a steam bath, Belli told reporters. While they were both steaming, he said, Tonahill had turned to him and said, "Let's fold up." Still elated with Guttmacher's testimony, and confident he had proven his case, he agreed. He also had noticed that the jury was getting restless and fidgety with all the technical testimony, adding, "There's a limit to human endurance." Yes, he continued, he had discussed it with Ruby, who had "mumbled agreement."

Unlike the prosecution, which must establish guilt beyond a reasonable doubt, the defense only needed to show by a preponderance of evidence that the defendant was legally insane. In Belli's word, if "the weight of the evidence can tip the presumption of sanity…toward the likelihood of insanity" the jury should acquit.

Dr. Guttmacher's testimony, he believed, had tipped that legal scale. His one regret about his case was that he had not been able to convince Dr. Frederick Gibbs, the nation's leading expert on interpreting electroencephalographs, to testify, nor had he been permitted to enter a report from Gibbs stating flatly that Ruby suffered from psychomotor epilepsy into evidence.

After the defense rested, Tonahill made a motion for a directed verdict, asking Judge Brown to instruct the jury that the facts of the case were so clear they must return a verdict of not guilty. Oddly though, as Tonahill made this plea he pointed out that "Your Honor's own selected, impartial medical specialist, Dr. Martin Towler, had made findings that the defendant had psychomotor epilepsy and some organic brain damage at the time of the crime."

Judge Brown rewrote history, instructing that "the record reflect that the court had nothing to do with Dr. Towler…he was appointed at your insistence, Mr. Tonahill."

While the defense's decision to call psychological experts at the second bail hearing had certainly spurred the court to appoint independent experts, it was not done at the insistence of the defense and Tonahill was astonished at that claim. "Why did you take our report…" he asked, "and conceal it from us and everyone else and restrain us from utilizing it…"

Judge Brown was adamant; the report was not going to be allowed into evidence and the jury could not consider it.

Belli then made a motion requesting any testimony concerning statements made by Ruby after he had been arrested be struck from the record, pointing out that there wasn't a single case in Texas law that would allow their inclusion.

No one was surprised when the judge said, "The Court overrules your motion." There was no indication from Belli that he realized how those few words would make such a significant difference.

CHAPTER THIRTEEN

As the morning session began, the courtroom settled into its established routine: Judge Brown was relaxed on the bench, from time to time turning to the side and utilizing his spittoon. Melvin Belli, clad in his finery, from his shoes shined to mirrors to his perfectly knotted tie, was busy reviewing documents at the defense table. Next to him big Joe Tonahill was hunched over his own notes, his shoulders rounded over that material as if offering protection. At the prosecution table the stout Henry Wade slouched way back in his chair, rolling his cold cigar stub from one side of his mouth to the other while his long, lean assistant Bill Alexander looked as if he was tensed to spring forward. The jury was upstairs in the deliberation room, reading, playing board games, listening to music, waiting to be called down when the prosecution was ready to begin its rebuttal.

To maintain a schedule, often the opposing sides in a trial inform their opponent when they intend to rest. That provides the other side the opportunity to make sure its witnesses are present and prepared to testify. But even that small dose of legal courtesy had disappeared. As the prosecution scrambled to locate its rebuttal witnesses and get them to the courthouse, Wade killed time by offering meaningless evidence into the record, efforts that were immediately withdrawn as soon as the first witnesses arrived to be sworn in.

The prosecution's first witness was WBAT-TV sound technician Ira Walker, who testified he had been sitting in the station's mobile truck outside the city jail, waiting for Oswald to be transferred, when Jack Ruby knocked on the window two different times and asked, "Have they brought him down yet?"

The defense objected, claiming this rebuttal witness didn't rebut any direct testimony.

"I'm going to let it in, Counsel," Judge Brown said.

And Walker's testimony did directly rebut the defense contention that Ruby just happened on the scene coincident to the time Oswald was being moved. If Walker was correct, Ruby was at the location well in advance and was waiting for Oswald to be moved.

But there was one glaring issue for prosecutors; why would Ruby have suddenly left the area and gone into the Western Union office if he was anxiously awaiting Oswald's transfer? On cross-examination Tonahill quickly established that Walker hadn't looked at his watch and did not know what time Ruby approached the truck. "It could have been 11:20 then?" It could. Nor had he ever met Ruby before. "How was he dressed?" Tonahill asked.

"I could only see his face."

"Was he wearing glasses?"

"I don't think so."

"Did he have a hat on?"

"I don't know." But he was certain it was Jack Ruby.

And when he asked "Have they brought him down yet" he didn't specify who he was talking about?

"No," the witness admitted, "he didn't say Oswald."

Simple questions and answers like this must have been a pleasant change for the jurors, media and spectators after several days of medical testimony.

UPI photographer Frank Johnson next testified he was in the basement as Oswald was being moved and saw Ruby leap out of the crowd. "I heard him yell, 'You s-o-b,' and the gun went off." Tonahill made quick work of him. "Do you know who yelled 'You s-o-b'?"

"I heard it from my right."

"You don't know who yelled it then, do you?"

"No sir. I didn't see it."

The prosecutors knew they had to clarify that he meant he didn't "see" Ruby say those words but he heard them. Tonahill then asked specifically, "You can't tell the jury that Jack Ruby ever said, 'son-of-a-bitch' that morning, can you?"

The chastened witness agreed, "No, sir."

Just after 11:00 a.m. the prosecution called its first of five medical witnesses, fresh-faced, pink-cheeked neurologist Dr. Sheff Olinger, who took to the stand exuding all the confidence of a young and somewhat inexperienced doctor. A neurologist, he explained, "is concerned primarily with the diagnosis and treatment of the organic diseases of the nervous system; that is the brain, the spinal cord and the nerves." He had been trained in electroencephalography and witnessed a portion of Ruby's neurological examination. In his opinion, these EEGs did not indicate any organic brain damage. There were occasional changes in the speed and amplitude of the waves, he continued, but they were dismissed as "non-specific changes." And while they would support an epilepsy diagnosis they were not sufficient to establish it.

He was aware of Dr. Gibbs's article describing the psychomotor variant but, he made clear, he didn't think much of it. "...it is the name...of a brain wave pattern rather than a clinical disease or specific disease...

"The reports of Dr. Towler's examination and the EEGs combined would not allow me to make a diagnosis of psychomotor epilepsy."

He was quite familiar with psychomotor epilepsy. Echoing earlier testimony, he said a person having such an attack could function normally without conscious memory of his actions. But he could not make a diagnosis of either psychomotor epilepsy or psychomotor variant in the case of Jack Ruby.

It was clear Belli could barely wait to have his turn at Dr. Olinger. He'd been chewing up far more experienced doctors on the witness stand long before the young doctor examined his first patient. More than any other aspect of trial law, this was his area of expertise. He began by establishing that Olinger would not be eligible for certification to the Board of Psychology, meaning he lacked sufficient training to be approved. Dr. Olinger admitted, "I don't believe there is a Board but if there were, I would not be eligible."

"I assure you," Belli informed him, "that there is... You are not certified in psychiatry either. Are you?"

"No, Sir."

Or in electroencephalography?

Again, no.

"There is an electroencephalography board..." Belli continued, "and I think Dr. Frederick Gibbs was the establisher of that board... Isn't he called the father of electroencephalography—like George Washington is called the father of our country?"

"Well, I am not sure about it."

Moments later Belli asked if Dr. Olinger recognized Gibbs as the outstanding authority on conducting and interpreting EEGs. "I don't," the witness responded, "...because I disagree with him."

That set up a situation that might be characterized as a Catch-22, a phrase that had entered the language only three years earlier with the publication of Joseph Heller's World War II novel of that name, meaning an illogical situation. The defense tried to enter Dr. Gibbs's report into record; the prosecution objected because they couldn't cross-examine Gibbs and Judge Brown upheld their objection—but he did permit the witness to testify whether or not he agreed with Gibbs's diagnosis, which the jury was not permitted to hear.

Question by question Belli attempted to strip Dr. Olinger of his reputation. "You are not certified in neurology either?"

"That's correct."

Belli continued his dissection, "Are you certified in any of the medical arts?"

"I am not certified in any specialty." He had been practicing neurology for four years, he said, or as Belli's curious tone indicated, *only* four years.

Having slipped in the dagger, Belli began twisting it. "So that we will be clear, you are not certified by any board in any branch of medicine of any kind, and have taken none of the examinations for certification." He then asked sarcastically, "So that I won't be confused, and we won't confuse the jury, you are licensed to practice, aren't you?"

"Yes, Sir."

Having established Dr. Olinger's relative inexperience and lack of specialized training he then proceeded to pick apart his earlier testimony. To make sure the jury knew about Dr. Gibbs's opinions he simply included portions in his question. "Do you agree or disagree with this article," he began, then read salient paragraphs.

Moments later the prosecution objected to that. "He is reading an article of Dr. Gibbs," Wade complained. Still confident that Gibbs would not appear as a witness he added, "When Dr. Gibbs testifies we want to cross-examine him."

Sustained.

While this questioning was in progress, Jack Ruby was sitting at the defense table, head bowed, completely engrossed in Dr. Guttmacher's book, *The Mind of the Murderer*. For the only time in the entire trial, he had put on reading glasses and was balancing the book before him on the defense table.

As Belli concluded his questioning of this witness, he asked him almost as an aside, if a person suffering from a psychomotor attack "can drive a car and they can do complicated mental problems, can't they?"

Olinger disagreed with previous witnesses. "No sir. They may drive a car...but if a person has a seizure, if he is driving he will have to continue driving. But if he must make a decision to stop, or to avert another car...he would not be able to do that, and he will not be able to carry out complicated mental activity. It's usually a situation of 'What have you done?'"

"And they don't have control of themselves during that time, do they?"

"No."

Belli had finally gotten the response he had been probing for. No further questions.

Assistant District Attorney Jim Bowie questioned the next prosecution rebuttal witness, the far more experienced and qualified Dr. Robert Stubblefield, chairman of the Department of Psychiatry at The University of Texas Southwestern Medical School and Chief of Psychiatry at Parkland Hospital. He was not, he admitted, "a qualified expert in EEG." And who did he consult when using an EEG in his diagnosis? "Dr. Sheff Olinger."

Stubblefield had been invited to examine Ruby by the Court and was not being paid by the prosecution for this appearance, presumably making him a neutral witness.

Bowie started at the end. "Were you able to form an opinion as to whether or not the defendant was sane, knowing the difference between right and wrong and the consequences of his act at the time of [examination]?"

"In terms of his competence to assess the situation and cooperate, I felt he was competent to stand trial."

"And would have been legally sane at that time?"

"That's correct."

Bowie then posed what arguably was the longest single question of the entire trial, a hypothetical question encompassing just about everything that had previously been testified to about the events of November 24, including all of the supposed comments made by Ruby, ending by asking if Stubblefield thought Ruby had been legally sane.

Stubblefield qualified his response. "If I assume the facts as you state them, in my opinion he would know the difference between right and wrong and would know the nature and quality of his act."

The prosecution handed the witness to the defense. "Doctor," Belli began, "you have to assume that everything was said…by Jack Ruby in a full state of consciousness, don't you?"

"That is correct."

And "if it wasn't said in a full state of consciousness he wouldn't know what he was saying, would he?"

"…he would not have."

Unlike his somewhat derisive manner when questioning the self-important Olinger, Belli was respectful, conversational and collegial with Dr. Stubblefield. "One of the components of [a psychomotor state] is automatic action, isn't it?"

Stubblefield agreed "with or without loss of consciousness."

And all Dr. Gibbs did was identify an already existing condition of "something that was always with us, like America, before it was discovered on this world?"

"That's my understanding."

Belli shifted his line of questioning. Throughout the trial he'd been mentioning the awkward way in which Ruby had been holding his gun when he fired it. It finally became clear why he had been so interested in that: Showing a photograph of the killing he wondered if that would "give you some indication that this might have been an automatic act?"

"It would confuse me," Stubblefield replied. "It might be an attempt to stabilize the gun or it might be an automatic act."

During his redirect examination, Bowie pointed out the difference between a sleepwalker who gets up to get a glass of water, which was a conditioned reflex in which the subject performed an ordinary activity, as opposed to purposeful behavior with intent and knowledge. Stubblefield refused to characterize that difference, saying he had no opinion about it.

Bowie also tried to nudge the doctor just a little bit further in his conclusion about Ruby's sanity, not just at the time of trial, but when the incident occurred. "At the time of the shooting… you found him to be…legally sane?"

"I have no opinion about that because we didn't discuss it."

During Belli's recross exam, rather than focusing on sanity or understanding right from wrong, he asked a broader question: "I want to ask you…did you find him to be, him being Jack Ruby, to be an unstable person."

"On the basis of history," Stubblefield agreed, "I would say that he is and was an emotionally unstable person." Under further questioning the doctor agreed Ruby was the kind of individual who, in a stressful situation, would have a lower breaking point than other people.

Although no one could know it at that time, Dr. Stubblefield's widely reported testimony had a far greater impact on the trial than his brief appearance on the witness stand might indicate.

Dr. John Holbrook came next in the battle of the medical experts. The round-faced, bespectacled psychiatrist had been the third member of the court-appointed panel along with Stubblefield and Towler. On the day after Oswald was killed, November 25, Bill Alexander had brought Dr. Holbrook into Ruby's cell for testing, and he had examined him several times subsequent to that first meeting.

The prosecution immediately established that it was Dr. Holbrook's professional opinion that Ruby "did know right from wrong, and he knew the nature and consequences of his act at the time."

Asked by Alexander if he had asked Ruby about the shooting he admitted he had not, "a physician's job is not to determine if someone had committed a crime or not…and in addition to that, very often answers you get from a person who is charged with a crime…are highly unreliable. That in a psychiatric evaluation of a criminal type one has to use more devious devices to…get some idea of their mental status… I was more concerned about whether he was mentally sick or able to tell right from wrong…"

When Dr. Holbrook was asked what Ruby had told him, the defense objected, calling it a violation of Ruby's constitutional rights.

Surprisingly, in this instance the prosecution backed off; instead asking if Ruby had displayed a good memory of the shooting. Holbrook answered simply, "Yes." In fact, he concluded in a soft voice, "There's no real, good medical reason to assume that he's not able to know right from wrong and the nature and consequences of his act at this time."

The fact that Dr. Holbrook disagreed with previous testimony on certain points was less important than the overall impression the prosecution was trying to convey to the jurors: don't pay too much attention to the defense experts. When legally acknowledged experts can't agree on a diagnosis, it is difficult for a juror to reach a decision based on the testimony of any one of them. Holbrook's real purpose in the courtroom, like Stubblefield or Olinger, was to prevent jurors from being swayed by Guttmacher or any other defense witness. Even if the jurors were uncertain or unconvinced one way or another, that would be a win for prosecutors since the defense had the burden to prove that Ruby was legally insane.

The best way for the defense to counter that would be to

demonstrate that this expert is not quite as qualified as the pros-ecutors would have jurors believe. When Belli got to question Holbrook, the two men sparred a bit over who each of them considered the experts in various aspects of the growing science. When Belli asked him if he had read Dr. Carl Menninger's recent book, the man Belli considered an authority, Holbrook topped him, saying he had read the original study and it had been given to him by Dr. Silvano Arrietti—whom he considered even more of an expert!

Well, wondered Belli, "Have you read any papers that were first done, the first one in 1956 on episodic control, on the ir-rational, impulsive criminal act that is sometimes identified as the psychomotor equivalent of a convulsion?"

Point, Belli: "No, I haven't read those." Holbrook had lost his cockiness, and hesitated. "I would like to just—if you don't object, and I'm sure you want the truth and I'm trying to give you an honest opinion."

Belli pressed his advantage. "The best way to get the truth is from you, under oath, in answer to my question... Would you answer my question?"

"Well, I can only answer your question by quoting author-ity on this."

"Don't you know yourself?"

After some additional hedging the doctor finally agreed with Belli's supposition, testifying "If you have an unstable personal-ity superimposed over a person who has psychomotor epilepsy, one would expect an increased frequency of these episodes. Now I do not wish to imply that it would increase the sever-ity, in any way."

"All right," Belli asked several minutes later, "now with Jack Ruby there's no question about it in your mind, that you found an unstable person, didn't you?"

"Absolutely."

Belli wanted to make certain the jurors understood the implications of that answer. "What?" he asked loudly.

"Yes." But unstable did not mean that Ruby was suffering from psychomotor epilepsy, and Dr. Holbrook made clear he still did not believe the diagnosis applied to Ruby.

Belli also made sure jurors learned that during Dr. Holbrook's examination Ruby had expressed his love for Dallas. In a death penalty case in particular, the more an attorney can humanize a defendant, the more difficult it may be for jurors to vote for his execution. And as has been known throughout the ages, a little flattery never hurts. "He volunteered this information to me," the doctor said. "I think he has a great feeling for the community. It has given him a lot more than anyplace else he's ever been…"

Alexander, concerned that Belli may have made some progress with his witnesses, began his redirect exam by repeating his initial question: Was Ruby legally sane when he murdered Oswald? He was, Holbrook also repeated. The seemingly frustrated prosecutor focused on the ability of a man in a psychomotor fugue state to carry out purposeful behavior, shouting his question, "Do you feel that a man suffering a psychomotor seizure could pick an individual moving target out of a crowd of two hundred people…and hit that target with a pistol?"

"It's rare," the doctor testified, "and probably never really happens, and if it does it's very rare that murder or some act of violence of some purposeful nature…that a person cannot remain organized in this state of confusion long enough to carry out a purposeful act…

"I do not feel [Ruby's actions] are possible in a fugue state."

When Belli got his chance, he went after the witness far more aggressively than in his earlier questioning: "Mr. Alexander put the question to you as to whether an epileptic could zero in on a moving target that was directly in front of him and five feet away…you don't feel an epileptic could go out into the forest and hunt his uncle down and shoot him while he was in a convulsive state, do you?"

"I don't think it would be true. I think that someone else might be able to believe it to be true."

That someone else, Belli explained, was Dr. Earl Walker, the state's next scheduled witness. "Have you read his report with reference to the patient who stabbed his wife thirty times while in an epileptic attack?"

"I think that could be done very easily."

Belli seemed incredulous. "Thirty times?... He wouldn't miss her in any of the thirty times..."

The courtroom rocked with laughter as Dr. Holbrook said, "Well, I don't know how many times he might miss her."

Rather than putting Dr. Walker on the stand, as scheduled, the prosecution called a firearms expert, retired Army Lieutenant Colonel Alfred Breninger. Lieutenant Colonel Breninger had instructed troops in the use of the pistol and had participated in shooting competitions. The man knew guns. His job was to assure the jurors that it was not at all unusual for a shooter to use his middle finger to fire a weapon rather than the more traditional index finger—as Ruby had done. The fact he had fired the gun with his middle finger was not proof that he was in an automatic state.

Holding up a pistol for the jury, Breninger demonstrated what he explained was known as "instinct shooting, or shooting in a hurry where you don't have time to use the sights... The idea is that in shooting with this middle finger that wherever your index finger is pointed your barrel to will be pointed... You point and shoot at the same time."

Tonahill got the witness to admit firing the weapon with the middle finger could result in the shooter's hand being burned by escaping gases. He then asked the witness to "stand up and let's see how fast you can get off three passes." The lieutenant colonel demonstrated how quickly he could fire an unloaded handgun three times. "Do it again," Tonahill instructed, then when it was done observed, "That is almost as quickly as you could by taking aim, is it not?"

"Probably so."

And in a friendly tone Tonahill asked if it was true that "People hesitate to use the middle finger..." as Ruby did, "...when there's the possibility of burning themselves, is that right?"

"That's possibly true."

Tonahill livened up the session by asking the witness to pretend fire several more times. While it proved little, it was a welcome diversion from opinions concerning the depth of a fugue state or even more interpretations of brain waves.

That entertainment was short-lived; the prosecution called Dr. Peter Kellaway, the director of the laboratory of clinical encephalography at Baylor University Medical School. He read, he explained, as many as twenty-five hundred EEGs annually and in preparation for this appearance had reviewed the Ruby charts. Alexander asked if there was anything in those EEGs that enabled him to make a diagnosis of organic brain damage, epilepsy or psychomotor epilepsy.

"No." Simply, firmly, "No."

He did acknowledge there was an abnormality in the reading, but explained it was "non-specific. They merely indicate that there is some dysfunction in the region from which they arise."

Dr. Kellaway agreed with the prosecution contention that an EEG is "merely a diagnostic aid," explaining "The electroencephalogram never provides, in itself, a diagnosis." There could be several causes for brain wave irregularity, he continued, and in his opinion there was no way of determining the origin of it.

The problem with his testimony came when Alexander asked him if medical experts believed "there is such a thing as purposeful behavior in epilepsy?"

To which he demurred, admitting, "I do not consider myself as a medical expert in this field."

Belli began by cutting down Dr. Kellaway's experience, pointing out that the defense expert, Dr. Towler, conducted almost twice as many examinations annually as he did.

"Actually," Kellaway countered, "my laboratory is one of the biggest in the world. We do about a thousand EEGs or more per month…under my direction."

Belli simply narrowed the frame of his question. "How many have you done where you have kept track of episodic, four, five and six waves of patients in the fifty year age bracket?"

Dr. Kellaway responded that his lab had not done any specific studies with those parameters.

"In fact," Belli pointed out, "Gibbs did the only study in the world of fifty thousand consecutive cases with this type of abnormality."

Kellaway had done a strong job fending off his questions and as the cross-exam continued, Belli became more confrontational. Kellaway dismissed the defense claim that Dr. Gibbs had reviewed fifty thousand cases, pointing out accurately that Gibbs might have looked at fifty thousand charts but actually had found this abnormality in only 253 cases. In fact, Kellaway didn't even agree with Gibbs's interpretation of Ruby's charts. "I think Dr. Gibbs must be expressing an opinion here… That is not my opinion."

Dr. Kellaway was an experienced witness; he apparently had mastered the art of answering questions to his own satisfaction without leaving a trail to be picked up and exploited by the defense. He continued to insist that while the slow waves seen on Ruby's charts indicated some abnormality, "It's a non-specific wave. It would just be slow activity." And unlike some other witnesses, he was willing to admit the limits of his expertise. When Belli asked him if it was possible the unusual waves were caused by vascular insufficiency, he shrugged and admitted, "I think you're going beyond my competency now," and after another question, "I think I am not competent to discuss this as an expert witness." Belli finally surrendered, limiting the damage this witness had done.

On redirect Kellaway stated simply and unequivocally: "There is no evidence in the EEG of any psychomotor epilepsy."

Belli got him off the stand as quickly as possible, asking him to confirm that in those cases Gibbs's studied he "found spells of bizarre behavior with uncontrollable temper and unconsciousness for one minute and two minutes…and they found also some gross antisocial behavior?"

"That's right."

The prosecution's final rebuttal witness was Dr. A. Earl Walker, the neurosurgeon in charge at the esteemed Johns Hopkins Hospital, the author of several books on brain damage and a qualified examiner of EEGs. In other words, an expert in all of the areas on which Belli had based his defense. As expected, he disagreed with Dr. Gibbs's interpretation of Ruby's brain waves, telling the jury, "These runs of waves are not seen ordinarily in a normal record. They need not be necessarily abnormal. The significance of them is not apparent at this time…"

They might have been caused by previous drug use, he suggested, or several other conditions including hypothyroidism, cerebral arteriosclerosis or convulsive disorders. He went even further. "There is no evidence from these tracings that this individual has epilepsy at this time."

His testimony was brief but damming to the defense, concluding by telling the jury, "One could not say that a psychomotor variant is a disease."

Rather than approaching the witness with the blunt force of a logger going into a forest to cut down trees, Belli treated him with the care of a landscaper doing some minor pruning. He got Dr. Walker to agree that the bursts seen in Ruby's tracings were unusual.

The real question was how much impact any of this was having on the jury. Almost 350 years earlier Sir Francis Bacon had noted in his classic book, *The New Organon*, "The human understanding when it has once adopted an opinion...draws all things else to support and agree with it...." In the vast majority of trials, jurors are called to decide cases about which they have no previous knowledge, have no relationship to anyone involved in the case and no personal or emotional stake in the outcome. But this case wasn't one of them. The facts here were widely known, and as residents of the greater Dallas area they had an emotional stake in the verdict. So had the jurors already made up their minds and were they just hearing facts and opinions that supported their preconceived positions? Scottish journalist Charles Mackay described broadly what became known as confirmation bias in his 1852 book, *Extraordinary Popular Delusions and the Madness of Crowds*. "When men wish to construct or support a theory, how they torture facts into their service!"

In this case, confirmation bias would suppose that many jurors had formed an opinion concerning Ruby's guilt or innocence even before the trial began and this parade of expert witnesses simply provided the facts they needed to confirm what they already believed.

By this point, journalists, jurors and spectators had become far more knowledgeable about epilepsy than they might have ever imagined. Few people knew, for example, as Belli asked Walker, "If we were to look at the brain of an epileptic, very carefully at autopsy, we wouldn't see any damage, would we?"

That was possible, the witness agreed. But Walker finally balked when asked if Dr. Gibbs's psychomotor variant seizure pattern had been recognized and accepted by the broader field. "No," he said firmly.

Dr. Walker had a pleasant manner, and Belli assumed the jury liked him. As he admitted later, he liked him. So the attitude he took was important. Belli wanted to leave the jury with the impression that the two professionals were in agreement. So he asked him if it was true that an experienced doctor could examine the results of a complete battery of psychological tests and from that diagnose brain damage of a particular kind.

Dr. Walker countered that it would depend on which tests were chosen but finally agreed, with some hesitation, "He might be able to."

After a few more questions, Belli thanked the witness. He later would write that he had gotten what he wanted from Walker, including testimony that Ruby's EEG pattern could prediagnose rage states. But the headlines in the next morning's *New York Times* were clear: "2 Psychiatrists Call Ruby Sane."

With the end of Dr. Walker's testimony, Wade announced that the State rested its case.

Damage had been done to the defense. Now Belli had to figure out how to deal with it.

CHAPTER FOURTEEN

It was possible for the trial to go on forever. After Wade's prosecution had completed presenting its rebuttal, Belli's team was entitled to a surrebuttal, the opportunity to respond to witness testimony or evidence presented during the rebuttal. This is a chance for an attorney to repair or patch up any damage the opposing side has done to their case or, as Belli explained it, "plaster in all the little holes." While technically a surrebuttal is limited to issues raised during the rebuttal, in practice judges often are lenient and new witnesses and evidence can be presented. Once the defense has concluded its surrebuttal, the other side may be allowed to counter that argument. The number of times a case can bounce back and forth is up to the judge; in theory it literally can keep going forever.

But this case was moving slowly, to a verdict. Belli's client, he believed, was getting increasingly detached from the proceedings, his temper was beginning to show and, he was convinced, the jury had enough and wanted to go home.

The defense put police lieutenant Jack Revill on the stand. The objective was to refute the testimony of Detective Mc-Millon, who claimed he had seen Ruby come out of the crowd screaming, "You rat son of a bitch. You shot the president." Tonahill showed Revill a photograph of the instant Ruby fired, showing McMillon apparently looking in a different direction, and asked, "I know you wouldn't want to call a fellow officer a liar, but if he said he was looking at Ruby when he came up with the gun, he just wasn't looking at him, was he?"

Objection. "The thing [photograph] speaks for itself," Alexander shouted.

Sustained. But the point was made to the jury; McMillon was not looking at the defendant.

The prosecution erupted again when Tonahill wondered if Revill would be willing to give Jack Ruby a polygraph test. Wade leaped up and shouted, "Have you already offered him one?"

The detective instantly responded, "Yes sir, I have!"

The defense next called Eileen Kaminsky, Ruby's younger sister. She was an attractive, prim woman and in a different trial this could have been the dramatic highlight during which the defendant's sibling spoke directly to the jury about her troubled brother. But the purpose here was just a bit of legal bookkeeping. Under Texas law, a defendant could be found guilty of murder and still be set free if the jury believes that is appropriate—but only if that person had not previously been convicted of a felony. Belli asked one question, "Whether your brother, Jack, has ever been at any time in his life, convicted of a felony?"

"No."

As she left the stand, she paused for a moment and asked her brother in a compassionate tone, "How do you feel?"

He did not respond.

The defense was moving rapidly now. Ruby's longtime house-keeper, an African-American woman named Eleanor Pitts, testified she had called him the morning of Oswald's murder to tell him she was coming to his apartment that day. "He sounded strange," she said, so strange that she even asked him, "Is this Mr. Jack Ruby?"

They agreed she would come in the afternoon. The defense point was obvious: No one who expects to be in jail needs to pay for their apartment to be cleaned.

Another Dallas detective, B. H. Combest testified he also was in the city hall basement when Oswald was scheduled to be moved. He was, he said, standing "approximately three feet away off his right hand shoulder." Suddenly, he saw Ruby move forward. He had often worked on the Vice Squad, which covered nightclubs, so he recognized him. "Did you hear him say anything at the time immediately preceding the shooting?" Phil Burleson asked.

Combest could see Ruby's lips moving but didn't hear him say anything, but "just in conjunction with the shooting I said... the best I can recall, I believe I said, 'Jack, you son of a bitch, don't!...

"Actually, it already had happened by the time I said it."

Several of his fellow officers had testified they had heard Ruby shouting threats as he shot Oswald. Combest's testimony offered an alternative possibility; rather than lying about what they had heard, they were mistaken about who had said it.

The defense was giving jurors a plausible alternative that they might want to believe. It was a good place to end a long day in court.

The twenty-first day of the trial, Thursday, March 12, began promptly at 9:00 a.m. America was slowly emerging from the shock of losing its beloved young president. The once commonplace was once again becoming commonplace. The two escaped courthouse prisoners remained at large, and the FBI officially entered the case on the "reasonable assumption" that the men had crossed a state line, making them federal fugitives. Attesting to the growing importance of Dallas as a business center, Delta advertised it now had three jet flights directly to Los Angeles every day. In New York the drama *A Case of Libel* opened on Broadway starring Van Heflin; reviewer Ann Holmes wrote that audiences "conditioned to *Perry Mason*, *The Defenders*, Percy Foreman in Houston and Melvin Belli with the Ruby case, Heflin lacks color, wit, and a real sense of drama" in a play as exciting "as a dish of tapioca."

But the aftermath of the assassination still filled the newspapers. In Washington, the Warren Commission was taking testimony from Lee Harvey Oswald's neighbor, a nineteen-year-old who had driven him to work the morning of the assassination. At Texas Southwestern Medical School, only a few miles from the courthouse, Governor John Connally, who had been seriously wounded in the assassination, finally had the cast removed from his right arm; "My arm seems okay," the governor said, "but it looks like the devil." The *Morning News* announced a fund to benefit slain officer J. D. Tippit's family had raised more than $600,000, with the largest donation coming from Dallas manufacturer Abraham Zapruder, who had contributed $25,000 paid to him by *Life* magazine for his 8 mm footage of the assassination. And Oswald's mother, Marguerite, who had sold interviews to European magazines, announced she would begin a lecture tour.

When the trial resumed, the defense continued its surrebuttal, calling Dr. Walter Bromberg, a practicing psychiatrist since 1928 and currently clinical director of the Psychiatric Hospital in Westchester, New York. Dr. Bromberg was a well-groomed man with neatly trimmed white hair and mustache. It actually took Belli about fifteen minutes to run through his expert credentials, director of this, chairman of that. During his long career he had treated many epileptics, a personality, he explained, "characterized chiefly by emotional instability."

Once again, Belli began by asking the question at the heart

of the defense. After examining Ruby for eighteen hours over four separate occasions, Dr. Bromberg concluded, "My opinion is that this man is mentally ill. He did not know the nature and quality of his acts; that his acts were in a state of suspended consciousness based on a complicated mental illness…

"…His emotional stability was severe and expressed itself in impulsive actions, triggered by emotional stimuli of intense type."

This affirmed the defense strategy: Ruby was a sick man; he couldn't help himself. Dr. Bromberg continued, "…agitation and the excitement triggered off an episode…his acts were of a distinctive, automatic nature, not voluntarily controlled."

And confabulation? Was that typical behavior of people with this diagnosis? "You find it in any organic brain illness," Bromberg explained, "where there is amnesia, loss of consciousness. The patient fills in the details." He put it in terms a lay person might relate to; "An alcoholic, for example, if you ask them where they have been and they don't remember, they fill in the detail. That is called a fabrication or a confabulation… They make up a story which is designed to make it appear they didn't have the unconsciousness, to make it appear normal…"

Henry Wade questioned Dr. Bromberg for the prosecution. Since Bromberg had testified at the bail hearing, the prosecution had taken time to completely examine his long history, and Wade was ready to bludgeon him. This was his Perry Mason moment. He began by asking about some staff conflict the doctor had experienced while working at a Mendocino hospital. "I believe it was your recommendation that [sex criminals] be released in the community and run around loose, isn't that right?"

"No—no," he protested. "It was a conflict of ideas…"

"Isn't it a fact that your idea was that in rehabilitating them they should have furloughs out among the citizens there?"

"That was the interpretation put upon it by the Department of Mental Hygiene… I said they shouldn't be locked up behind

stone walls if they were better…and that the process of treatment involved some freedom on the grounds…"

In fact, Wade continued, isn't it true that you were given notice and "rejected as a permanent employee in this clinical job."

Bromberg tried to fight back. "After fourteen months' activity the conflict between myself and the director was such that
I had to stop work. I was not rejected. I had the job, but there
was a conflict, so I ceased working there." There was a Civil
Service hearing and, he admitted, "I lost the hearing."

The dissection continued. "I believe they [Belli's firm] pays
you $350 a day." In 1964 dollars that was a significant amount
of money.

Belli had to do something to deflect this broadside. He
launched a counterattack. When Wade pointed out that Bromberg was so far out of the mainstream that he even disagreed
with the M'Naghten rule, Belli interrupted and claimed, "I
think there are a lot of people who don't agree with…"

Alexander cut in, "Your Honor, he doesn't need any coaching from Mr. Belli."

Belli turned on him. "You timed it right. Let's have it out
insulting friend, who uses the word 'peasant'…"

Bowie joined the ruckus. "Oh, we object to this, Your
Honor."

"…Jew boy!" Belli continued, "—the name of God in vain."

Belli took a long and deep calming breath, musing, "I am almost to the limit of human endurance."

Judge Brown leaned across his desk and squinted. "Just a minute, Mr. Belli!"

When order was restored, Wade continued his take down,
quoting from books Bromberg had written that seemed to contradict his testimony. The doctor tried to fight back, insisting
"This man is a basic psychotic personality… He has an epilep-
toid personality, with occasional psychomotor seizures…" Then

he added, with an unfortunate word choice, "That's the total diagnosis in a nutshell."

Bromberg explained that he based that diagnosis on his examination of Ruby. Wade suggested Ruby's memory of the event was selective, wondering, "Would it change your thinking about him any—assuming he did remember all this and didn't tell you about it?"

The doctor pointed out, "Well, if he remembered it and didn't tell me, I wouldn't know that he remembered it..."

Wade then spent the next several minutes painting his own long and winding alternate scenario, what he believed were the facts of the case couched as a hypothetical question: Suppose this, suppose that, then suppose this and that. He went on and on, finally concluding, "and suppose when he gets to you, he can't remember anything about it..."

"The trouble with that question..." Tonahill interrupted, "...is that all those facts aren't so. Some of them are complete misrepresentations."

"Just assume they are, Doctor."

Before Bromberg could answer, Tonahill loudly continued pointing out inaccuracies in the question. There was so much fighting back and forth that when Judge Brown sustained the objection, it wasn't clear what he was sustaining. Finally, the witness answered the question with the only logical answer, however ridiculous, "If he didn't say the things he said to me, that he did say, and his behavior was not what he said that it was, the situation being entirely different, it is conceivable a different conclusion would come from that material."

Belli's redirect went right to the point. "Is there anything I could have said to him as a lawyer, or a doctor, a psychiatrist, a priest or a holy man, or a legal man that could have changed his electroencephalogram?"

"No. Definitely no." In fact, there was nothing anyone could have done to change the results of any examination.

In this battle of the experts, the goal was to make your expert's opinion become the one that jurors remember when reaching their verdict. Belli referred to Dr. Holbrook as "Mr. Alexander's friend." When Mr. Alexander objected to that, as Belli probably suspected he would, Belli suggested, "Let's assume this psychiatrist who was retained by Mr. Alexander went up to see this man, Jack Ruby...and Mr. Alexander told him, 'We have been friends for a long time, Jack, relax and be at ease, I won't do anything to damage our long friendship.' Even under those relaxing soporific expressions by Mr. Alexander the psychiatrist for the state still said that this man was an unstable person...if he were living in a city like Dallas and the events that happened here, would that agitate anybody with that type of personality?"

"Yes. I feel it would."

Belli, just like Wade or any competent trial lawyer, fed suggestions to the jury disguised as questions.

The nastiness between the two sides continued during Wade's recross examination. He cited Bromberg's report when he pointed out Ruby remembered standing two feet from Oswald. The witness objected, explaining that was his own interpretation of Ruby's comments, "He didn't say that—I was writing that."

"I guess," Wade said, as sarcastically as had become common, "that was what your Dr. Belli called your 'confabulation.'"

Belli's elbow was on the table, his head resting on his palm. He waved wearily and said, "I am just too tired to respond to that one, Judge." Knowing laughter rippled through the courtroom.

Later in this examination Wade reminded jurors there was another possible motive for the killing. "He had a feeling of wanting to be a hero, is that right?"

"A martyr, rather," Bromberg corrected. "He had a definite Messianic trend, his motto being to rescue the Jewish people from the charge that they haven't got the guts, to put it in his words."

When Belli followed up, he asked if a boxer knocked out but

still on his feet or a football player who leaves the sidelines and runs onto the field to tackle an opposing player can be explained "by organic brain damage...blood withheld from a particular part of the brain."

"Yes," Bromberg agreed, "there is a suspension of or impairment of consciousness then."

In his follow up to Belli's follow up, Henry Wade asked about that boxer "that gets hit, that has nothing to do with psychomotor epilepsy, does it?" Actually, the doctor responded, the fugue state that occurs when someone is concussed "is not unlike the fugue state in psychomotor epilepsy."

Belli came back, asking if that boxer could follow his opponent "around the ring, do complicated acts, feinting, throw an uppercut, a left hook, duck, go back and drink out of a bottle... come into the ring again, fight the whole fight and then get dressed, talk to the press and wake up a day later and not know what he was doing?"

Objection. Hypothetical outside the scope of evidence previously presented.

Sustained.

Wade landed the final blow in this series of jabs over boxers and fighters: "you never have seen one [a fighter] in that state jump out of the ring and shoot someone in the audience, have you?"

"I can't say that I remember that," the doctor agreed, causing spectators to chuckle.

The witness was excused.

Joe Tonahill called Ruby's rabbi, Hillel E. Silverman of the congregation Shearith Israel in Dallas. Rabbi Silverman was an imposing figure, a handsome, tanned, fit man with close-cropped dark hair and a deep, commanding voice that might be seen to be strong enough to carry the word of God. Because the defense had decided it was too risky to put Ruby on the stand, they wanted to get into the record personal details that could only come from people like his sister or his rabbi.

While religious leaders may not be experts in a subject, they bring gravitas with them to the stand. Most jurors assume they are telling the truth. As one of the Ten Commandments warns, "Thou shalt not bear false witness against thy neighbor." Rabbi Silverman was testifying voluntarily. For more than 150 years, conversations between clergy acting in their professional capacity and parishioners has been recognized as privileged speech. After a Protestant minister was forced to testify against a defendant in the 1811 case, *People v. Smith*, the New York state legislature passed laws granting special protection for men of the cloth. That law became the model eventually adopted by every state. But here any privilege was waived because the defendant was allowing him to share those conversations.

The square-jawed rabbi played his solemn role perfectly. He had known Jack Ruby for several years, he said, and had visited Ruby in his cell as many as seventy or eighty times since the incident. He also had seen him at the end of the memorial service for the president. Over one thousand people had attended but Ruby had stood out. "I remarked to myself...that there was something peculiar...he seemed to be in sort of a trance. There was not a tear in his eye."

That did not surprise him, the rabbi explained. Two months earlier, during the Jewish High Holy days, Ruby had called him. "He talked to me for about forty-five minutes. He was completely distraught, completely emotional, he was crying and he was screaming." For years, Ruby told Rabbi Silverman, he had been attending services with his sister, but "something had happened the night before, and he told me...he didn't remember what it was. He thought it was some sort of an argument, some sort of altercation, some sort of misunderstanding and he felt so guilty..."

Ruby asked him to call his sister, which he did. "In the conversation she told me it wasn't only a misunderstanding or argument but that he had shoved her, pushed her and actually struck her... Jack had no memory of that when I called him back. He didn't remember that at all."

That was precisely the evidence the defense needed to prove that Ruby had previously suffered from blackouts, triggered by a highly emotional state during which he was capable of committing violent acts about which he had no memory.

The rabbi recalled other bizarre episodes. On another occasion, Ruby had come to his home with his then-six dogs. As those dogs ran on the rabbi's front lawn, "I made a remark about them and suddenly he began to cry for no reason at all. And he began to tell me, 'I'm unmarried, I have no children, this is my wife,' and he pointed to one of the dogs, and 'these are my children,' and he began to sob and cry and moan and then in five or ten minutes he forgot about it completely and went on to another subject..."

In perhaps the single greatest understatement of the trial, Tonahill asked, "You considered that abnormal?"

"I have found that on many occasions Jack has been most emotional; very rational one moment, very logical, very precise and then suddenly would begin to cry...and then suddenly come right out of it and would return again to emotional stability... He will suddenly stop in his conversation, with a blank stare, again, almost a trance. It would last maybe a minute..."

The prosecution objected when the defense asked the rabbi to relate his jail-cell conversations with Ruby, essentially slipping the defendant's testimony into the record without having to put him on the stand. "It's part of the res gestae," Belli claimed, perhaps facetiously.

"Res gestae two months later?" Wade responded somewhat incredulously.

Although the rabbi was not a doctor, Tonahill put the M'Naghten question to him. "It is my opinion from the de-

Ruby had a bizarre relationship with his dogs, keeping as many as twelve dachshunds and referring to them as his "children." He had brought his favorite dog, Sheba, whom he referred to as his "wife," with him on that fateful morning and left her in his locked car. For some, that was evidence that he had not planned the shooting, knowing he would be apprehended and the dog would be left alone in the locked car for some time.

scriptions to me by him," Rabbi Silverman replied, "that at the time of the shooting he did not know the difference between right and wrong…"

Cross-examining clergy can be difficult. A lawyer has to show respect for the person and their position while trying to undermine their sworn testimony. Wade wondered if in the past the rabbi had suggested to other members of his congregation that they seek psychiatric help? He did indeed, he said. "Did you ever recommend to Jack Ruby that he go to a psychiatrist?"

"It is not an easy matter for a clergyman of any faith to recommend to anybody that he see a psychiatrist, because once you mention this to a person, you've put into his mind that he's a psychotic or a neurotic or a manic depressive." Two months before the assassination, he recalled, "I said to myself, 'One more episode and I will definitely recommend that he see a psychiatrist.' I didn't see him since that time, and that's why the answer is no..." He explained further, "I'm afraid sometimes to use the word psychiatrist to people. After all, unfortunately it has a stigma, and therefore I talk in terms of medical help and medical counsel and before he knows it I've sent him to a physician who happens to have had psychiatric training."

After the rabbi stepped down, the defense seemed to be plastering some chips in its case when it called Curtis "Larry" Crawford, the twenty-three-year-old man who had driven Ruby and roommate George Senator on the middle-of-the-night mission to photograph the Impeach Earl Warren billboard. Crawford described himself as "kind of a footloose character," and had hitchhiked back to Dallas when asked to testify. His "financial situation" he explained, "was none." But he wanted to help Ruby. He did general chores at the Carousel Club, he said, including taking care of Ruby's dogs. In fact, a dog Ruby had given away had been returned and he had been preparing a crate to ship that dog to California. It was somewhat jarring testimony: this man who literally was crazy about his dogs was planning to give one of them away. To prevent the prosecution from suggesting this showed Ruby was making certain his "family" would be cared for when he was in prison, Ruby attorney Phil Burleson emphasized that this dog had been given away previously and returned and the plan to ship it to California was in progress before the president was assassinated.

Sam Pate, a furniture sales and sometimes radio reporter, was present on Saturday, November 23, when Oswald had been moved. He saw Ruby "standing on a table...less than ten feet from Oswald."

Tonahill asked, "...Was he in a position where he could have killed Oswald if he had wanted to?"

"Yes, sir."

Timelines matter. To support its contention that Ruby's act

had been spontaneous, the defense was showing that he'd had other opportunities but had not taken advantage of them.

During the cross-exam, the witness further embarrassed the Dallas PD by mentioning "They were supposed to have some security in the place as far as press passes, getting in, and I left my press pass home that day and I walked in."

Jack was a hustler, Pate suggested, always handing out cards from the Carousel Club. Pate himself had never been there, he said, "because I don't drink and...my wife wouldn't care for me to go down to a burlesque place."

"You don't believe in going to burlesque places?"

The entire courtroom burst into knowing laughter when he admitted, "Well, if I could get by without my wife knowing it, it would be fine."

Wade showed a photograph to the witness, asking him to identify Ruby. He couldn't, the witness said. Ruby wasn't in the picture. The defense demanded to see the photograph but the prosecution refused to show it to them because it hadn't been entered as evidence. Judge Brown did not require them to turn it over, causing Belli to shout out in frustration, "This is the worst type of groundhog evidence that I've ever seen." Waving his hands up and down he added, "I mean, it comes up and then it goes back down into his hole."

Tonahill did have some fun with the prosecutor, asking his witness, "Was Ruby there when Mr. Wade made a statement that Oswald murdered the president, the case was broken..."

"Judge," Wade appealed instantly.

"Get on some other subject," Judge Brown warned Tonahill.

Wade told the judge, "Tell the jury not to consider it."

"Ladies and gentlemen, don't consider it for any purposes."

When that was done, Tonahill looked at his witness and asked, "Did Mr. Wade express..." Judge Brown practically screamed at him to move on to another subject. And then, after asking a few other questions Tonahill wondered, "And you saw Mr. Wade acknowledge some gesture..."

Objection.

Tonahill's last question raised some other questions. "Did you hear Mr. Wade turn to Jack Ruby when he was on the phone talking and say, 'Who is it, Jack? The Weird Beard?'"

The Weird Beard? "No."

The morning session ended with that exchange. During the lunch break, as often had been the case, the defense team was followed to a restaurant by protestors carrying antipsychiatry signs, trying to block their movement and screaming at them. Belli warned them that he was going to ask Judge Brown to find them in contempt of court. When court resumed Tonahill suggested, "The State would join with us" in condemning these people. "Ain't that right, Hank?"

"I don't care nothing about them," Wade snapped.

In the afternoon session, the defense put a series of witnesses on the stand to make minor points. A trial that had meandered along at a pace of a lazy summer afternoon suddenly regained speed as if racing to meet a deadline. One by one the defense called nine people to answer only a few questions: KLIF disc jockey Kenneth Dowe testified that Ruby had called the station saying "He knew Mr. Wade and that Mr. Wade would probably help us get the story." *Dallas Times Herald* printer Arnold Gadash had seen Ruby the afternoon of the twenty-third and remembered that Ruby had tried to sell him "some sort of twistboard apparatus" that was "good for the waist and he said it was good exercise for the hips...it swivels and you get on it and the upper part of your body goes one way and the lower part goes the other...which he let me have for two dollars" and then had been "very emotional...upset" when he took out ads announcing his clubs would be closed that weekend. At a bar that same Saturday afternoon, Ruby had bumped into "a casual acquaintance," jewelry designer Frank Bellocchio, who remembered Ruby "was not coherent;" both of them were "pretty emotional," he said, furious that people were blaming Dallas for the assassination. Ruby showed him the photograph of the billboard then confided in him that he had "a scoop" for the FBI, which later made Bellocchio wonder if he was referring to his own plan. Bank teller Mrs. Ingrid Carter gave minimal help to the defense by telling the jury she had seen Ruby in the bank a week earlier and "He seemed very depressed," then added he told her he was taking stimulants and "I am all by myself, nobody loves me." Alexander was able to suggest Ruby was making preparations for the killing when he asked her if she was "the teller that he got $4100 in dollar bills from, just shortly before the assassination"—she was not.

The defense continued with American Airlines pilot T. R. Apple who testified he had been with Frank Bellocchio in the bar and had heard Ruby say he was going to give the photograph of the Impeach Earl Warren billboard to an unnamed agency because, "I want it to be a scoop." Jack Ruby had phoned respected Dallas attorney Stanley Kaufman, who had handled some civil documents work for him, on Saturday afternoon. Now, Kaufman testified Ruby had asked him how he might locate the person whose name was on the anti-Kennedy newspaper ad that had appeared in the *Morning News*. Kaufman recounted Ruby saying "whoever put that ad in must have known that the President was going to be killed." Kaufman was not able to help him.

All of these minor witnesses testifying about Ruby's anger and sadness in the wake of the president's death were simply there to support the defense's portrait of a man in despair and mentally crumbling. But they also worked against the growing theory that he was part of a larger conspiracy. After all, if Ruby was a conspirator in a plot to kill the president, why not lay low before finishing his part of the job? Was he just pretending to be so shaken? These are questions that would be asked for years to come.

According to Belli, moments before his next witness, a Dr. Ulevitch, (who had seen Ruby for an upper respiratory infection several weeks earlier,) took the stand, he had told the defense that "Ruby was absolutely unstable and I can honestly say that," but on the stand he said his examination "was so cursory it would have been impossible to correctly evaluate the personality of this person... My examination was limited to the chest." Another physician, dermatologist Dr. Coleman Jacobson, testified he had known Ruby as a friend and patient for nine years and that Ruby had called him hours after the assassination and asked in a voice "quite agitated and full of emotion" what time services started that night at the synagogue.

The "Weird Beard" mentioned previously was explained when popular KLIF disc jockey Russell Lee Moore, who used that nickname on air, took the stand. He told jurors he was at city hall after midnight on the twenty-second and Ruby had introduced him to Henry Wade. He had taped a brief interview with Wade, and although he believed he had that recording with him, ("You called me so fast this could be an air take of The Beatles for all I know") Judge Brown was adamant he would not allow it to be played in the courtroom.

With that, the defense rested its unfocused, wide-ranging surrebuttal, having at the least provided some entertainment for the jurors by presenting the very popular radio DJ. Even Henry Wade had been pleased to meet him. "The Weird Beard," he'd said. "My kids listen to you!"

It appeared that the defense had presented its case but there was one major surprise coming—and it would come as a great surprise even to Melvin Belli.

CHAPTER FIFTEEN

The trial raced through the afternoon into the early evening and then the night. The prosecution had more experts lined up to refute the defense's refutation, but everyone inside that courtroom also recognized the jurors were losing patience. Wade called Dr. Robert S. Schwab, a professor at Harvard Medical School and the director of the EEG laboratory at Massachusetts General Hospital. Dr. Schwab, a thin, balding man with a thick mustache, had examined Ruby's charts and declared in a booming voice that the EEGs might "be found in a person who had a mild history of head injuries, or previous brain damage, but it could also be found in people who had no brain damage. I would not make the diagnosis at all." He suggested the findings could also be the result of regular drug use or even sleep deprivation.

During his cross-examination, Belli tried desperately to get Dr. Schwab to agree to other possibilities but the witness remained firm: These EEGs did not allow for a diagnosis of epilepsy. Belli cited the esteemed but absent Dr. Gibbs's work several times, and each time Dr. Schwab disagreed with those findings. At best, he said, "The records suggested a non-specific, mild abnormality" that could be the result of many different things.

Next up was Dr. Francis Michael Forster, the former president of the American Board of Psychiatry and Neurology, who had attended to then-President Dwight Eisenhower in 1957 when he'd suffered a serious stroke. He had conducted what was essentially a blind test, mixing Ruby's tracings with others run on the same machines and recording his reaction to each of them before learning which were the defendant's. His finding was that Ruby's EEGs "would not" support a diagnosis of any type of epilepsy or psychomotor epilepsy.

Asked by Alexander to explain what psychomotor epilepsy is, he told the story of a patient of his, a doctor who also was an accomplished musician. "He always played the Christmas carols on Christmas Eve," he related. "And he was playing 'Oh Come Let Us Adore Him' when in the middle of this he had one of these seizures and for a few minutes did an unusually fast rendition of be-bop. He played be-bop music, fast music… Then he came right back to 'Oh Come Let Us Adore Him'…"

Alexander then described Ruby's actions, emphasizing his comment, "I thought I could get off three shots," and asked if that person could have been suffering psychomotor epilepsy at that time.

"No." Dr. Forster emphasized that after the fact, someone suffering an epileptic seizure would not recall the incident at all.

Belli tried to right ship with his first question, asking the doctor to define "confabulation," a term that the jurors had heard many times now.

But Dr. Forster challenged what they had heard from defense experts, saying that confabulation is *not* associated with epilepsy: "If a patient has the disease which is causing epilepsy and which is also causing a memory defect which he will fill in with confabulation, he may have confabulation, but it is not part of the epilepsy."

Belli's questioning became confrontational. "Would you agree there are islands of amnesia in psychomotor epilepsy? Is that clear to you, what islands of amnesia are?"

"I said," Dr. Forster repeated, "there is amnesia of the episodes in the seizure. Therefore, if you wish to call that an island, that's quite all right."

"I didn't ask if it was quite all right. I asked your opinion on that." Belli suggested that a patient recovering from an attack may recall some of the things that happened and not remember other things.

Dr. Forster seemed to agree, pointing out "In some of these seizures patients will disrobe to some extent and obviously as they come out they see they have disrobed, and they would have recall... I would say that is good deductive reasoning."

Belli then returned to the work done by Dr. Frederick Gibbs; the witness agreed that Gibbs was among those who had done the most work on the psychomotor variant, and said that he had read his report—but that he disagreed with it. Belli feigned incredulity. "You disagree with the report of the man who knows more about this than anyone in the world? Is that correct?"

"Dr. Gibbs has done the most work on this. These are his findings. They are not completely accepted by the profession." The EEG pattern Gibbs described as a psychomotor variant were actually common, he said, and he would not diagnose them as such.

Unable to get Forster to budge, Belli changed tack. "You say what you saw in Jack Ruby's electroencephalogram could not be due to organic brain damage of any kind?"

"I can't say that... I can't say from that EEG that there is organic brain damage."

Belli pounced. "Could there be?"

Objection.

Overruled!

Gleefully, Belli told the witness, "You've got to answer that."

Dr. Forster conceded, "There could be."

"Say it louder," Belli told him, "so we can hear it."

"I say there could be." Finally Belli had introduced some doubt into Forster's testimony.

The prosecution's next witness was presumably the final expert witness. Judge Brown was determined to conclude the testimony before recessing for the evening. Dr. Roland MacKay, the oldest expert to testify in the trial, had served as president of both the American Neurological Association and the American Epileptic Society and was presently a professor of Neurology at Northwestern University. Perhaps more telling, he had known Dr. Gibbs for many years and had been with him on the staff of the University of Illinois Medical School.

He had examined the EEGs, he told Alexander, and "These two tracings are both within the limits of normal, except that they look to be the record of a sleepy person, or a person in some light sleep, or perhaps some medication."

"Are these EEGs even suggestive that the patient has any type of epilepsy or psychomotor epilepsy?"

"Not to me, sir, no."

Alexander asked if a person in a psychomotor seizure state could have done what Ruby did, pick out a target, move in on him, and shoot him at close range?

"No, sir."

"That's all," Alexander said. "Pass the witness."

Belli's only path was to demonstrate that this expert was not as expert as the defense experts. But there was so much of this expert testimony that it risked becoming confusing. Too many experts had testified for too long about too much, and their professional disagreements had clouded the picture.

Belli aggressively questioned Dr. MacKay, who said firmly he didn't have much use for clinical psychologists; as a research method psychology was valuable but "it doesn't serve me very well in my work."

So, Belli wondered, "You're of the school of thought that we ought to throw the psychologists out?"

MacKay objected to that, stating he believed sitting with a patient, questioning that person is much more valuable and informative.

It was 5:30 p.m., nearing the end of the long and final day of questioning when Belli finally brought MacKay's attention to Dr. Gibbs, whose work had been the foundation of the defense case. It was an odd situation, with so many witnesses on both sides giving strong opinions about his report—but the jury had not been able to read it themselves or hear from its author. Dr. MacKay acknowledged cautiously that Dr. Gibbs had done more work with EEGs than any other American and was the author "of the only paper" about psychomotor epilepsy variant.

Do you agree with his report to the court, Belli asked, knowing that MacKay hadn't read that report and the court would not allow him to comment on it. But, he wondered aloud, how MacKay could disagree with Gibbs if he hadn't read the letter?

Jim Bowie confidently repeated the prosecution's legally correct position once again. "We object to his reading any letter and asking whether or not he agrees with some doctor who's not present, who's not testified, who's not been in this courtroom…"

Tonahill then stunned the courtroom; he leaped to his feet and proclaimed, "We assure you Dr. Gibbs will be here to testify to the contents of that letter, Judge."

Belli was incredulous; later he recalled that he was so surprised he wondered if Tonahill had "flipped."

"Did you just call him?"

Tonahill nodded, grinning broadly. "We assure you he will be here."

Gibbs's reputation had been firmly established. To varying degrees every expert had acknowledged their respect for him.

The prosecution hadn't objected or even fought back very much about those comments, secure in the knowledge that Gibbs had refused to testify. Suddenly, the posse was racing to town, ready to save the day.

Dr. Gibbs had been in Chicago reading reports of the trial, growing angrier as the prosecution's experts lauded him but attacked his findings. Dr. Towler had phoned him to complain that the prosecution was dismissing the diagnosis both men had agreed upon. A lifetime's work had gone into that report, and finally Gibbs had decided to defend it. He told Towler, "I'd feel very bad if the truth did not come out." So when Tonahill phoned him again, he finally agreed to testify for the defense and stand up for his work.

His flight was scheduled to arrive in Dallas at 12:05 a.m.— and Judge Brown had demanded testimony end earlier that day. Meanwhile, knowing Dr. Gibbs was on his way, Belli finished with this witness. "What does Dr. Gibbs look like?"

"Gibbs is a dark man—fairly slender, tall. I'd say about five feet ten," MacKay said. Pressed further, he reiterated his disagreement with Gibbs's interpretation of EEG waves. "I can't find myself in complete academic agreement with Dr. Gibbs as to…the validity of what he calls an abnormality. I think Dr. Gibbs' case has not been proved and it has not been verified by anybody else…

"I agree with Dr. Gibbs wholeheartedly on almost any point, he's an eminent man, but I think Dr. Gibbs is in error on this particular point."

As MacKay finished his testimony, the prosecution announced, firmly, "Your Honor, ladies and gentlemen of the jury, the State rests its case."

The stage was set for the leading expert to make his climatic appearance the following morning.

Except that Judge Brown was being ornery about it. The defense explained Dr. Gibbs would arrive at midnight and would be the first and only witness the following morning, the morning of Friday the thirteenth of March, 1964. That wasn't good enough for the judge. "No. We're going to close this case tonight, gentlemen. I told you today we were going to go on through testimony till we finish it."

Belli objected.

Wade objected to the objection.

Tonahill stood and shouted above them all, "He'll be here on the midnight plane, Judge."

Judge Brown pointed angrily at Tonahill. "Be quiet until I get rid of...get the jury out, will you." He took a deep breath. "You have to bull your way through everything."

The damage was done though. After hearing about the eminent Gibbs for weeks and learning he was on his way to testify at last, the jury had to be anticipating his appearance.

As the jury left the courtroom, the legal arguments began. Belli warned, "We're in the South! We'll just have a filibuster," meaning he'd keep finding and questioning witnesses, dragging out the evening session until Gibbs arrived. "We'll have the damndest filibuster you've ever seen."

Wade made his own threats, promising to go on "all night if we have to, to get this thing done."

Judge Brown finally retreated into his chambers, trailed by the platoon of lawyers. They all squeezed into the room and the angry shouting continued. Reporters pushed up against the door, trying to hear the arguments. When Frank Watts, a member of the prosecution team, stuck out his head, members of the media asked what was going to happen? "It's definitely indefinite," he assured them.

Judge Brown finally relented, agreeing to allow Dr. Gibbs to testify the following morning. Before court was dismissed though, the defense presented one more witness. A woman who with any other type of defense would have been the star witness, rather than a doctor known for academic papers on a relatively obscure topic. Her name was Alice Nichols, a striking strawberry blond secretary.

For days Jack Ruby had sat silently as the parade of doctors debated his sanity, dispassionately discussing testing and charts and interpretations. He seemed like nothing more than an observer. But this witness was going to be different. Alice Reaves Nichols had been Jack Ruby's longtime girlfriend.

Nichols was chicly outfitted in a fur-trimmed black dress accessorized by two strands of white pearls, her hair partially covered by a beribboned, floppy black hat. "I've known him since the latter part of 1949," she testified, looking directly at Tonahill rather than the defendant. "We talked about getting married." Ruby sat stoically, staring straight at the witness. They had dated regularly, she said, then sporadically for over ten years and then their relationship at last ended. Supposedly he had told friends that he had stopped dating her because he'd promised his late mother he would never marry a gentile. "The only time I talked with him in 1963," she continued, "was after the president's assassination... He called me..." There was something poignant about that admission. On a day when every American—including every juror—was reaching out for consolation to those people closest to them, Jack Ruby had reached out to an old girlfriend with whom he hadn't been in contact for more than a year.

She was on the stand only briefly. Her memories about him were vague. After his business failure in the early 1950s she recalled, "He was very despondent during that time. He lost quite a bit of weight and he looked very bad."

Her testimony did little to help the defense. If anything, she aided the prosecution, confirming she previously had told Henry Wade that when dating Ruby "I never could see any indications of insanity."

Nevertheless, she was a jarring reminder that Ruby was a human being, a real person, a man who had loved and been loved, a somewhat sad character who had been reduced to sitting alone and ignored at the defense table in a great murder trial. She reminded jurors what was at stake when they voted on life or death for the defendant.

As she left the stand, she glanced at Ruby. Their eyes met for an instant, then she turned and walked quickly out of the courtroom.

As soon as she got outside, the horde of photographers descended on her, flashbulbs popping in her face. Jack Ruby's only serious girlfriend had brought a human element that had been missing into the trial, and the media needed pictures of the woman he might have loved. With tears flowing, she started walking away from them rapidly but they wouldn't let her go. More than a dozen surrounded her; she pushed through the crowd and began running. A half block away she stopped, realizing an escape from the photographers was impossible. So she stood there, sobbing and shouting incoherently, until they had their fill of pictures and left her standing alone on the sidewalk.

Court was adjourned. After Judge Brown ended the long session, Belli returned to his hotel determined to get a good night's sleep. While he could not have known the following day would become one of the longest days and nights in Texas judicial history, he knew he would have to give his closing argument after questioning Dr. Gibbs.

Belli was acknowledged as a master of the closing argument. He often would spend several emotional hours dominating the courtroom, brewing a mix of facts and feelings into a compelling argument. It took its toll though, and he wanted to get sufficient rest. But his phone rang at nine o'clock.

"This is Gibbs," the caller said. Impossible. Gibbs was on an airplane at that moment. He'd caught an earlier flight. "I hear you're a good guy," he said with light laughter in his tone.

"I've admired you for a long time," Belli responded. While

they had never met, he had been aware of Gibbs's pioneering work for more than two decades. While Belli was graduating law school in 1933, Dr. Gibbs was at work perfecting America's first EEG device.

When Belli met Gibbs for breakfast the following morning, he asked bluntly, "Doctor, will you say from the EEG of Ruby's that he is definitely epileptic?"

"Unqualifiedly."

Belli shook his hand, telling him, "You might be saving a man's life."

Dr. Gibbs had previously testified at almost a dozen murder trials, although none of them involved epileptics. The only concession he had demanded from the defense was that he not be subpoenaed or held in Dallas so he might return to Chicago later that afternoon.

Dr. MacKay's description of Dr. Gibbs was not quite accurate. It was as if he had been cast for this role as a distinguished authority. The thin fifty-six-year-old man was considerably taller than five foot ten, and his full head of dark hair was punctuated by patches of gray. Belli later described him as "square-jawed" with "deep-set flickering eyes" that reminded him of the actor Henry Fonda who only a few years earlier had starred in the classic courtroom drama *12 Angry Men*. The *Dallas Morning News* reported that Gibbs "reminded numerous courtroom spectators of actor Gregory Peck," who had won a Best Actor Academy Award for his portrayal of a noble attorney in 1962's *To Kill a Mockingbird*.

There was great anticipation in the courtroom as Gibbs swore to tell the whole truth and took his seat. As the *Dallas Morning News* reported, "Belli had built [Gibbs] up into such a mythological figure...that the only way Gibbs could live up to his billing would be to materialize into court in a puff of smoke."

Instead, Dr. Gibbs sat forward intently in the witness chair and replied in a soft but firm no-nonsense voice. As Belli began his questioning, the courtroom was absolutely silent, understanding the importance of this testimony. "You are by choice and profession an electroencephalographer," Belli began. That was correct. He worked at it full-time, both researching and interpreting EEGs for clinical purposes. He had been doing it since 1932, when he, along with his wife and an associate, had been the first Americans to use this German-developed technology and had authored the standard work on the subject. The psychomotor variant epileptic discharge was first mentioned in his 1952 book, *Atlas of Electroencephalography*.

He also said that he had flown to Dallas at his own expense and would receive no payment for his appearance. He had requested to testify, he explained, after reading about the trial in Chicago newspapers. From reading tracings sent to him by Dr. Towler, "I determined that Jack Ruby had a particular, very rare type of epilepsy; one that does not manifest itself usually in convulsive seizures... The pattern occurs in only one-half percent of epileptics..."

"When you say this is a rare thing, could we say it is something like...leprosy is rare, but when you find it you know you've got it, is that right?"

"Approximately correct." Jack Ruby, it was obvious to the doctor, had it.

Dr. Gibbs joined Belli standing directly in front of the jury. For the first time he put on his horn-rimmed glasses as he went through Ruby's tracings for the jury, pointing out what he considered the telltale notches of psychomotor epilepsy. "This whole configuration is extremely rare," he told them.

Eventually he was asked about one of the prosecution experts who had disagreed with his conclusion. "Did you teach Dr. Olinger to read the electroencephalograms?"

No, he hadn't, he said, then added casually, "I taught his teacher."

In his own, calm manner, Dr. Gibbs conducted a seminar

on that part of the human brain associated with epilepsy, telling them, "It's the part of the brain that has charge of the internal workings of the body, it is the first relay station on the way to the cortex... It is also the control center for emotion, and when an epileptic type of discharge occurs in here you can have symptoms of the sort that would be expected of a sudden malfunction...pains and dizzy spells...headaches...nausea and vomiting. Then you can have sudden rage outbursts, you can have sudden illusions..."

Dr. Gibbs had been researching epilepsy since 1946, he continued; he had studied entire prison populations and had found no relationship between epilepsy and criminal behavior. In fact, "You are safer from being murdered in an institution for epileptics...than you would be in your own neighborhood." Unfortunately, because of a few unique cases, or movies, or novels "the notion goes rocking down through the years that epileptics are wild, dangerous people." But, he cautioned, murder does happen in "a very, extremely rare, unusual event...

"...and the proper kind of epilepsy."

To identify this kind, the psychomotor variant, Dr. Gibbs had examined fifty thousand tracings of epileptics and found it in only 253 cases. "And," asked Belli, "this one of Jack Ruby is unmistakable and within that group, is that correct?"

"It is."

The lesson extended through the morning, sometimes seeming little more than a casual conversation between Belli and Gibbs, a brief course on epilepsy. While it was spoken of in the Bible, there was little understanding of the condition until "the encephalograph showed us just what we were dealing with...[which] shows living activity." He made clear that this unique type of epilepsy could only be detected through EEGs and even clinical psychologists would not be able to detect it.

Belli finished his direct exam in just twenty-four minutes

believing, he said later, that he had proved the defense case "beyond a shadow of a doubt." When he was done, Dr. Gibbs started to get up but Judge Brown caught him, telling him he wasn't done. It was time to be cross-examined.

Sitting comfortably at the prosecution table, Bill Alexander handled this witness respectfully. In a sense his job was to cut down a tree without damaging the bark. He began by establishing that Dr. Gibbs was firm in his conviction that an EEG was the only possible way to diagnose this variant. More than a clinical diagnosis? he wondered.

"Most emphatically," Gibbs responded.

The two men bantered back and forth about whether or not electroencephalography is an art or a science, or even if the psychomotor variant was a disease ("It is a disease in the same sense that diabetes is a disease."). Alexander proposed that it actually existed mostly on paper. Gibbs corrected him, "What's on the paper comes from the brain."

Alexander got a little tougher, attacking the entire field in which the witness had spent more than three decades. "As a matter of fact, you can soak a rag doll's head with salt and hook up these wires and get an EEG reading…"

"Not what I call an EEG."

After making several additional mostly unsuccessful attacks on the value of EEGs, Alexander abandoned that path and fell back to the main question, asking in a loud voice, "Do you have an opinion from your electroencephalogram as to whether Jack Ruby knew the difference between right and wrong and understood the nature and consequences of his acts on November 24th?"

"I have no opinion," Gibbs responded. That was not the function of an EEG, and the charts he examined were done at an entirely different time and place. In fact, this was well outside Gibbs's field of expertise; he simply could not know Ruby's mental state when he shot Oswald. And that the response was exactly what the prosecution wanted. As juror Max Causey later remembered, "Dr. Gibbs's answer absolutely floored me… I had expected more from this great man."

The prosecutor went after Gibbs's credentials, his reputation and his standing in the medical community. In response to Alexander's questions, Gibbs confirmed that after graduating from medical school in 1929 he did neither an internship nor a residency and, in fact, did not obtain his license to practice until 1957. He was not a member of any professional boards and had even resigned from the American EEG Society—which he had helped organize. Taken together these details had an impact, and even sounded somewhat ominous. In fact, Dr. Gibbs had, during that time, conducted ground-breaking research and helped develop the field.

Listening to the prosecution's questioning, Belli was furious at this attempt to diminish Dr. Gibbs's professional qualifications and to do so in front of media from around the world. But Alexander plowed forward, asking the witness to confirm that he had resigned from the society he had helped found because of a conflict with a colleague. "You consider yourself a heretic in this field," he asked, "do you not, and have referred to yourself as such?"

"That's correct," Dr. Gibbs replied evenly. The tone of the questioning didn't seem to bother him.

Alexander concluded his cross-exam by asking once again if it was possible for Dr. Gibbs to determine Ruby's legal sanity from the tracings. He was putting on a show for the jury.

"No, I cannot."

Belli quickly went to work repairing any damage done. As a result of Gibbs's and his associates' work, he asked, "did they start putting these machines in all of the hospitals in the United States?"

"Yes."

In response to the prosecution's attacks on Dr. Gibbs's reputation, he responded angrily to an objection by practically shouting, "I think we should all pause, even in the pursuit of justice, to give a man his due, after they have done as much for the human race as he has..." His fury quieted the courtroom like a blanket had been laid over it. For several seconds it was eerily silent.

Then, in almost a whisper, Judge Brown overruled the objection and nodded to the witness, telling him, "You may finish, Doctor."

Belli then established that Gibbs's laboratory was so well-respected that it was sent tracings to be examined from "all over the country" and "all over the world," and from neurosurgeons who "send these to you for diagnosis and collaboration," often before "opening a man's skull in a life or death operation."

Gibbs was, he made clear, world-renowned. And with that the defense rested.

The state was done too.

It was a few minutes after ten o'clock in the morning.

The next step in the trial was for Judge Brown to "charge" the jury. This is essentially an instruction manual telling jurors how to reach a verdict. It defined the applicable law and provided a range of options. What were the possible verdicts? How might they go about deliberating? What procedures apply to their debate? In Texas, the district attorney, without input from the defense, would draw up an initial draft of the charge and present it to the judge. After the language was formally drawn up by the court, the other side then had an opportunity to comment and suggest changes.

There were a common set of rules that most states generally followed; for example, jurors were instructed not to consider the failure of the defendant to testify as an indication of guilt. But the defense was stunned early in the afternoon when they received a first draft of Judge Brown's charge. Tonahill called it a road map to a verdict of guilty of "cold-blooded murder." After studying it, Phil Burleson realized it was nearly identical to the charge in a murder trial in which he had served as the court-appointed defense attorney a year earlier. In that case an insanity defense had been completely truncated and his client had been convicted and sentenced to death. Burleson went to work, adding thirty-six pages of requested corrections, amendments and greater legal options for the jury to consider.

Meanwhile, the trial remained on hold. Journalists milled around in the corridors as they waited for final arguments to begin. And waited. And waited. In chambers Belli pleaded with Judge Brown to begin closing arguments the following morning, claiming the defense would need five, six, even seven hours. Wade, meanwhile, pleaded with Judge Brown to get this going, get it finished. Judge Brown, claiming later that after twenty-two days he was worried about the condition of the jury if the trial went even a day longer, decided the trial would resume at eight o'clock that night. He told Belli "The case will go to the jury tonight and I don't give a damn when you finish arguing it." Each side would get two and a half hours to make its case. He also announced that he would permit a TV camera in his courtroom when the verdict was read.

Belli prepared for his presentation with a steam bath and rubdown. He skipped dinner.

The courtroom began filling up in the early evening. This final session had been transformed into a social event. Spectators dressed for an evening out piled into the courtroom, many of them from Dallas society. After all the seats were taken, people were permitted to stand against the walls. While the elite of Dallas filled the courtroom, Judge Brown sat casually on the front steps of the courthouse, as usual chewing on the stem of his pipe and watching several evangelicals loudly voicing their own opinions about heaven and hell and Jack Ruby. Finally Judge Brown told a reporter, "Mighty interesting, ain't it?" and went back inside.

At a few minutes after eight o'clock, the session began. To the horror of the defense, Judge Brown had made very few, mostly meaningless changes to his instructions, crossing out several words. The main issue to be decided, he told the jury in a sing-songy manner was Jack Ruby's mental state when he committed the crime, and if they found him to be sane, whether or not the crime had been committed with malice. Depending on that decision, the possible sentences ranged from the death penalty to confinement for "not less than two years."

Most important to the defense, Judge Brown instructed the jury that "every person charged with an offense is presumed to be sane...until the contrary is shown by proof." In essence, the defense had the burden to prove insanity and if that proof was presented, "no act done in a state of insanity can be punished as an offense."

It took the judge seventeen minutes to read his charge to the jury. The jury listened attentively as he defined the law, instructed them on the definition of certain legal terms and told them which forms needed to be filled out when they had reached the verdict. Several jurors smoked cigarettes as they listened. When Brown was done, he leaned well back in his chair, looked at the prosecution table and nodded.

The prosecution would present its argument first. At 8:22 p.m., Bill Alexander said, "We have come to the end of a long... trial," but the longest night had just begun.

CHAPTER SIXTEEN

As lawyers on both sides began rehearsing their closing arguments and the jurors began preparing to go home, history was being made outside Judge Brown's borrowed courtroom. In Washington, the Department of Justice had asked a federal court to order Alabama governor George Wallace to immediately allow integration in the state's public schools. Secretary of State Robert McNamara announced that our military forces would begin pursuing Viet Cong guerrilla fighters into North Vietnam. At newly named Cape Kennedy, the fourth stage of a Blue Scout rocket failed, and its thirty-three-pound gold-plated scientific probe plunged back into the Earth's atmosphere and was destroyed.

But in Dallas, all attention was focused on Judge Brown's courtroom. This was a wounded city, linked forever with the murder of the beloved young president, and putting the trial of Jack Ruby behind them would be another important step in what was certain to be a long healing process. The city's reputation was at stake, and there was no public consensus as to what verdict would be the most beneficial.

The long trial had created a sizable record. Sixty-six witnesses had testified. A pile of exhibits had been entered into the record, including almost twenty-feet of EEG readings. It was now the task of each side to take precisely the same facts and evidence and mold them into two entirely different narratives. Presenting a closing argument is as much an art as a learned technique. It requires a knowledge of the law, a bit of theatrics, and sufficient sensitivity to read a jury, to know when to press an issue and when to stop. Each lawyer is given the spotlight for a brief period, mostly without interruption, to seduce the jury. It also provides the setting for great trial lawyers to make their reputations. It is an old tradition, easily traced back to the Founding Fathers. Alexander Hamilton, for example, was said to be among the first great courtroom orators. His voice was melodious, his eyes riveting, his passion intense. When it came time to make the closing argument in a property trial, wrote jurist James Kent, "He rose with dignity and spoke for perhaps two hours in support of his motion. His reply was fluent and accompanied with great earnestness of manner and emphasis of expression."

Hamilton's weakness though, a familiar weakness that has bedeviled lawyers through centuries, was that he would become entranced by the brilliance of his ideas. Often, he was guilty of the greatest sin of a trial lawyer: he didn't know when to shut up. Judge Robert Troup recalled, "I used to tell him that he was not content with knocking [the opposition] in the head, but he persisted until he had banished every little insect that buzzed around his ears."

That evening in Dallas, Bill Alexander rose to his full six-foot-four-inch height and in the dramatic tones of a tough, experienced trial lawyer, with an occasional burst of revivalist furor, began by laying the foundation for the presentations that would follow: "The prosecution must prove beyond a reasonable doubt every element of the indictment...that Jack Ruby...shot and killed Lee Harvey Oswald. I tell you we have proved that.

"...If the defense injects insanity...he must prove insanity by a preponderance of believable evidence, because the law presumes every man to be sane..."

Each member of the prosecution and the defense had a role to play. Alexander's job was to guide the jury through the long line of witnesses, to remind them what each of them had said and where necessary challenge the testimony of defense witnesses. Or, as jury foreman Max Causey explained it, "Each member of the team retraced the evidence as they had been previously presented to us, while belittling that which their opponents had presented...designed to sway the jury one way or the other with pure emotion, with the eloquence of a college debate team..."

Alexander was to knit together all of the disparate testimony into one coherent story. For example, the gist of prosecution witness Detective Sims's testimony was that on Friday night Ruby had offered to bring sandwiches to the Homicide and Robbery Bureau. This seemingly innocuous, maybe even compassionate offer actually was far more sinister, according to Alexander. "I think this evidence showed an unnatural wanting on the part of this defendant to be in the presence of Lee Harvey Oswald!"

When witness testimony conflicted, he cast an ominous shadow over defense claims. The two men who had accompanied Ruby on his nocturnal visit to the Impeach Earl Warren billboard said he had not gotten out of the car, while two workers at the *Herald* said he had been there at roughly the same time. "What is it," Alexander asked suspiciously, "that George Senator and Larry don't want us to know about?

"George Senator and Larry Crawford are either mistaken—or they are not telling the truth."

Where that testimony did not square with the prosecution's case he offered alternatives. If Ruby actually sent a telegram at 11:17 a.m., it was difficult to believe he intended to be shooting Oswald at that same time or earlier, so "perhaps that [tele-gram] could have laid there for a minute or two before he put the time stamp on it...whether it laid on (clerk Doyle Lane's) desk while he made changes... I do not know." His inference was that perhaps the important time stamp should not be considered entirely accurate.

Alexander used testimony to show how the prosecution had satisfied all the requirements of the law. "We must prove the identity of the person we have alleged to have been killed..." Dr. Rose testified, "Oswald's mother and Oswald's wife came to the hospital and identified the body...the man named in the indictment, Lee Harvey Oswald... Dr. Rose told you also... that Lee Harvey Oswald died as a result of the gunshot wound, which was no surprise to us, but...is part of the record and necessary to be proved."

Refuting defense claims, Alexander reminded jurors that "As they got off the elevator, Ruby said, 'I meant to shoot three times but you guys stopped me.' So the defendant had perfect recall. He knew what he was doing, there is no question about fugue or epilepsy or any one of these weird psychomotor variants they seemed to have developed for this man."

Alexander remained standing throughout his entire presentation, his booming voice echoing throughout the courtroom. Spectators leaning against the walls shifted weight from one leg to another without taking their eyes off him. They listened attentively. He was touching each base: Jack Ruby killed Lee Harvey Oswald. He did it knowingly. "The only question, if there is a question—there's none in my mind, is malice and intent."

Life or death.

"I am not going to defend Oswald to you. But I tell you this, American justice is on trial. American justice had Oswald in its possession... Oswald was entitled to the protection of the law... Oswald was a living, breathing American citizen...entitled to be tried in a court of justice..."

At that moment Alexander whirled around dramatically, pointed directly at Ruby and screamed, "...Just like YOU, Jack Ruby, who was his judge, his jury and his executioner!"

Ruby seemed startled. For the first time throughout the proceedings, everyone in the courtroom turned to look directly at him. Ruby stared straight ahead, his eyes locked on the man he had once considered a friend.

Still pointing, Alexander chastised him. "You denied him the very thing that you demand through your lawyer the loudest." He turned once again, making eye contact with the jury as he continued, "Jack Ruby killed a man who was in handcuffs... that is 'Judge Lynch' at its worst...the very thing our law is designed to prevent."

Lawful or not, there remained a sizable number of people who believed Ruby had done the right thing. He had killed a man who deserved to be killed, and if he had to be punished for it, well, make it an appropriate punishment. The prosecution was in an odd position and Alexander acknowledged that, "I am not going to defend [Oswald] but I will say this, Lee Harvey Oswald loved life and he had a right to draw every breath that God, and Dallas County government, the government of Texas and of the United States would let him draw. Lee Harvey Oswald... is dead, he is silent. And the Lord alone knows what secret..."

Objection! This was the first hint in the closing of some deeper conspiracy, a conspiracy to protect the real killers of President Kennedy, and Belli refused to let it stand. "There is no issue here whatsoever, and my friend knows it, that Lee Harvey Oswald took secrets to the grave with him."

Sustained.

Having presented evidence supporting the prosecution's version of the murder and Ruby's arrest, Alexander began his assault on the defense experts, mocking them by suggesting, "I wonder if they get their psychomotor variant from the psychomotor pool." He derided their tests, "they probably tapped his knees to see if his feet would click," and their expertise, "Dr. Roy Schafer, who thinks he can diagnose everything with ink spots." The prosecution's experts, conversely, were so renowned "You could have had a world congress on neurology and psychiatry right here in the Dallas County Courthouse." Even the doctor called for the past president of the United States, Dwight Eisenhower, when his life was at stake "told you he does not believe in this Gibbs psychomotor variant."

Finally, he provided a motive for the murder. "Jack Ruby misjudged public temperament. He thought he could kill Oswald, that perhaps he would be a hero by doing it... I submit to you [he] wanted to become famous and make money out of the act..." His voice rising to a crescendo, he railed, "He is nothing but a thrill killer seeking notoriety!"

He concluded by asking for the death penalty "not only for the life of Lee Harvey Oswald, but because he has mocked American justice while the spotlight of the world is on us."

In a theater there might have been applause, but in the courtroom there was only silence.

Texan Phil Burleson made the first argument for the defense. In contrast to Alexander's loud and lively presentation, Burleson became the voice of reason. He addressed the jury in a mannerly fashion, as if he were explaining a theory to invited guests in his living room. He simply wanted to clear up a few of Alexander's statements, knowing "after this trial is over Mr. Alexander and I will still be friends." But it was necessary, he explained so "you won't be misled by statements and conclusions of these lawyers."

There were simple explanations for actions the prosecution made seem nefarious. Going to the police station? Perhaps it was as simple as curiosity, a chance "to see, to be around the man who was charged with the assassination of the president of the United States... I personally wouldn't want to see him, but then again it might be a piece of history…is it so bad that this man wanted to see a piece of history?"

Burleson described the prosecution's case as one of suspicion and obfuscation. Their witness had testified to the time stamp on the telegram, "and they are bound by his testimony, except if they can try to throw some doubt into it in another feeble, yes feeble attempt to conjure up some malice…that wasn't there." Burleson was homing in on the weakest part of Wade's case: malice. Even if these jurors believed that Ruby was sane at the time he shot Oswald, if it could not be proved that he had acted with evil intent or malice, he could be released in a few years.

"The only malice," he continued, "comes from the blistering lips of police officers, who…didn't even put in their report[s] to their chief the things they testified to down here." That curious testimony, he suggested, could easily be explained by the fact that they were "now prosecuting the man who broke their security." His meaning was obvious: they were lying to cover their own hides.

Attacking the claim that Ruby had shouted a slur at Oswald as he shot him, Burleson showed the jury the photograph in evidence in which Detective McMillon was caught looking in another direction at that moment, then reminded them that only one detective testified he'd heard that cry. Why didn't other people hear it? "Because it didn't happen."

Burleson knew he was fighting on the legal undercard before the heavyweight championship bout between Hometown Henry Wade and Big-time Belli. But legally his argument was as important, or more so, than any other. No need for doctors or electroencephalograms, just practical and rational reasoning. Ruby just had gotten caught up in a moment with no planning or premeditation. The defense that many believed Belli should have pursued from day one.

Frank Watts, whose work for the prosecution had been mostly in the trenches rather than in the spotlight, spoke next. The short, balding assistant prosecutor was the opposite of Alexander physically and professionally; rather than loud and forceful, he was soft and suggestive, asking jurors to "do your duty to protect society from the ravages of criminals who would break our laws." He seemed to have been shoehorned into this phase, and his objective was little more than responding to Burleson's response to Alexander. Addressing the question of who had called Oswald a son-of-a-bitch, for example, "The evidence is this, that Combest did use the word but he also saw Ruby's lips moving."

Those words, he claimed, proved malice. "The law says that malice may be inferred from acts done and words spoken." As he rattled off a series of quotes attributed to Ruby by various police officers he crouched, then suddenly sprang up, pointed his forefinger at Ruby and startled the courtroom by crying out that Ruby's words "show a black wicked heart!" Then building to a grand crescendo he shouted, as if preaching from a pulpit, "I say to you that he was sane when he shot Lee Oswald and he is sane today. The blood is still red on the hands of Jack Ruby." His reputation as soft-spoken and retiring had been loudly erased.

Joe Tonahill next stood to his full six-foot-four-inch height and addressed the jury. He spoke calmly about the passions the trial had raised, admitting the "actions and conduct of the attorneys have produced…sparks and high feeling… We have all done things in a much louder voice than was necessary for anyone to hear us… I felt that on my part I have responded to some instances because I was shocked; shocked beyond disbelief, dismayed because I have seen…a concerted, concentrated deliberate effort to distort facts, to deny which is right, that which is fair, that which is just."

It is not at all unusual for lawyers to remind jurors that their sworn obligation was to be honest, which could be translated to mean finding for their client. By taking the oath, Tonahill said, "You and each one of you shook hands with the Lord…" He continued, "Mr. Alexander says that Oswald loves life, loves life, just like you do. I never thought I would live long enough to hear a prosecuting attorney tell a jury or tell twelve people in Texas that Oswald loved what they love…they said Oswald wants to live like you, that Oswald wants to be a good Dallas citizen." Then he went a step further: "They would have you take Oswald by the hand and walk with him."

"Objection!" Henry Wade interjected. "Nobody said they should take Oswald by the hand."

Tonahill continued impugning the motives of the prosecution for trying a "sick man" for murder, "to gratify nothing but political ambition, embarrassment, humiliation, a need to satisfy…" his voice rising, "…an innate feeling of frustration…this desire and this demand that you do something to Jack Ruby to make up for this great political opportunity that Mr. Wade might have had to prosecute Lee Harvey Oswald!" He added, "My brother lawyers are so wrought up in this thing that they feel so deeply that they have to get somebody as a substitute for Lee Harvey Oswald." This was clearly a stinging attack on Wade's integrity and Wade responded in kind, telling reporters Tonahill was "uncouth, unsavory, ungentlemanly, undignified" and the ultimate insult, "un-Texan!"

Tonahill returned to Ruby's mental state, describing a severely damaged person, "highly emotional, unstable…having dogs, calling them…his wife and children. Just going completely berserk over nothing, terrible fights, throwing people down the stairs, jumping on them and suddenly saying, 'Oh, did I do that' when he comes out of his seizure… One right after another, violent, outrageous things, violent eruptions of his mind, violent discontrol… Blackouts, fugues, loss of consciousness, loss of mental control…

"And then, when he could come out of those…psychomotor variant seizures he would be calm."

But there is reason to save this poor man, Tonahill suggested. He had the crowd in his grasp now. "Spectators forced back tears," wrote the *Times*, when told "Jack is a patriotic man and a good man, the best he can be. Limited? Highly limited, of course, because of his mental problems…"

Tonahill went on and on and on, well past ten o'clock. Several jurors were struggling to stay awake. One female juror did fall asleep. And still Tonahill continued. The case must "stand or fall…on McMillon's testimony… This boy says he saw Ruby come up with the gun…" but the photograph in evidence showed him looking away. "McMillon lied in his teeth, because he didn't see what he swore on that witness stand… This is the perjury that Mr. Wade must digest."

On he went, covering mostly familiar territory until suddenly, out of nowhere, he made the astonishing claim that to decide that Ruby had acted with malice jurors had to also agree that the Dallas Police Department was in cahoots with him. The Kennedy conspiracy industry was growing rapidly, and Tonahill fed into it when he suggested that if the shooting happened as the prosecution claimed, the Dallas PD had to be working with Ruby. "There would be no way in the world for Jack Ruby to arrive there [the basement] simultaneously with that man coming out there unless there was a two-way radio between him and Captain Fritz telling him. No human possible way…"

After more objections and more fighting among the lawyers, Tonahill made clear that he didn't actually believe that. It was a coincidence, "probably the greatest coincidence in the history of the world." But for the prosecution to prove malice they had to show, Tonahill argued, that Ruby knew when Oswald was being moved, and that was only possible if he had been "tipped off by somebody in the police station when he was coming… He couldn't have had malice without help—and he didn't have any help."

It had been a nasty, bitter trial marked by personal attacks and asides, and Tonahill's antipathy spilled out again: the prosecutors "would have you bring in a political verdict…" he shouted, "because Jack Ruby's scalp added to Henry Wade's belt would mean something maybe. Bill Alexander likes to travel. He would like to see the rolling hills and the bluebonnets and the tall pines over in east Texas on his way to Huntsville to watch the execution…he'd watch it and he'd love it… Have you watched his… tarantula-like eyes and seen the terrific pleasure that he would derive." He contrasted that with his cocounsel Melvin Belli: "A great man to sit at the elbow of, a wonderful humanitarian, a kind thoughtful, considerate man…"

"Objection" Wade interjected. "Judge, I don't think that's in the record either, what a great man Mr. Belli is."

Tonahill concluded with a heartfelt plea; he talked Texan to the jury, telling them about his own struggle to become a lawyer, "working all day in Washington, going to school at night. I have a great love and feeling for the law. And it hurts me to see it twisted, distorted and abused. It hurts me deeply, hurts me bad. And I can't help being who I am and what I am… I can't do anything about me. If I get shocked at what I see, I just have to get shocked…"

He walked over to the jury box and continued his appeal in a low, respectful voice, telling them, "When you look at your face in the mirror each morning…remember you dealt with a tremendous precious thing; you dealt with justice. You walked in majesty, as kings…you won't be taken in, you're not that kind of people. You're good people, God fearing people… I just want to look at you a minute." He paused and silently met the glances of each jury member. "I see great courage in your eyes. I have great faith that you will rise to the occasion."

It was after 11:00 p.m. when he concluded. Judge Brown called a brief recess. Every person in the courtroom stood and stretched—except Jack Ruby, who remained seated impassively at the defense table.

Several jurors lit cigarettes as Jim Bowie began his closing, which consisted primarily of refuting Tonahill. Bowie obviously was tired and spoke without the bluntness of Alexander or the passion of Tonahill. His presentation was marked by odd gestures: he bounced around the courtroom on the balls of his feet, whirled his arms out of sync with his words and would suddenly crouch or do several deep-knee bends as he stopped in front of the jury box railing, then moved away.

Bowie dismissed Tonahill's argument as "the oldest defense known to the defense...if you can't defend the defendant, prosecute the prosecutor."

He did some nit-picking, finding contradictions or loopholes and bringing them to the jury's attention. The defense claimed Ruby was carrying cash to pay back taxes he owed; Bowie wondered who pays taxes on a Sunday morning. He pointed out the various disagreements among all the expert witnesses until finally he reached his emotional closing: he stood straight in front of the jury, staring in turn at each juror for a few seconds, locking on to their eyes. In a soft voice he told them, "There is something here, much more important than you and I and Jack Ruby. It is the law. The law of this state... It protects human life, it deters others.

"We ask you as a juror, under the Court's charge and under the law of this state, to write a verdict that will deter others from doing the same. The law against murder. And the State of Texas today is no stronger than the weakest heart that sits on this jury."

It was minutes before midnight when he sat down.

And then, finally, Belli stood. He paused for a moment to gather his thoughts. The courtroom remained absolutely silent with anticipation. This was the star turn. As Belli later recalled, "I walked the five miles from counsel table to jury rail, it took me several hours. I felt like Alice in Wonderland falling down the hole. My feet didn't seem to touch the floor. I was about to make my plea for Jack Ruby's life."

He stood in front of the jury and began. "My mother always told me when I came to a strange place if I was treated graciously to thank my hosts, and that I do first," he said, smiling his appreciation. Rule number one: smile for the jury. Make nice to them.

He continued in a tone described by *Houston Post* reporter Harold Scarlett as "a velvety, hypnotic voice that could charm cobras out of their baskets... He played that voice like a symphony. It was by turns a Stradivarius, a bugle, an oboe, a snare drum racing at breakneck speed... Then slowing, taking on a sob and a throb..."

Considering what was to come, his opening plea was truly ironic. "Let us see now in the beginning small hours of the morning when great discoveries in the history of the world have been made in garrisons and basements if here in a temple of justice we can't rediscover something that was never lost in your great city of Dallas, that we may rediscover justice."

They faced a great dilemma, he pointed out. "You've heard from everybody from the 'Weird Beard' to the great Gibbs. How shall you know who to believe? Think of your own life," he suggested, "and if your child needed an expert neurological opinion to whom would you turn?" His answer, of course, was the man who invented the EEG, Gibbs.

The real difficulty they faced was how to look into a man's brain to determine "whether this man was sick, whether he was well, whether he did an act that was responsible or irresponsible... What I am trying to tell you here is the justice that you can discover is the justice of science and the law... We are not here to try the shooting. We are here to look into this mind with the help of our doctors.

"Gibbs is the only man in the world who can give you that answer. Gibbs is the only man who has done the work... No one peered into Jack Ruby's mind over their television sets when he shot Lee Harvey Oswald. But Dr. Gibbs has..."

In the quest to make jurors empathize if not sympathize with a defendant, lawyers often try to put those jurors in the defen-/

dants place: What would you do in that situation? After looking into Ruby's mind, Belli was asking them to look into their own souls. Think back, he told them, remember "this tousled-haired young president" and asked jurors, "what were your feelings when that young man was assassinated?"

He paused dramatically and mused, "Each of you must think of some one thing in this man's career that gave you the most pride. For me... I remember him standing in front of the Berlin Wall saying, 'I am a Berliner,' his hair flying in the wind and the roar of a million German people filling the air to echo into East Germany. So here is the one man I am defending. A normal Texan, a Dallasite who had shot the assassin of the President.

"If one of you, a normal human being with a high breaking point shot the assassin, could we not ask then...that you suspend the sentence because of the tragedy of the three days?" But then, "Let's take the second case of the man who has an unstable personality... I often say to myself, with this event that happened here, had I been there, had I been so situated, there but for the grace of God and a stronger constitution of mind, could go I."

So who is Jack Ruby? How to describe him, Belli wondered. "In the old days we used to call them...the village clown, the village idiot? There's the chained wolf, there's the hunchback of Notre Dame..."

Ruby did not show any response to this.

Jack Ruby, he continued, was "The man who is always around the police station bringing the coffee, the man who brings the donuts...this poor sick fellow, and sick he is, and you know in your hearts he's sick...there cannot be any doubt that there is something wrong here."

According to the Post's Scarlett, Belli's "marvelous voice glided and soared and dived—never faltering, never stumbling, never pausing except for effect."

A major problem the defense was forced to deal with were the array of threatening or boastful comments prosecution witnesses had testified they had heard. Burleson had dealt with McMillon, whose face was turned in a different direction when the shot was fired. Belli dealt with Detectives Archer and Leavelle; "Even if all those things were said...confabulation. Those big words don't throw you now. The mind abhors a vacuum. It abhors the insult to the ego of not remembering what went on..."

But did Ruby actually say those things? Belli reminded the jurors that Archer had been instructed by his superior officers "to write out everything that happened," and in his affidavit "there is not one word of anything Jack Ruby is reported to have said by this officer when he was on the stand." Belli quoted Archer's statement at length, pointing out how different it was from his testimony.

The evidence was clear, he continued, that Jack Ruby, the "unstable personality" who came from "bad stock" had not planned to kill Oswald. "That man would not have been there if he hadn't sent Little Lynn that twenty-five dollars... He left the dog in the car across the street... The cleaning woman was coming in...but he walks down the ramp..."

The proof that he was in a fugue state when he shot Oswald, Belli said, was that even after being grabbed by police officers "his finger kept trying to pull the trigger... These were his friends, those policemen. He wasn't trying to shoot them...yet his hand was still contracting..."

It was Saturday morning as he neared the end of his presentation. He'd shown them loopholes in the prosecution's case, he'd given them alternative possibilities, he'd asked questions that had not been answered and finally he began his emotional appeal. The only thing he hadn't provided, he said, "The only thing we don't have in there and which jurors are told that they can't consider, is that which we could not live without. Faith."

He cited Rabbi Silverman "who says he thinks the man is insane at the present time...if you will, put him some place for treatment..." Again and again, Belli seemed to close off any potential for compromise: "It would be an incongruity to compromise and say one year, two years or five years...where do you have the right to take a man's liberty when he is one of the afflicted?"

Rather than focusing on the more practical and immediately understandable defense presented by Phil Burleson in his closing, that there was no premeditation and no malice, Belli argued that even a suspended sentence would be unjust: "If you put a felony of any kind on him, he won't be eligible for Veteran's Administration... He is sick. Give a just and fair verdict compatible with modern science. That's what the world wants to see in justice from this community... You're an intelligent jury, and I don't butter you up... I tell you, use your God-given intelligence in this case...don't stigmatize the character, the village clown, a sick man, by any jail sentence.

"Be true unto yourselves."

Belli thanked the jury and took his seat. Tonahill, having been brought to tears, leaned over and patted his back. Ruby said nothing. "I did my best," Belli would say, admitting he was not pleased with his remarks, "but the hour was too late."

"The jury had been assailed by too much noise and emotion."

While some reporters praised the address, many others questioned his insistence that the jury acquit his client without offering viable alternative verdicts like murder without malice or guilty without the death penalty. It was all or nothing. A very risky proposal in a case where death was an option. In response, Belli later claimed those options were not really there. The district attorney wanted this conviction for political purposes and "24 of the 25 cases [Wade] tried before the Ruby case that had gone to the electric chair...mercy had been asked in those cases."

Wade went last. It was 12:45 when he began his final remarks. He began by saying out loud what everyone knew to be true: "I know you are tired and I am tired and everybody else is tired." He would be quick, he said. Judge Brown had put all the participants in an awkward situation. This was the most public murder trial in Dallas history. The world was paying attention. The defendant was facing the electric chair. And yet court was still in session at one o'clock in the morning and the prosecutor was promising to be brief.

Admittedly there was pressure on the judge. Texas law had not provided for an alternate juror. If anything should happen to one of the jurors, the weeks of work would be in jeopardy. Judge Brown did not want to risk keeping the jury sequestered for another weekend so he had pressed forward. The result was a hurried end to a vitally important, high profile trial.

Wade's presentation was brief and workmanlike. He zipped through the list of witnesses, he mocked Belli's claim of "confabulation, or whatever that word is…nobody said they killed him I know of other than Ruby."

As for the defense arguments, "Mr. Tonahill mentioned the Communists… You can bet your life's dollar the Communists would be happy to know that you could commit murder of a handcuffed man, in police custody and walk out a free man.

"I don't think you're interested in that."

Wade too, excited conspiracy theorists when he told the jury, "Ruby robbed the people of Dallas of knowing more about Oswald…" now it was Belli shouting an objection which was sustained and Wade corrected himself. "What I was going to say is that it robbed them of the right to try Oswald…" but then quickly added, "It robbed him of the right to see whether anyone helped him or not…"

The conspiracy theorists would savor every word: the defense had suggested the police department might have been involved. The prosecution wondered if he had assistance? The gates had been opened.

Just as Belli did, Wade stood in front of the jury box and told those twelve men and women what he expected of them. After admitting the police department may have made some

BETTMANN/GETTY IMAGES

Henry Wade had been serving as district attorney of Dallas County since 1951 and would have gained more national renown prosecuting Lee Harvey Oswald—had not Jack Ruby changed history. On the night of Kennedy's assassination, Wade recalled receiving a call from a key Lyndon Johnson aide, warning him, "Any word of a conspiracy—some plot by foreign nations—to kill President Kennedy would shake our nation to its foundation. President Johnson was worried about some conspiracy on the part of the Russians... It would hurt foreign relations if I alleged a conspiracy—whether I could prove it or not... I was to charge Oswald with plain murder." His revelation added another fascinating fact to the growing conspiracy theories.

mistakes he said, "Ladies and gentlemen of the jury, our laws are no stronger than the weakest link. And in this case it is you twelve jurors. You are the ones that are going to put a price on this sort of thing. You put an approval or a price and our laws against murder of a handcuffed and manacled man is no stronger than the weakest heart on this jury..." And he made clear that this was not happenstance, that Ruby "wanted the limelight, he wanted publicity, and he wanted to go down in history as the man that killed an alleged assassin. And my question to you ladies and gentlemen is what would you want the history books to say about you?"

Most lawyers who have tried capital cases will agree that jurors find it difficult to condemn a defendant to death. No matter what jurors have told lawyers during voir dire, voting for a man to die it is a hard thing to do. Screenwriter Reginald Rose dealt with that in *12 Angry Men*, putting these words in a juror's mouth: "It's not easy for me to raise my hand and send a boy off to die without talking about it first." Henry Wade understood that and dealt with it. "Jack Ruby, and his murder, was the Judge, the jury and the executioner. Now he and his lawyers ask you for mercy and sympathy and compassion." Waving at them with his index finger, shaking his head, frowning, he dismissed that. "I ask you…to show Jack Ruby the same mercy and the same compassion and the same sympathy he showed to Lee Harvey Oswald in your police department and mine.

"You wonder probably why we, why anybody should give the death penalty, why anybody should give it… There are a lot of reasons given, but the greatest one is the deterrent to others who would do the same…people who would take the law into their own hands…people who would kill…"

His voice rising, he emboldened them. "You can write a verdict in this case that will ring out all over this nation…and you want the whole world, and you want Communism to know that we believe in the rule of law here, that we believe that democracy and the Bill of Rights, the things we have all been raised on, still exist."

He took a long, deep breath, finishing softly, "I appreciate your service as jurors, and I know that you will write a verdict of twelve strong men and women."

The courtroom, which had remained quiet for hours, let loose a wave of noise it had been holding in. The sounds of a large restrained room coming suddenly to life. Wade returned to his table and was congratulated by the prosecution team, but he too was dissatisfied with his argument, later calling it "the worst closing argument I've ever made."

After this long trial, his closing remarks had lasted less than a half hour. It was minutes after 1:00 a.m. Judge Brown began giving instructions to the jury but decided it was too late, instead telling them to return to the cells in which they had been living, and be prepared to begin deliberations the next afternoon.

Dallas was not an all-night town. The bars closed at midnight. Belli and a British journalist found an open lunch counter. He had a chicken sandwich then walked back to his hotel.

No one sleeps well the night before a verdict is announced.

CHAPTER SEVENTEEN

The concept of an American jury voting to determine a defendant's fate was more than three hundred years old. In 1630, a jury in the Plymouth Colony of Massachusetts found pilgrim John Billington, a man who had signed the Mayflower Compact, guilty of the "willful murder by plain and notorious evidence" of John Newcomen, and he was hanged by the neck until dead.

The jury that would decide whether Jack Ruby would live or die began the day with breakfast at the Dallas-Jefferson Hotel. The eight men and four women had to finish the job before going home. As they walked the two blocks back to the courthouse, they passed a small roundish white-haired woman. There was no indication they recognized Lee Harvey Oswald's mother, also on her way to the courthouse.

The media had filled the courtroom and the corridors outside by the time the jury arrived there slightly before 9:00 a.m. Throughout the trial the media had been running its own "ghoul pool," wagering on the verdict. Initially the betting had been spread, but in the last week just about every journalist had come to believe Ruby was highly likely to be convicted and receive a long sentence. Thirty, even fifty years was mentioned. Few believed he would receive the death penalty. Bob Considine told other reporters, "I can't conceive of them killing him." The *Times*'s Homer Bigart agreed, saying sarcastically, "I'd be shocked to death if they gave him the electric chair."

In its editorial that morning, the *Dallas Morning News* reminded readers that no matter how long the sentence, according to Texas law "Jack Ruby would become eligible for freedom on parole within ten years." That of course, presumed that he would live.

Belli remained hopeful. He had begun his morning by visiting Jack Ruby in his cell. Then he walked to the courthouse, strolling past high school bands tuning up for the St. Patrick's Day parade scheduled to start before noon. He paused along the way for a brief conversation with a priest wearing a green paper hat.

As Henry Wade entered the courthouse, a reporter asked if he believed Ruby should be sentenced to death. "I would vote it if I were on the jury myself," he replied, but perhaps revealed his own expectations by adding, "but I'd regard a life term or a long sentence as a victory."

His deputy, Bill Alexander, seemed less conciliatory, boasting to journalists, "If they're so curious about Ruby's brain, I'll be happy to deliver it to them."

The jury closed the door to the deliberation room at 9:15. A small, joyless space painted dreary green on the third floor, its only window looked out onto a brick wall. The rooms in which juries deliberate are often spare, with very few amenities; this room was not designed to be a comfortable place to relax. It served one function only: reach a verdict as rapidly as possible.

The jurors had four verdicts to consider: guilty of murder with malice, which carried the possibility of the death penalty; guilty without malice, which called for two-to-five years in prison; not guilty by reason of insanity; and not guilty of committing the crime at all. There also was the possibility that the jury would be unable to reach a verdict, that it would be dead-locked and have to declare a mistrial, in which case Ruby would have to be tried again.

The jury began by electing the first juror selected, Max Causey, as foreman, a vote taken while he was in the bathroom.

As the jury began deliberating, the prosecution team was watching preparations for the St. Patrick's Day parade, being held on a Saturday three days early so Dallasites could enjoy it. Looking out a window Jim Bowie mused, "Dallas is sure crowding its luck holding another parade for an Irishman."

After just two hours and nineteen minutes, Causey went downstairs and informed Judge Brown that the jury had reached its verdict. He went back to the deliberation room as the trial participants were told to return to the courtroom, and final preparations were made to nationally televise the verdict as it was rendered. The one TV camera being shared by all three networks was focused directly on Judge Brown. It would not move during the reading of the verdict.

In the deliberation room, the jurors agreed they would not discuss the particulars of their decision-making process with reporters. They also agreed that while the verdict was being read they would look directly at Jack Ruby.

It took almost an hour before the judge and trial participants returned to the courtroom. A large crowd gathered on the sidewalk across the street, awaiting the verdict. Inside, the courtroom and corridor were jammed, spectators standing two-deep against the walls. As Bill Alexander walked into court, he looked directly at the defense team—then lifted his necktie behind his right ear. The hangman's gesture.

"Have you reached a verdict in this case?" Judge Brown asked at last.

Judge Joe B. Brown ran a casual courtroom, a down-home place where lawyers got to speak their piece. In this photo, the jury is to the right of the defense table at lower right, close enough to hear whispered conversations. In his memoir, Judge Brown wondered, "Did Jack Ruby receive justice?" Avoiding an answer, he decided, "The question of justice is as old as the ages and who knows what real justice is?"

"We have," the jurors replied in a chorus.

The bailiff handed a single folded sheet of paper to the judge. "Is this your verdict?" he asked. All twelve jurors raised their hands in affirmation. Judge Brown then warned everyone that he would not permit any demonstrations or outbursts, cautioning everyone to remain seated until he had dismissed the jury.

Belli glanced at Tonahill, who nodded grimly. Then he leaned over and whispered to Ruby, "It's bad. Take it easy. We expected it all along and we tried this case for the appeal court. We'll make it there." He continued speaking to him, trying to soften the blow.

Judge Brown adjusted his glasses, wet his fingertips and read as if reciting some boring bill details, "We the jury find the defendant guilty of murder with malice as charged in the indictment and assess his penalty as death."

"Oh God!" Ruby's sister Eileen Kaminsky cried out.

Jack Ruby did not respond in any way. He just sat still, absorbing the verdict.

Belli, who seconds earlier had tried to calm Ruby, nevertheless was stunned by the imposition of the death penalty. He leaped to his feet, pointed at the jury and screamed, "May I thank this jury for a verdict that is a victory for bigotry!" The legendary Melvin Belli, known for his cool manner in the courtroom, was losing it. And he was only getting started. "I want to assure you we will appeal this to a court where there is justice and impartiality," he continued shouting as the jury filed out. As the jurors returned to their quarters, the courtroom doors burst open and the media poured in. Reporters and cameramen scrambled for position, climbing over tables and chairs, sticking microphones in front of all the lawyers, turning on floodlights. Two cameramen jumped up on the defense table. Belli was irate, screaming as loud as possible as deputies escorted Ruby back to his cell, "Don't worry, Jack, we'll appeal!" Then he proceeded to yell a few nasty comments into every microphone. "This is one of the most shocking things I've seen in my lifetime. We have a little bit of Russia." He focused his criticism on the city. "The festering sore that is now the most shocking place in the nation. If this venomous infection spreads throughout the country, God save us all!... I hope the people of Dallas are proud of this jury...this was a kangaroo court, a railroad court and everybody knew it... We are back a thousand years. The jury has made this city a shame forever... You talk of the shame of Dallas; now you see it in full glory..."

Tonahill leaned into the scrum and called it "A violent miscarriage of justice. I'm about to throw up."

Other reporters had gathered around Eileen Kaminsky, who was sobbing, "He didn't get a fair trial..."

Judge Brown, who had left the room after the verdict was announced, returned to his bench; he had taken off his robes and donned a fedora. He stood there for an instant, taking in the hectic scene, then began screaming at the guards to clear the courtroom. "Get those people off the table. Clear those damn cameras outta here right now." The guards immediately began shoving journalists toward the door.

Belli wasn't budging. "We will appeal to every court in the land... Judge Brown went down the line for every motion the District Attorney made," he bellowed. "He committed 30 errors."

A few feet away Henry Wade also was speaking to reporters, telling them, "I just thanked the jury for what I thought was a fair and impartial verdict."

Eventually Judge Brown pushed his way through the crowd to Belli and offered him his hand. Belli shook his head. "I can't shake hands with you, Judge," he said coldly. "You've got blood on your hands."

Judge Brown looked at him evenly. "I'm sorry you feel that way about it, Mel. Come back and see us again." Then he turned quickly and walked away.

While Tonahill also had his difficulties with the judge, he knew, as a Texan, that chances were darn good he would be standing in front of Judge Brown sooner or later. He couldn't afford to ride with Belli. Earlier, while awaiting the return of the jury, he'd slung his arm over the judge's shoulders and asked friendly-like, "Judge, when this is over why don't you come down to Jasper for some catfishing?"

After watching Belli's explosion, Alexander told reporters, "I think this little display shows Mr. Belli is sicker than his client."

While the verdict had been expected, the sentence had come as a surprise. As Judge Brown later admitted, "It shocked even me." The fact that the jury had reached its verdict so quickly stunned a *United Press* reporter who called it "gross and vulgar to spend so little time to kill a man." Maurice Carroll of the *Herald Tribune* agreed. "Just for appearances sake, they should have stayed out a little longer." *Dallas Times Herald* editor, A. C. Greene said, "The town's a little bit shaken. The verdict was almost as shocking to everyone as Ruby's own shooting had been."

In the jury room, with little discussion or debate, the jurors had agreed unanimously that Jack Ruby was guilty of murder. They agreed unanimously he was sane when he shot Lee Harvey Oswald. They agreed unanimously that he was sane at the present time. They agreed unanimously that he had committed the murder with malice. When they began debating the sentence, however, the initial vote was nine to three for the death penalty. Foreman Causey was one of those three minority votes. As he later explained, "There should have been more latitude within the law as it would apply to an unstable personality than there was within the M'Naghten rule."

The second vote was ten to two. Causey said he intentionally slowed down deliberations to give "each juror more time to challenge his own conscience that it was the right decision." But it didn't take much longer for all of the jurors to reach agreement on the sentence, as well.

Ironically, several jurors received death threats even before they got home. Their names were known, most of their phone numbers were listed. A caller told Causey's wife, "Your son-of-a-bitch husband should be shot between the eyes." Some of them moved out of their homes for safety for the next week. But other callers thanked them for doing a difficult job. Public opinion in the city generally was mixed, as it was nationally. The National Epilepsy League publication, *Horizon*, published a story with the headline "Epilepsy 'Not Guilty.'"

Within an hour of the verdict being delivered, the defense team visited Ruby in his cell. He was calm, but distant, as if he didn't completely understand the impact of the verdict. "Just think," he reportedly said. "If they can do this to me, think how many others they've railroaded in Dallas." But he seemed far more upset that police officers he considered to be his friends had testified against him.

DAN ABRAMS AND DAVID FISHER

For Bill Alexander, the issue wasn't the jury or the city of Dallas but the defense. He later said of Melvin Belli: "He took a good five year murder without malice case and made it into a death penalty for his client. He put on this god awful defense and day by day Jack melted—he just looked worse and worse. He was a pitiful object by the time the trial was over. Instead of being a hero, Belli was bringing out all this stuff about Jack's mother being in an insane asylum and how Jack himself was sick. He just wanted to get on the stand and say 'I shot the guy because he killed my President,' but Belli hacked away at his family in public. It was humiliating for Ruby. I actually felt sorry for him. It took away whatever dignity he had left."

While the trial was over and the jury had spoken, this was only the first stop on a long legal road. And much of what happened after the trial was as important, if not more so, than what occurred during the trial itself. From the legal maneuvers and rulings to the words of Ruby himself, many additional questions were addressed—and some answered—in the months and years to come.

This trial was simply the end of the beginning.

As Belli left the courthouse later that afternoon, he told waiting journalists that he would immediately be filing an appeal asking Judge Brown to throw out the verdict and schedule a new trial. The defense had ten days to file that request and they were entitled to a hearing. If that motion was turned down, which seemed certain, the defense could then turn to the Texas Court of Criminal Appeals and eventually to the highest court in the state, the Texas Supreme Court. The job of any appellate court is generally to determine if a petitioner received an unfair trial rather than to reevaluate guilt or innocence.

The system of appealing a legal wrong can be traced back at least to the kingdom of Babylon, when Hammurabi created a system in which anyone who felt they had been mistreated by the courts might appeal to the king or his counselors for redress. Romans were granted appellation, the right to appeal to a magistrate to reverse a perceived legal wrong or protect themselves from a legal action. In ancient England an appeal was settled by physical combat: if that person making an appeal was defeated before the nighttime stars appeared, he was hanged; if he lasted the fight into the night or won the battle, he was acquitted. As British law developed, the right of appeal was enjoyed by both the prosecution and the defense. By the early fourteenth century, the common pleas and King's Bench was hearing appeals in civil cases, but it took until 1673 for the court to grant a new trial in criminal convictions. That appeal was granted if the court found the jury's verdict was not justified by the evidence, if the admission or exclusion of that evidence was questionable, if the jury had been given erroneous instructions or simply if a new trial would further justice.

While Texas established an appellate court for criminal cases in 1876, in the federal system, it wasn't until 1889 that Congress gave the US Supreme Court jurisdiction to hear appeals. That may have been sparked by the actions of Texas Judge Isaac Parker. Known as "The Hanging Judge," he presided over the vast Indian Territories and sentenced 160 people to death, at times ordering multiple condemned men to be executed at the same time. For his first fourteen years on the bench, Parker's court functioned as both a trial and appellate court, meaning the only avenue of appeal was directly to the president of the United States—although on several occasions Parker was sufficiently moved to order a new trial. The judge believed strongly that sentences once given should be carried out, even death sentences, saying, "in the uncertainty of punishment following a crime, lies the weakness of our halting justice."

Before Melvin Belli could file the appeal, he was fired by Ruby's family. In dismissing him, the Ruby family said it was "dissatisfied with the defense presented by Belli and shocked at the tirade he delivered…" which was aimed at "…promoting only Belli's personal fame and fortune." By so publicly attacking the court, the judge, the city and the state, Belli had ruined any chance he could represent Ruby successfully in any Texas legal proceeding. Belli and Tonahill had also supposedly smuggled a camera into the jail where they took photos of Ruby that they later offered to sell to *Life* magazine. When Ruby's sister found out about it, she was furious and stopped the sale. By firing him the family also made it clear it did not share Belli's opinions.

Belli was also condemned by the American Bar Association for questioning the integrity of the court and jury. In response to the ABA's threats to take disciplinary actions against him, the still boiling mad Belli said, "Being barred from the ABA would be like being banned from the Book of the Month Club."

A day later the Texas attorney Percy Foreman, nationally known for his expertise in capital cases, was hired. "My clients may not always be right," he once said, "but they are never wrong." While Foreman was busy on another case, Joe Tonahill and Phil Burleson filed a motion for a new trial with Judge Brown. First among the 182 legal errors cited in that motion was that Brown erred by not allowing a change of venue. Also questioned was the fact that eleven of the twelve jurors had "witnessed" the killing and that the court had allowed police officers to testify about statements supposedly made by Ruby after being arrested.

A day after the appeal was filed, Percy Foremen met with Jack Ruby for the first and last time. After a dispute arose about his fee, he resigned from the case. Several other attorneys were hired and fired over the next year as Tonahill and Burleson led the appeal. One of them, Hubert Winston Smith, even withdrew after being informed by his employer, The University of Texas Law School, that he would "not be included in the budget" if he continued representing Ruby.

Judge Brown heard the request for a new trial at the end of April. By that time the number of alleged errors had grown to 205 and now included claims that the judge had allowed the media to turn the trial into a public circus. "Their activities and sensational news releases not only destroyed the atmosphere of dignity and decorum that should surround a trial if an accused is to have vital issues of his case heard and determined free of passion and prejudice..."

The one-day hearing was as contentious as the trial had been. Within an hour Tonahill and Bowie were shouting, accusing each other of having "no guts." When Brown ruled against the defense motion to hear five witnesses, Tonahill roared, "Your Honor has a tremendous burden in this case, and for God's sake do your duty."

The most obvious difference between this hearing and the trial was the deteriorating condition of Jack Ruby. He appeared in court looking nervous, gaunt and haggard and throughout the hearing muttered to himself. The weekend before the hearing he had twice made futile suicide attempts, slamming his head into the wall of his cell and then attempting to fashion a noose from mattress filling and prison clothing. An abrasion about the size of a half-dollar was visible on his head, presumably where he had smashed into the cell wall. Joe Tonahill told reporters that Ruby had tried to fight him when he visited Ruby's cell. A court appointed psychiatrist said Ruby had delusions he was personally responsible for "the slaughter of millions of Jews." After interviewing him that doctor had diagnosed Ruby as paranoid, which was manifested by delusions, and potentially suicidal. The proof he was not mimicking this condition, the doctor reported, was that he "vigorously rejected every suggestion he was mentally ill," while a person faking the condition "usually grasps eagerly at such an explanation." Another Catch-22.

As deputies escorted Ruby out of the courtroom during a recess, he turned to his sister Eva Grant and told her, "Goodbye, I'm not coming back."

It was a bizarre, completely out of context statement. When reporters asked Joe Tonahill what Ruby meant, he told them, "He's a sick man, a sick, sick man. He's cracking up completely and he's going to get worse unless he's put in a hospital where he can receive proper treatment."

His sister was hysterical, pleading with anyone who would listen, "He's so sick, he's so sick. Why can't they do something?"

The prosecution team suggested Ruby was "putting on an act" to convince Judge Brown to deem him insane. Wade said later that he did not doubt Ruby needed treatment—but his mental condition was caused by his actions rather than causing them. "He's been under a strain, sitting up there knowing he'd been sentenced to the electric chair." He described it "death-house psychosis."

As widely anticipated, Judge Brown refused the defense request to hear new witnesses then rejected the defense motion for a new trial, ruling that Ruby had received a fair trial. But as was required by statute, he did agree to schedule a sanity hearing to determine if Ruby had become insane or incompetent since the end of his trial.

As Ruby left the courtroom, he turned to his sisters and told them repeatedly, "I won't see you again, I won't see you again." The next step in the legal process was an appeal of the verdict to the Texas Court of Criminal Appeals.

Before that took place though, Jack Ruby agreed to testify in front of the Warren Commission. Conspiracy buffs, as they were becoming known, suggested Ruby was part of a larger plot and had killed Oswald to prevent him from naming those people who had hired and paid Oswald—and may have even been shooting at the president on that Dallas afternoon.

Several people had claimed to have seen Oswald and Ruby together prior to Kennedy's assassination. Henry Wade had made the controversial decision not to call any of these witnesses during the trial. "We knew the testimony from these witnesses could have had a big impact on the jury, one way or another," he said. "But I felt then that there had been no proof Ruby and Oswald knew each other." In addition, he added, he just didn't believe their stories, pointing out "Three of them had failed lie detector tests."

But claims and rumors persisted that Ruby had played a role in the Kennedy conspiracy. To confront those accusations, both Ruby's lawyers and his sister Eileen had sent a letter to the Warren Commission informing them that he wanted to testify.

They were certainly interested in hearing his account, so, on Sunday, June 7, Ruby met with them in the interrogation room of the Dallas County jail. Ruby was not just familiar with Supreme Court Justice Warren, but convinced that an "Impeach Earl Warren" billboard was connected to the murder of President Kennedy. In addition to Warren, Congressman Gerald Ford and several attorneys, including Arlen Specter, Leon Jaworski, Jim Bowie and Joe Tonahill were all present. This was Ruby's opportunity to tell his own story of Oswald's murder in public for the first time. But Ruby did not make it easy, often failing to respond directly to questions, at other times ignoring them or seemingly plucking answers out of thin air. One thought often was interrupted by leaping to a completely different thought. He began by repeating a request to be allowed to take a lie detector test, pointing out to them that without that they would have no way of knowing if he was telling the truth. "I would like to be able to get a lie detector test or truth serum of what motivated me to do what I did at that particular time."

He became increasing desperate. "Gentlemen, unless you get me to Washington, you can't get a fair shake out of me... Do I sound dramatic? Off the beam?"

"No," the chief justice said, "you are speaking very, very rationally."

"I am not a crackpot, I have all my senses. I don't want to evade any crime I am guilty of..."

Chief Justice Warren finally agreed to arrange for Ruby to be tested at another time, a decision Warren would later say he came to regret.

Ruby started his tale on the morning of Kennedy's assassination "Mr. Belli did not go into my case thoroughly, circumstantially," he explained. "If he had he wouldn't have tried to vindicate me on an insanity plea to relieve me of all responsibility, because circumstantially everything looks bad for me... had Mr. Belli spent more time with me, he would have realized not to try to get me out completely free."

He had wanted to testify at his trial, he insisted, but Belli had told him, "When the prosecution gets you on the stand, they will cut you to ribbons."

His story contained numerous details that completed a picture seen in part during the trial. He carried cash, he said, because "I owe the government quite a bit of money (unpaid taxes) and it is doing business out of your pocket."

On the day of the Kennedy assassination he had cried and called people; his family, his friends around the country, his old girlfriend. "You want other people to feel that you feel emotionally disturbed the same way other people do," he explained. He would not open his clubs that night, he decided, even though he needed the money. He finally went to his sister's apartment. "Eva and I have a very complex personality. Very rarely can I be with her... I wanted to be with her."

He wandered that night. He heard the police were working late so he bought sandwiches for them. He went to the station that Friday night, "and I am carried away with the excitement of history... I went down to the assembly room in the basement... I got up on a little table where I knew I wasn't blocking anyone's view...and they brought the prisoner out... There was a lot of questions thrown back and forth and this District Attorney Henry Wade was answering them to the best he could. From the way he stated, he let reporters know that this was the guilty one that committed the crime."

Ruby paused here and asked once again to go to Washington "to take all the tests that I have to take. It is very important." He was certain somebody was preventing him from taking a lie detector test.

He skipped around, telling a story he had previously forgotten that took place the night before the killing. He had run into a police officer with a young lady who had worked at one of his clubs. "I felt I didn't want to involve them in anything because it was supposed to be a secret that he was going with this young lady. He had marital problems… They stated they should cut this guy [Oswald] into ribbons… They were crying and carrying on…"

At this point, Ruby noticed that Tonahill was taking notes and paused to ask to see the notes. Ruby then read them aloud: "'This is the thing that started Jack in the shooting.'"

Tonahill had written, "[The young girl] was talking about Oswald."

Ruby was furious at Tonahill for suggesting that he had been set off on Friday by this couple and threw the pad on the table. "This is untrue. That is what I wanted to read.

"You are lying, Joe Tonahill. You are lying because you know what motivated me. You want to make it that it was premeditated."

Tonahill quickly tried to defend himself. "No… I don't think there was any premediatation."

"Why go back to Friday, Joe?" Ruby responded. "That set me off… Because it never entered my mind when they talked about cutting him into bits…that is not it…you want to put that into my thoughts, but it never happened…" Ruby became increasingly reluctant to tell his story, upset that there was no way to prove he was telling the truth. It was pointed out to him that after he told his whole story, the polygraph, which responds only to yes or no answers, could be used to confirm it. That seemed to soothe Ruby, who said, "I wish the President were right here now. It's a terrible ordeal, I tell you that."

Jack Ruby paused and requested almost all the law enforcement officers leave the room, including Joe Tonahill. When it was pointed out to him that Tonahill was his lawyer, he was adamant. "He is not my lawyer." After they had left he again told Warren, "You will have to get me to Washington soon, because it has something to do with you, Chief Justice… I want to tell the truth and I can't tell it here." Looking at Warren he warned him, "Chief Warren, your life is in danger in this city, do you know that?"

"No, I don't know that," Warren replied, trying to get the witness back on track. "If that is the thing you don't want to talk about, you can tell me, if you wish, when this is all over, just between you and me."

Ruby was difficult to follow, acknowledging, "I bet you haven't had a witness like me in your whole investigation. Is that correct?"

Warren responded, "I came here because I thought you wanted to tell us a story, and I think the story should be told for the public… [But before arranging for a polygraph examination] we must first have the story we are going to check it against."

Warren finally asked the most important question: "Did you know Lee Harvey Oswald prior to this shooting?"

The increasingly frustrated Ruby tried to explain. "That is why I want to take the lie detector test. Just saying no isn't sufficient…the only thing I want to get out to the public, and I can't say it here, is with authenticity, with sincerity of the truth of everything and why my act was committed, but it can't be said here…it's got to be said amongst people with the highest authority that would give me the benefit of the doubt…"

At various times during this interview, Ruby's paranoia surfaced. In addition to his own life being in danger, he said, the chief justice also was in danger and "my whole family is in jeopardy. My sisters, as to their lives…my brothers—my in-laws… they are in jeopardy of loss of their lives just because they are blood-related to myself…"

Ruby continued to skip around until finally he returned to the issue of premeditation: "…that thought never entered my mind prior to that Sunday morning when I took it upon myself to try to be a martyr or some screwball…but I felt very emotional and very carried away for Mrs. Kennedy…that someone owed it to our beloved president that she shouldn't be expected to come back to face trial of this heinous crime… Consequently, right at this moment I am being victimized as part of a plot in the world's worst tragedy and crime at this moment…

"At this moment Lee Harvey Oswald isn't guilty of committing the crime of assassinating President Kennedy. Jack Ruby is. How can I fight that, Chief Justice Warren?"

Warren fumbled for an answer as Ruby continued to claim that his action "has put a lot of people in jeopardy with their lives… I won't be living long now… My family's lives will be gone." Once again Ruby stopped on a random moment that November weekend; as he remembered a rabbi's sermon after Kennedy's death he started crying, completely losing control. When his tears finally stopped, he said with obvious embarrassment, "I must be a great actor. I tell you that…[the sermon] created tremendous emotional feeling for me… I was carried away."

Finally, he began to address the supposed conspiracy. That Sunday morning, he read a newspaper column, a letter to Caroline Kennedy "the most heartbreaking letter…that caused me to go like I did… I don't know Chief Justice but I got so carried away. I remember prior to that thought there has never been another thought in my mind; I was never malicious toward this person. No one else requested me to do anything. I never spoke to anyone about attempting anything. No subversive organization gave me any idea. No underworld person made any effort to contact me. It all happened that Sunday morning…

"…suddenly the emotional feeling came within me that someone owed this debt to our beloved president to save her [Mrs. Kennedy] the ordeal of coming back. I don't know why that thought came through my mind…"

He had received the phone call from Karen "Little Lynn" Bennett asking for money, he said. "I drove past Main Street, past the County Building and there was a crowd already gathered there. And I guess I thought I knew he was going to be moved at 10:00…and I took it for granted he had already been moved… My purpose was to go to the Western Union—my double purpose but the thought of doing, of committing the act wasn't until I left my apartment." After leaving the Western Union office he walked toward the ramp. "I didn't sneak in, I didn't linger in there. I didn't crouch or hide behind anyone…

"…I realize it is a terrible thing I have done, and it was a stupid thing, but I was just carried away emotionally do you follow that?"

"Yes I do indeed every word," Warren responded.

"I had the gun in my right hip pocket and impulsively, if that is the correct word here, I saw him, and that is all I can say. I didn't care what happened to me. I think I used the words, 'You killed my President, you rat.' The next thing, I was down on the floor. I said 'I am Jack Ruby. You all know me.'"

Finally having the opportunity to tell his story, it flowed out of him. "I never used anything malicious, nothing like s.o.b. I never said that I wanted to get three more shots off, as they stated."

He had recently been under additional pressure, he continued, accused of "unfair competition" and violating union regulations, which had impacted his business. "I was being insolvent because of it."

Once again he rambled on about various underworld figures

who some conspiracy buffs had suggested were involved in the plot with him. He wanted to make clear he simply made brief contact with them "to try to solve business problems...that is the only reason I made those calls."

The chief justice asked again, "Did you ever know Oswald?"

"No... The first time I ever have seen him was the time in the assembly room when they brought him out, when he had some sort of shiner on his eye."

He backtracked, asking Warren, ironically, "I recall seeing a sign on a certain billboard 'Impeach Earl Warren.' You heard something about that?"

"I read something in the paper, yes, that is all."

Mostly forgotten in the chaos of events was Oswald's shooting of police officer J. D. Tippit along with the president and governor. Some conspiracy theories had dragged Officer Tippit into it too, claiming bizarrely that he was the actual assassin and had met with Oswald in Ruby's Carousel Club a week before the shooting. "I knew there were three Tippits on the force. The only one I knew used to work for the special services, and I am certain this wasn't the Tippit."

Another member of the investigation team, attorney J. Lee Rankin, said, "The man that was murdered. There was a story that you were seen sitting in your Carousel Club with Mr. Weissman [Bernard Weissman, who had signed the anti-Kennedy ad in the newspaper], Officer Tippit and another man who has been called a rich oil man, slightly before the assassination. Can you tell us anything about that?"

"I'm the one that made such a big issue of Bernard Weissman's ad," he pointed out in response, then accused the Commission, "Maybe you do things to cover up, if you are capable of doing it."

Asked directly about his knowledge of a conspiracy, Ruby finally gave a simple, direct answer, "I am as innocent regarding any conspiracy as any of you gentlemen in the room... I want you to dig into it with any biting, any question that might embarrass me…" Despite Ruby's often disjointed and at times paranoid testimony, he never wavered in his vehement insistence that he acted alone and impulsively. His descriptions of, and explanations for, shooting Oswald remained consistent.

As for his supposed underworld contacts, Ruby claimed that while he had known some minor crime figures years earlier while still living in Chicago, "I have never been a bookmaker. I have never stolen for a living. I am not a gangster. I have never used a goon squad for union activities… I never knew what a goon looked like in Chicago… I never belonged to any subversive organization."

Rankin asked, "You have never been connected to the Communist party?"

"Never have."

Rankin cited trial testimony that Ruby had been carrying a gun when he first saw Oswald on Friday night. "I will be honest with you," Ruby replied. "I lied about it… I didn't have a gun." That undercut one of the arguments Belli had made that if Ruby had wanted to shoot Oswald on the Friday night after the assassination, he could have. He also insisted he never made several of the statements attributed to him, essentially accusing several prosecution witnesses of perjuring themselves: "I never inquired from the television man what time is Lee Harvey Oswald coming down. Because really, a man in his right mind would never ask that question. I never made the statement, 'I wanted to get three more off.'

"'Someone had to do it. You won't do it.' I never made those statements… I never called the man by an obscene name…because there was no malice in me. He was insignificant to my feelings for my love for Mrs. Kennedy and our beloved president… I never made a statement to anyone that I intended to get him. I never used the obscene words that were stated."

When it seemed they had completed their questions, Chief

Justice Warren looked around and asked, "Congressmen do you have anything further?" Ruby jumped in, convinced that there were more subjects to cover, more conspiracies to debunk: "You can get more out of me. Let's not break up so soon." And then, he rambled some more.

As the interrogation wound down, Rankin said he remained puzzled by Ruby's claims that his life and his family members' lives were in jeopardy and asked him to explain that. "As I stated before," he said, "some persons are accusing me falsely of being part of the plot. Naturally, in all the time from over months ago, my family has been so interested in helping me…" The men in the room listened without commenting. "…when your family believes you and knows your mannerisms and your thoughts, and knows your sincerity; they have lived with you your whole life and know your emotional feelings and patriotism…by helping me like they have, going all out… My brother who has a successful business, I know he is going to be killed. And I haven't seen him in years…"

He went on and on: "…Now if I sound screwy telling you this, then I must be screwy."

Justice Warren responded pleasantly, assuring Ruby "There has been no witness before the Commission out of the hundreds we have questioned who has claimed to have any personal knowledge that you were a party to any conspiracy to kill our president." He offered that if such a claim was made, he would give Ruby an opportunity to refute it and to take any tests he desired. "Does that seem fair?"

"No. That isn't going to save my family… I'm in a tough spot, and I don't know what the solution can be to save me… I am making a statement now that I may not live the next hour when I walk out of this room." Then he made a comment seized on by those who believe in a conspiracy, that if the president had learned of his "true story" months earlier, he might have been able to save him, because "a certain organization wouldn't have so completely formed now, so powerfully, to use me because I am of the Jewish extraction...to commit the most dastardly crime that has ever been committed...

"That goes over your head, doesn't it?"

Warren admitted, "Well, I don't quite get the full significance of it, Mr. Ruby..."

Referring to the far right John Birch Society, Ruby bemoaned the fact that President Johnson had not found out "the truth about me before he relinquished certain powers to these certain people."

Warren was trying to be kind. "I am afraid I don't know what power you believe he relinquished to them. I think that it is difficult to understand what you have to say."

"I want to say this to you," Ruby responded. "The Jewish people are being exterminated at this moment. Consequently, a whole new form of government is going to take over our country and I know I won't live to see you another time. Do I sound sort of screwy—in telling you these things?"

"No. I think that is what you believe, or you wouldn't tell it under your oath."

Ruby pleaded with them, "If you don't take me back to Washington tonight to give me a chance to prove to the president I am not guilty, then you will see the most tragic thing that will ever happen..."

Congressman Ford asked what more he might reveal if he was taken to Washington.

"All I know is maybe something can be saved. Right now... I am used as a scapegoat, and there is no greater weapon you can use to create some falsehood about some of the Jewish faith... if I am eliminated, there won't be any way of knowing... In all fairness to everyone, maybe all I want to do is beg that if they found out I was telling the truth, maybe they can succeed in what their motives are, but maybe my people won't be tortured and mutilated."

Chief Justice Warren assured him "that the President and his whole Commission will do anything that is necessary to see that your people are not tortured."

Joe Tonahill asked Ruby who he believed was going to kill him. "I have been used for a purpose," Ruby said. "And there will be a certain tragic occurrence happening if you don't take my testimony and somehow vindicate me so my people don't suffer for what I have done."

"But we have taken your testimony," the chief justice told him. "We have it here...for the President...for the Congress... for the courts...for the people of the entire world."

Again and again Ruby repeated, "All I want is to take a polygraph to tell the truth..." As this interview ended, Ruby told Warren, "You are the only one who can save me. I think you can... There was no conspiracy."

It was impossible to grasp any rational meaning in many of Ruby's statements. But in his own world he seemed to be resigned to his fate—even if exactly what they mean remained unclear. "By you telling them what you are going to do," he warned, "and how you are going to do it is too late as of this moment."

This interview lasted slightly more than three hours. The question that could not be answered was, what might have happened if Belli had put Ruby on the witness stand? But even after this interview one thing was certain: the jury's verdict could not possibly have been worse.

CHAPTER EIGHTEEN

On July 18, 1964, forty-one days after his testimony to the Warren Commission, Jack Ruby sat facing a blank wall in the Dallas County jail. This was done to eliminate any distractions as he finally took his polygraph test. His attorney at that moment, the president of the Dallas County Criminal Bar Association, Clay Fowler, had strongly advised against it. As he pointed out, since his client's sanity was in question his answers would have no value. Officially, the FBI said, "The polygraph technique has a number of limitations, one of which relates to the mental fitness and condition of the examinee to be tested."

But Ruby desperately wanted this test, believing that Americans would finally believe his account of what happened. The "box" as the polygraph is known, had a long and mixed history. For centuries societies had been searching for an infallible way to determine if someone was telling the truth. The ancient Chinese, for example, made suspects chew dry rice while being questioned; believing their mouth dried up when lying so they could not spit it out. Of course that still was considerably safer than the "ducking stool," in which an accused person was pushed underwater until he told the supposed truth. The so-called modern lie detector was invented to record emotional responses. The "Father of the Lie Detector," William Moulton Marston—who also created the comic book character Wonder Woman—based his turn of the twentieth century invention on the theory that blood pressure rose when people lied. Questions have to be answered simply yes or no while the subject is monitored. The first attempt to introduce lie detector results as trial evidence took place in 1923, when the US Supreme Court in *Frye v. United States* rejected it—and by doing so set the accepted standard for the introduction of scientific evidence in the courtroom that was followed for decades. Basically, if the relevant scientific community accepted a process or test as reliable, it might be introduced in a trial. The polygraph never received that universal acceptance.

But it still has proved to be a valuable law-enforcement tool. Rather than being used to determine guilt or innocence, it provided a good starting point for investigations. Sometimes just the specter of taking the test led suspects to come clean.

But Jack Ruby didn't know that. He believed it would convince the public that he was telling the truth. With electrodes attached to Ruby's fingers to determine his sweat level, a cuff around his arm to assess blood pressure movement or changes, and a rubber tube around his chest to monitor his breathing patterns, the test began.

"Is your first name Jack?"

"Yes."

FBI special agent Bell Herndon conducted the test. He quickly got to the important questions: "Did you assist Oswald in the assassination?"

"No."

"Have you ever been a member of the Communist Party?"

"No."

"Did you shoot Oswald in order to silence him?"

"No."

There was one wistful moment. When asked if he were married, Ruby replied, accurately, he was not, but the question had triggered an emotional response. Asked about that by Herndon, Ruby explained, "I was thinking of a young girl, that had I been married I wouldn't have been in this trouble."

To assess Ruby's responses, Herndon interspersed questions that had an objectively accurate answer like "Do you have any brothers?" and "Were you in the Army Air Corps?" with questions about the incident:

"Did you ever meet with Oswald and Officer Tippit at your club?"

"No."

"Did you first decide to shoot Oswald on Sunday morning?"

"Yes."

There were many starts and stops as they broke down the examination into separate parts and attempted to clarify any ambiguities in the breaks. During one of the conversations between questions, Ruby made it clear it was most important to him that people understood he was an American patriot who acted out of emotion. But Ruby increasingly became frustrated that the questions were limited to yes or no answers and that he was not being asked to explain more about his mindset at the time. "The most important question you haven't asked me yet, why did I shoot Oswald." Ruby then proceeded to repeat his previous testimony to the Commission that he "felt so carried away. I felt somehow... I could save Mrs. Kennedy the ordeal of coming back for trial here..." Arlen Specter finally interjected that they would address that issue later in the proper format for a polygraph.

Throughout the session his responses supported his previous statements. He did not plot the killing in advance, had no prior knowledge of when Oswald was to be moved. He did no business with Cuba. He was not influenced by foreign governments, labor unions or underworld connections to shoot Oswald. He acted alone.

At one point during the examination, Ruby had asked that his attorney Joe Tonahill leave the room while prosecutor Bill Alexander be permitted to stay. When asked about it afterwards by an FBI agent, Ruby explained, "After all this legal business is over with, Alexander or Wade will call the governor and tell him to spare my life and he will. My lawyers can't do this."

Agent Herndon concluded, in testimony to the Warren Commission, that assuming "Ruby was mentally competent and sound, the charts could be interpreted to indicate that there was no area of deception present with regard to his response to relevant questions during the polygraph examination."

That was a big assumption. The official government investigation into the Kennedy assassination would involve interviewing 552 witnesses before releasing its 888-page report, supported by 26 volumes of transcribed interviews and evidence in late September 1964. The Warren Commission concluded that Lee Harvey Oswald was the lone gunman. Part of the finding that there was no wider conspiracy was the interview with an obviously mentally deteriorating Jack Ruby: "The Commission found no evidence that either Lee Harvey Oswald or Jack Ruby were part of any conspiracy, domestic or foreign, to assassinate President Kennedy." Nor was there "any evidence to support the rumor that Ruby may have been assisted by any members of the Dallas Police Department in the killing of Oswald."

Around the same time, Belli's book *Dallas Justice* was rushed to publication. He traveled the country denouncing the judge, the Ruby family for failing to properly appreciate him and the trial proceedings, calling it a "kangaroo court." His book and comments were covered around the world, leading the *Australian Law Journal* to set the record straight on his reference to their national animal, the kangaroo, assuring readers that his comment "was in no way intended to disparage Australian criminal proceedings..."

The official appeal of Ruby's conviction finally had been filed thirty minutes before the midnight deadline on July 28, 1964, by Burleson. The defense cited fifteen reasons the verdict should be thrown out, among them Judge Brown's refusal to grant their change of venue motion, the oddity that jurors actually were witnesses to the crime and the fact that the jury was permitted to hear Ruby's comments after his arrest—assuming those comments actually were made. To illustrate the massive amount of pretrial publicity, the defense submitted a several-feet-high pile of newspapers containing stories about the trial. Naturally that pile made a great photograph, which was published by those same newspapers.

But before the Court of Criminal Appeals would hear the case, it mandated that a sanity hearing be held. Ruby did not want Tonahill to represent him at that hearing so he tried to fire him. A prehearing hearing was held to determine who would represent Ruby. Like so much else in the trial, this hearing became utterly confusing: Tonahill refused to be fired. He claimed that Ruby had been sane before the trial but had gradually lost touch with reality, and as he no longer was competent he couldn't fire him.

During this hearing to determine if Ruby was sane enough to decide who would represent him at the sanity hearing, Ruby took the stand and claimed that on the morning of the murder he had taken thirty pills, including a dozen "antibiotics" that "make you want to do positive things." As for his mental condition, he argued he was able to determine who should represent him, saying, "If I am an insane person, the rest of the world is crazy." But then, for the first time in public, he made an emotional plea. "To the American people and the world. I'm going to be branded a part of a conspiracy with Oswald. You're going to forget how I felt about the beloved President Kennedy. There has been so much torment, so much hardship...

"I shouldn't have tried to play the part of a hero. My background wasn't clean enough to play the part of a hero." His great regret, he continued, was that he had not avoided the trial and thrown himself on the mercy of the court. As for his own fate, he appeared resigned. "Me, Jack Ruby, Jack Rubenstein, am the greatest scapegoat in the history of the world."

Judge Louis Holland finally ruled without formally determining Ruby's sanity, that legally he was still competent to pick his own lawyer, therefore he had the right to fire Joe Tonahill. That spurred the Texas State Senate to pass a resolution congratulating and commending Tonahill for his work on the case.

A few weeks later Judge Brown, who was scheduled to preside over Ruby's sanity hearing, voluntarily resigned from the case. In reality, he had no choice. It had become known that he had agreed to write a book about the trial entitled *Dallas, Ruby and the Law.* In a folksy letter to his editor obtained by the defense and eventually the media, he seemed prepared to lie about having already started to work on the manuscript: "I can refute that by stating that there has been no book published or that I have not begun to write a book," he wrote. Then adding, "We are coming along nicely. We have approximately 190 pages complete." Maybe even more troubling for the sanity hearing where he would be deciding the outcome, he had written, "It is my opinion they will never prove Ruby insane..." His voluntary resignation made the defense motion to disqualify him moot, and allowed him to avoid giving a reason, describing it as "a personal decision."

It became clear the prosecution was at least somewhat concerned about the appeal when in November 1965 Henry Wade suddenly made a public, unsolicited offer to Ruby's lawyers: he would request that the State Board of Pardons and Paroles reduce Ruby's death sentence to life—on the condition that the defense join him in that plea. Basically, he was asking them to drop the appeal in exchange for a sentence that could end up being as little as eight years, if he was released early. Instead, Phil Burleson insisted that the appeal would go forward until the defense ran out of courts without commenting on the offer.

While the defense initially had requested the sanity hearing, by the time it took place in June 1966, several of Ruby's lawyers had changed their minds. They did not want it to take place at all, and asked to withdraw the motion. When the court ruled it had to proceed, the defense chose not to participate. Ruby's lawyers selected no jurors, made no statements, put no witnesses on the stand and conducted no cross-examination. As Texas law puts the burden of proving insanity on the defense, and the defense refused to do that, the outcome of the hearing was predetermined.

Unlike the trial that took weeks to select a jury, this time it took the state forty-two minutes to seat an all-white jury of seven men and five women.

Bowie and Alexander appeared for the state. They presented six witnesses: four of them were county prison guards who had spent time with Ruby in his isolated jail cell. All of them agreed Ruby was aware of his situation and seemed to be of sound mind. One of them, K. H. Crory, testified he believed Ruby was sane because "He's a pretty good gin rummy player." Another guard said that on occasion Ruby cheated, and "if he got caught, he didn't like it very much." The prison doctor, Dr. John Calahan, stated that Ruby was in control of his faculties.

The sixth witness was Jack Ruby, who finally got to take the stand in a trial: ironically, as a witness for the state. His appearance was another extremely unusual episode in this legal fight. If he was found to be insane, all proceedings would be suspended—and he could not be executed. If he was deemed sane, his appeals would proceed but so could his execution.

Despite those risks, under oath he testified, "Never at any time have I tried to make anyone believe I was of unsound mind. I never tried to camouflage my mental capacities."

As expected, Ruby was adjudged sane. The Court of Criminal Appeals agreed to hear the appeal of the various issues from the trial. The long-postponed hearing finally would take place in late June 1966.

By the time the hearing took place, the legal landscape had evolved dramatically particularly on the issue of pretrial publicity. The perplexing question of how media attention might prejudice a jury against a defendant might be traced back in the United States to 1807, when Vice President Aaron Burr was tried for treason. The sensational trial was headline news throughout the young country. Burr's attorney, Luther Martin, raged that "the inflammatory articles which had been published against Colonel Burr in the *Alexandria Expositor* and other newspapers..." served to prejudice potential jurors against his client, essentially denying him the fair trial to which he was entitled.

Chief Justice John Marshall, presiding in this case, set the standard that access to pretrial publicity need not disqualify a potential juror as long as his opinion was not affected, ruling, "It would seem to the court that to say that any man who had formed an opinion on any fact conducive to the final decision of the case would therefore be considered as disqualified from serving on the jury, would exclude intelligent and observing men, whose minds were really in a situation to decide upon the whole case according to the testimony." That remained the accepted standard as the country grew from coast-to-coast and new technologies provided greater and faster media coverage.

The availability of television in the 1950s made the problem even more complex. In June 1963, several months before the Ruby trial began, the Supreme Court had overturned the murder conviction of Wilbert Rideau because a judge refused to grant him a change of venue after his filmed "confession" to the sheriff had been broadcast numerous times on local TV. The stage was being set for Ruby's appeal.

In June 1965, the Supreme Court overturned the 1963 Texas fraud conviction of Billy Sol Estes. Because Estes had business relationships with then Vice President Lyndon Johnson and Secretary of Agriculture Orville Freeman, the potential political scandal attracted nationwide media attention. Estes was tried on both state and federal charges. In throwing out the state conviction, the Supreme Court noted that "Massive pretrial publicity had given the case national notoriety." While in this case the judge had granted a change of venue, the court allowed a two-day hearing on a defense motion to prevent television, radio or photographers from covering the trial, to be carried live on television and radio. This hearing "emphasiz[ed] throughout the community the notorious character the trial would take. Four of the jurors selected later at the trial had seen or heard all or part of the broadcasts." The Court held that Estes's Fourteenth Amendment rights, that guaranteed no state shall "deprive any person of life, liberty, or property, without due process of law" had been violated.

Almost exactly a year later, on June 6, 1966, the Supreme Court upheld a lower court ruling that overturned the second degree murder conviction of Cleveland neurosurgeon Sam Sheppard. When Dr. Sheppard's pregnant wife was found bludgeoned to death in 1954, he became the prime suspect, even though he had supposedly suffered injuries fighting with the intruder. The case dominated national headlines for weeks. It had all the elements of a great murder mystery: Sheppard, it was revealed, had been having an affair with a nurse at the time of the murder. There was no evidence of a break-in. The family dog was not heard barking to warn of an intruder, and the couple's child slept soundly through the attack in another room. Meanwhile, the doctor was found with blood on his pants and no murder weapon was ever found, but the county coroner testified a bloody print found on a pillow could have been made by a surgical instrument.

It was the type of crime that sold newspapers even if many of those stories proved false. But the chief prosecutor was running for Municipal Judge and the judge in the case was running for reelection. The police and the judge essentially allowed the media unfettered access creating, as the Supreme Court noted, "A circus atmosphere." Newspapers were permitted to publish the names, addresses and photographs of the jurors. Apparently the trial judge told one reporter that Sheppard was "guilty as hell." Even with all that pretrial publicity it still took the jury thirty ballots to find Sheppard guilty.

That began a decade-long series of additional appeals. Finally the Supreme Court determined in an eight to one decision that Sheppard had been denied a fair trial: "Despite his awareness of the excessive pretrial publicity, the trial judge failed to take effective measures against the massive publicity, which continued throughout the trial, or to take adequate steps to control the conduct of the trial... The massive, pervasive, and prejudicial publicity attending petitioner's prosecution prevented him from receiving a fair trial consistent with the Due Process Clause of the Fourteenth Amendment."

The American legal system is built upon previous decisions or precedent, with each decision becoming part of the foundation and those recent rulings figured prominently in arguments before the Texas Criminal Court of Appeals in Ruby's case. The hearing, which took place on June 23, 1966, lasted four hours, substantially longer than most other appeals. It was heard by a three-judge panel that asked no questions. The largest crowd in the history of Court of Criminal Appeals packed the three-hundred-seat courtroom. The Ruby lawyer merry-go-round had continued, and now five different attorneys pled his case. They were all working without being paid and often battling among themselves or with other former Ruby attorneys. The family had long since run out of money and in yet another action filed a "Pauper's brief" with the court, which allowed the defense copies of transcripts and records without having to pay for them.

Ironically, while Ruby wasn't present for this hearing the lawyer he had fired, Joe Tonahill, was there. Tonahill had been invited to appear by the court as a "friend of the court," a person knowledgeable about the issues who could offer advice. With the shadow of the Sheppard decision hanging over the courtroom, Sam Houston Clinton Jr., an Austin, Texas, Civil Liberties Union attorney, told the panel that Ruby had received only the semblance of a fair trial. "First there was a trial by inflamed public opinion," he said. "Then there was a trial by newspaper and television. There was a trial by ritual—with 11 of the 12 jurors [who had witnessed the killing] going through the ritual of saying they could set aside their opinions. There also was a trial by ordeal with final jury arguments starting at 8:30 p.m. on a Friday night and continuing until 1:07 a.m. Saturday."

Judge Brown's conduct was brought up by Chicago attorney Elmer Gertz, who cited correspondence and passages from Brown's unpublished book in which the judge concluded "that Ruby did not get a fair trial but he wasn't going to lose any sleep over it," and that "the atmosphere in halls and around the courthouse resembled that of a circus" and "the press undoubtedly had an effect on the jury." Gertz cited numerous false claims published in the media including that Jack Ruby was a mobster, that he was connected to hoodlums and organized crime, that he was a Communist, that he had done business with Fidel Castro and that he had met Oswald before the Kennedy assassination. He told the judges, "Almost every type of story that would poison the atmosphere was played up."

Phil Burleson repeated the argument that "eleven of the twelve were witnesses" to the murder. "The fact that at least one of the 162 potential jurors had not seen a televised account of the killing was proof it would have been possible to seat a jury that had not been influenced by television."

Overall, the defense made sixteen different claims. Noted New York civil liberties attorney William Kunstler focused on several issues raised during the trial that showed "blatant disregard for due process," especially the testimony of Sergeant Dean. "The record is replete with Dean lying," he said flatly, pointing out inconsistencies in the policeman's testimony. "The only malice in this case comes from the lips of Dallas police officers." Kunstler contended that the prosecution "invented a fabrication" from Dean "that he [Ruby] intended to kill Oswald after he saw him Friday night." Otherwise there simply is no credible explanation for Ruby arriving in the basement more than an hour after Oswald had been scheduled to be transferred.

Kunstler finished the defense presentation by leaning on the wording of the Sheppard ruling. The widespread publicity both before and during the trial "aided and abetted by the district attorney and, admittedly defense counsel...should not be permitted to blot out due process of law."

Representing the state, Bill Alexander fought back, arguing "Jack Ruby killed Lee Harvey Oswald in full view of approximately 140 million people. The fact that hundreds of people with cameras were in the vicinity does not lessen his guilt one iota." Besides, he continued, the defense admitted that Ruby shot Oswald, claiming he was temporarily insane—but even television could not show to those millions of people the state of Jack Ruby's mind. Additionally, whatever prejudicial impact seeing the killing on television might have had was mitigated when those same moments were shown in both actual speed and slow motion during the trial.

As for the so-called "circus atmosphere," Alexander pointed out "Whatever the atmosphere might have been outside the courtroom, the jury was insulated and isolated from it."

None of the passions that surfaced during the trial, the yelling, the acerbic remarks, the snide insults were present now. The hearing remained calm and orderly, the two sides making prepared statements then sitting down. The rancor of the long bitter trial seemed history as the attorneys argued the law.

Unlike a trial, at which the verdict is delivered at the end, an appeals court takes the submitted briefs and the oral presentation under advisement, meaning it takes as much time as needed to consider the issue. The Criminal Court of Appeals adjourned for the summer shortly after this hearing, promising to deliver its ruling when the court resumed in the fall.

Meanwhile, Ruby sat in jail, waiting and, according to the *New York Times*, drawing pictures of nude women and playing solitaire.

During that period, Phil Burleson and Ruby's other lawyers filed yet another appeal, this time to the Supreme Court of the United States. When Burleson had learned that Judge Brown had signed a contract to write a book, he had filed a motion with District Judge Holland demanding that Ruby's conviction be reversed because Judge Brown had a financial interest in it. Judge Brown actually had appeared in that hearing as a witness to defend himself. After Judge Holland (and later the Criminal Court of Appeals) had rejected the motion, Burleson and the Texas Civil Liberties Union petitioned the Supreme Court, claiming Jack Ruby "has not had the remotest semblance of a fair trial."

The Court was in summer recess at the time. As the nation's final court of appeals, Supreme Court justices select the few cases they want to hear argued from among all the many appeals filed. Ruby's lawyers would have to wait until the Court began its next session in October to learn if the Court was willing to hear this argument.

That wasn't necessary. On October 5, 1966, the three-judge Texas appellate court panel unanimously overturned the guilty verdict and ordered that a new trial be held in a city outside

Dallas, Texas. In nine paragraphs the court tossed out years of legal wrangling, tens of thousands of dollars spent by the state, the family, spent emotions and the reputations of fifteen different lawyers. That was now history. The trial of Jack Ruby would begin from scratch.

Each justice had submitted his own opinion, and there were several minor points of disagreement. Writing for all on the court, presiding Judge W. A. Morrison began the decision. "The offense is murder; the punishment, death."

Judge Morrison stated the facts of the case, briefly summarized the change of venue and sanity hearings and finally got to the legal reasoning behind this decision: "During the trial, over the strenuous objection of appellant that anything that appellant may have said while in police custody constituted an oral confession in violation of the statutes of this state and was not admissible as res gestae, Sgt. Dean of the Dallas police testified as to a conversation which he had with appellant... The time element which elapsed between appellant's arrest and the conversation in question varies... Be this as it may, under none of the authorities cited...could this statement be held to have been spontaneously made... The test in this state is spontaneity and these facts do not fit the test... Obviously [Ruby's] statement constituted an oral confession of premeditation made while in police custody and therefore was not admissible. The admission of this testimony was clearly injurious and calls for a reversal of this conviction."

The court had ruled that it was "obviously" a mistake. Belli had been vindicated in his continuous objections to Judge Brown's admission of the statements, and those rulings had caused sufficient damage to Ruby's constitutional rights to require the entire case to be thrown out. But there was more. The court also found that Brown had been wrong in failing to grant a change of venue.

While both the Estes and Sheppard rulings had been decided

after the trial, "it is abundantly clear of a careful study of both opinions of the Supreme Court and the record of this case that the trial court reversibly erred in refusing appellant's motion for a change of venue."

In fact, the trial record was so marred that this opinion took the unusual step of rebuking Judge Brown who "has removed himself from any further connection with this case and, we have concluded, properly so.

"The judgement is reversed, and the case is remanded with directions that the venue be changed to some other county other than Dallas."

The court also appeared to agree with Belli's claim at the very beginning that the city itself was on trial. Justice W. T. McDonald wrote in his concurring opinion that there existed "such strong feelings in the Dallas County climate that it was not humanly possible to give Ruby a fair and impartial trial which is the hallmark of American due process of law."

One question remained in dispute: Could jurors who had seen the killing on television render a verdict based on the evidence? According to Justice McDonald, Texas criminal law "demands and requires that witnesses to the charged offense cannot serve as jurors. There can be no difference to the competency of a witness who has heard via telephone or radio or saw a matter through a mirror or field glasses and a witness who has viewed a matter on television." The third judge, K. K. Wooley, disagreed, concerned about its use as precedent. "In view of another trial or future trials," he wrote, "it should be also clearly understood that the majority does not hold that a juror who saw the shooting of the deceased on television is, for that reason alone, disqualified…" In some ways he was recalling Justice Marshall's opinion 150 years earlier: it isn't access to information that matters, it is whether the juror forms an opinion based on that material.

Phil Burleson broke the news to Ruby in his prison cell, shouting, "Jack! You won! You got a reversal today!" He was so excited that he forgot Ruby's response. He told reporters that the fact that the court had struck Sergeant Dean's testimony would make it difficult if not impossible for the prosecution to prove malice. And without that, considering the penalty for murder without malice was a maximum of five years and Ruby already had served three years, Burleson believed he could plead guilty to that and be out of prison within months.

Henry Wade calmly disagreed with the decision, telling reporters he intended to retry Ruby and would again ask for the death penalty. As for the possibility that Ruby might be free in a few months, he scoffed at that and said he would not accept any guilty plea—unless the penalty was life in prison.

Joe Tonahill was elated. "I'm going to tell [Ruby] to get a law school graduate to handle his business, because that's all he needs now."

Belli claimed to feel justified by the reversal although he made no comment about the fact that every court had found Ruby to be sane.

On December 8, 1966 Judge Holland announced the retrial would be held in Wichita Falls, probably to begin in February. While Wade remained firm that he intended to seek the death penalty, Burleson indicated in this trial the defense would plead guilty to murder without malice. The very defense that Burleson had focused on during his portion of the closing argument at the trial. It was suggested that Jack Ruby might be a free man by the end of 1967.

That retrial would never take place. On the ninth of December, Ruby complained he didn't feel well. He was diagnosed with pneumonia and admitted to Parkland Hospital, the same place where Kennedy and Oswald had both been pronounced dead. On the tenth, tests revealed his body was riddled with cancer; it had begun in his lungs and spread to his liver and brain. The cancer was inoperable and his condition deteriorated rapidly.

His attorney, Elmer Gertz, and his brother Earl Ruby recorded a deathbed interview with him that was then offered for sale. In this interview, Ruby repeated the story he had often told, but then mused, "The ironic part of this is had not I made an illegal turn behind the bus to the parking lot, had I gone the way I was supposed to go straight down Main Street, I would have never met this fate because the difference in meeting this fate was thirty seconds one way or the other."

Jack Ruby died on January 3, 1967. Phil Burleson, the only attorney who had been with him from the very beginning of the legal process until its end, pointed out, with satisfaction, that "Jack Ruby died an innocent man."

But his role in the Kennedy assassination remained unsettled. As years passed his notoriety grew. The fact that there has never been any hard evidence linking Ruby to a conspiracy has not stopped believers from attributing a variety of roles to him. The twist of him being diagnosed with terminal cancer before he could be retried fit into those theories, some people even claiming he had been injected with it to prevent him from "talking."

In 1979 a House Select Committee investigating the assassinations of Kennedy and Martin Luther King determined that there likely was a conspiracy to assassinate JFK and that Jack Ruby may have played a significant role in it. An initial six-hundred-page draft report would have confirmed that Oswald and then Ruby acted alone. In the controversial final version, the committee found no credible evidence against most of the most cited conspiracy suspects and could not identify who else might have been involved. But they did refer to circumstantial evidence linking Ruby to organized crime mobsters like Santo Trafficante and Johnny Roselli, and even suggested that he might have been running guns to the Castro regime.

As a result of the trial Belli became a certified American celebrity. The *New York Times* favorably reviewed his 1964 book, *Dallas Justice*, concluding, "One thing becomes clear in this always dogmatic book: the Ruby case is far from ended." The

Italian Sons and Daughters of America named him its Man of
the Year. And, as he said, he was asked to join in an array of interesting cases; some of them including "bare-bosomed waitresses and showgirls." The next year he was a guest star on the
hit show *Star Trek* where he played Gorgan of the planet Tria-
cus. With the ability to hypnotize children, Gorgan was almost
able to steal Captain Kirk's spacecraft the USS *Enterprise*. A few
years later, he even auditioned for the lead role in *The Godfather*,
which eventually went to Marlon Brando.

Ironically, while Ruby and Belli had captured the national
headlines, it was Henry Wade whose name would resonate in
history. In 1970, as District Attorney of Dallas County, he became the defendant of record in a case brought by a woman
known as "Jane Roe," who had been denied an abortion under
Texas law. When the U.S. District Court for northern Texas
agreed with Roe that the law was unconstitutional, Wade's office appealed and the case eventually ended up in the United
States Supreme Court. While Wade was never personally involved in case, and in fact never expressed any strong opinion
on the issue, the Supreme Court decided in the landmark Roe
v Wade that women had a legal right to abortion, thus ensur-
ing Wade's name would never be forgotten.

In death, Ruby proved to be a valuable commodity. The
weapon he used sold for $220,000 in 1991, and bullets for that
weapon were put on sale for $495 each. In 2009 the fedora he
was wearing when he killed Oswald was bought at auction for
$53,775; the handcuffs used to chain him to the bed as he lay
dying went for $11,054 and, in perhaps the last great irony of
this trial, an X-ray of his head was sold for $776.

★ ★ ★ ★ ★

BIBLIOGRAPHY

Case Closed: Lee Harvey Oswald and the Assassination of JFK, Gerald Posner, Random House, New York, 1993

Dallas and the Jack Ruby Trial: Memoir of Judge Joe B. Brown, Sr., Diane Holloway PhD, Editor, Authors Choice Press, Lincoln, Nebraska, 2001

Dallas Herald, various editions 1963–1964

Dallas Justice: The Real Story of Jack Ruby and His Trial, Melvin M. Belli with Maurice C. Carroll, David McKay, Publishers, New York, 1964

Dallas Morning News, various editions 1963–1964

Denial of Justice: Dorothy Kilgallen, Abuse of Power, and the Most Compelling JFK Assassination Investigation in History, Mark Shaw, Post Hill Press, New York, 2018

"Exorcising the Clergy Privilege," Christine P. Bartholomew, *Virginia Law Review*, Volume 103 Issue 6, October 2017, https://www.virginialawreview.org/articles/exorcising-clergy-privilege/

"History of Criminal Appeal in England," Lester B. Orfield, *Missouri Law Review*, Volume 1 Issue 4, November 1936, Article 3

Houston Chronicle, various editions, 1963–1964

"The Image of Truth: Photographic Evidence and the Power of Analogy," Jennifer L. Mnookin, *Yale Journal of Law & the Humanities*, Volume 10 Issue 1, January 1998, Article 1

The Jack Ruby Trial Revisited: The Diary of Jury Foreman Max Causey, John Mark Dempsey, Editor, University of North Texas Press, Denton, Texas, 2000

Melvin Belli: My Life on Trial, Melvin M. Belli with Robert Blair Kaiser, William Morrow and Company, New York, 1976

"Playboy: Alex Haley Interviews Melvin Belli," *Playboy*, June 1965

Reclaiming History: The Assassination of President John F. Kennedy, Vincent Bugliosi, W. W. Norton & Company, New York, 2007

"Revisiting the History of Scientific Expert Testimony," Tai Golan, *Brooklyn Law Review*, Volume 73 Issue 3, 2008, https://brooklynworks.brooklaw.edu/cgi/viewcontent.cgi?article=1312&context=blr

Rush to Judgment: A Critique of the Warren Commission's Inquiry into the Murders of President John F. Kennedy, Officer J.D. Tippit and Lee Harvey Oswald, Mark Lane, Holt Rinehart and Winston, New York, January, 1966

The Ruby Cover-Up (Who Was Jack Ruby?), Seth Kantor, Zebra Books, New York City, 1980.

TimesMachine: New York Times archive, https://timesmachine.nytimes.com/

The Trial of Jack Ruby, John Kaplan and Jon R. Waltz, Macmillan, New York, 1965

The Warren Commission Report: Report of the President's Commission on the Assassination of President John F. Kennedy, U.S. Government Printing Office, 1964

"Who Was Jack Ruby?," Gary Cartwright, *Texas Monthly*, November 1975

Report of the Select Committee on Assassinations of the U.S. House of Representatives, Washington, D.C. 1979

ACKNOWLEDGMENTS

In our three other books, David Fisher and I often felt like legal archaeologists uncovering trial transcripts almost completely ignored or lost to history. And it often wasn't just the trials themselves but the facts surrounding them that had been forgotten as well.

While the trial of Jack Ruby somehow became a historical footnote, the events surrounding it have been as well tread as almost any other topic in American history. This book was about the trial with the transcript as the centerpiece, but we also approached the project armed with the mountains of research already completed. That made some of the books in this bibliography that much more important. For me the long out of print The Trial of Jack Ruby by attorneys John Kaplan and Jon R. Waltz from 1965 was particularly useful for almost real time assessments of some of the legal strategies. It also served as a sort of rorschach test for what one thinks of a defense strategy the authors clearly disdained. I largely agreed with them while David felt they were unfairly critical of the defense.

And this exemplifies how David and I work so well together. We figured out a way to tell the story of a controversial defense in one voice. So let me once again thank David for his partnership and leadership on this project. I get the top billing. David deserves it.

Let me echo our thanks to our amazing editor Peter Joseph for all of his support and guidance and for living these books and stories along with us. And to Peter's intrepid team of Emer Flounders, Grace Towery and Eden Church.

I want to once again thank my father Floyd for his inspiration in so many ways. But not only has he always been a terrific father but he is a tireless and loving partner to my mother Efrat. Mom, if you could still understand the words here, I know you would agree.

My sister Ronnie, her husband Greg and their kids Dylan, Teddy and Finn remain so important to me, not just by blood but by choice. I love seeing them all and am so proud of the young women all the girls have become.

My son Everett remains my treasure. His energy, love and positivity simply makes me a happier person. I think about him in everything I do. I have been particularly impressed, although not surprised, at how quickly he has become a welcoming and warm big brother for his new sister Emilia who is almost nine years his junior. I know she will always cherish him.

And then there is their mother Florinka. Thank you for being such a valuable sounding board on all matters. Thank you for providing me the time and space to work on this project while our parental duties were magnified during the pandemic. And thank you for your tireless, and wildly successful, efforts to turn our children into thoughtful, happy little humans.

If Jack Ruby had been a little happier and more thoughtful, he certainly never would have become the subject of this book.

—*Dan Abrams*

My life was changed in grade school by a librarian named Herb Deutsch, and since then I have had the utmost respect and admiration for librarians. It is impossible to overstate the impact librarians have had on my career. In writing this book we were assisted by Christine Sharbrough, MSLIS archival studies Manager, Dallas History & Archives Division City of Dallas (www.dallaslibrary2.org). Navigating through the challenges of the pandemic would have been impossible without her joyful attitude, creative problem-solving, knowledge and ability to dig deep into existing material. We are tremendously grateful to her.

We also greatly appreciate the assistance we received from the Texas Court of Criminalized Appeals centralized court case files. Archives and Information Services Division, Texas State Library and Archives Commission.

We also want to thank Martha McDonnell, who helped us open the pages of history.

We also would like to express our continuing gratitude to our editor, Peter Joseph, who, in addition to being a consistent cheerleader, has put his own mark on these pages. He has his masters degree in the art of tact and displays it as we work together.

We are very fortunate to be published by Hanover Square Press. There are seemingly innumerable parts that bring a book from an idea to these pages; in this process we have been aided by the properly named Grace Towery, who does the nitty-gritty with such grace and competence, Emer Flounders who brings it to the world and Eden Church, who makes it all work. We are truly grateful to all of them.

The business of this book has been done by Frank Weimann, vice president of the Folio Literary Management, in his own quiet but extremely competent way. For that we are deeply grateful.

For several decades my personal business has been done by Alan Susskind. Alan, who smiles, always. My trust and confidence in him has enabled me to focus on the job of writing. Alan is retiring now, his role being filled by Alan Dworkin and AnnMarie Quinn. But I would be remiss if I didn't publicly thank him. Alan and I share so many memories of so many people for so many years, but knowing he was there has made a huge difference in my life.

I would also like to thank Jerry Wade, who generously offered important advice and cooperation when it was needed at the beginning of this project.

For me, David Fisher, it would be difficult to have a better partner than Dan Abrams. When working with someone, now on our fourth book, perhaps the greatest compliment I can give is, he does the work. Somehow, given his many ventures, Dan finds the time to do even more than the basic requirements. From the inception of a concept, through development, down to the words on the page, he is always there. I am so grateful for that, too.

And last but always first, my wife, Laura. It literally would be impossible for anyone to be more supportive (but if it were, she would be). Through this pandemic she has remained steadfast, creating the place that allows me to dig into history. (And obviously I need to mention her sidekick, Willow Bay, who does not obey but does find comfort on my lap as I work.)

—*David Fisher*

INDEX

Page numbers for photographs are indicated in *italics*.

INDEX

Page numbers for photographs are indicated in *italics*.

DAN ABRAMS AND DAVID FISHER

Bruce, Lenny, 35
Buchanan, James, 84
Burleson, Phil, 43, 59, 330–31, 372,
    378–79, 382–83, 384

Cabell, Earle, 73–74
Calahan, John, 374
Campbell, Don, 22, 114–16
Carney, Frederick, 56–60
Carousel Club, 37, 48, 120, *196,* 199, 363
Carroll, Ed, 79
Carter, Ingrid, 306
Causey, Max, 90, 141, 347
chain of evidence, 136
change of venue hearing
    about, 51–52
    Belli filing for, 50–52
    Brown on, 84–85, 381–82
    defense resting their case, 84
    defense strategies and, 59, 85
    evidence for, 55–56
    as minitrial, 52
    motion at start of trial, 111
    prosecution affidavits, 84
    prosecution objections, 78
    Ruby interviews during, 64, 80–81
    start of first day, 52–53
    start of second day, 70
    start of third day, 80
    witnesses for, 56–84
charging the jury, 322–23, 324
Citizens Council, 21, 55–56, 57–58, 60,
    73, 81, 86
clinical psychology, 217–18, 311, 319
Cohen, Mickey, 35
Combest, B. H., 293
Commentaries on the Laws of England
    (Blackstone), 51, 71
Communism, 20, 21, 26, 75, 76, 93,
    237–38, 343
confabulation, 231, 238, 295, 298,
    309–10, 339, 341
confirmation bias, 288–89
Connally, John, 21, 22, 28, 48, 52, 294
Considine, Bob, 199–200, 232, 346
conspiracy theories
    Kennedy assassination, 12, 13, 47–48,
        67–68, 76, 119–20, 198–200,

237–38, 306, 329, 334, 357, 371,
    384
    police involvement in Oswald
        shooting, 40, 146–47, 162–65, 341
    Ruby and Oswald acquaintance,
        25–26, 47–48, 62–63, 75, 356–57
Crawford, Curtis "Larry," 303, 327
crime of passion, 45–46, 47
crime reporting, scope of, 30
Criminal Courts Building, Dallas
    County, 87–88
Crisis of Confidence in Dallas (Carney), 57
Crory, K. H., 374
cross-examinations, about, 156, 255–57

Dallas, Texas
    criminal history of, 30
    growth of, 19–20
    homosexuality, Texas constitution
        and, 126
    as murder capital of Texas, 148
    political parties and, 20–21, 55
    reputation of, 24, 74–75, 79, 86, 110,
        144, 183–84, 325–26
Dallas County Criminal Bar Association,
    70
Dallas County Criminal Courts Building,
    87–88
Dallas Justice (Belli), 371, 384
Darrow, Clarence, 216
Dean, Patrick, 172–81, 379, 381–83
"death-house psychosis," 356
death penalty
    factors for, 139
    jurors and, 343, 348–49, 351
death threats to defense attorneys, 72
Decker, Bill, 69, 144, 196
defamation, 205
defense strategies
    attacking Wade, 127–28
    bail request for Ruby, 46
    change of venue hearing, 59, 85
    Communism and, 93
    Dallas being on trial, 74–75
    defendant as witness, 242–43
    extenuating circumstances, 45–46, 47
    filing motion for new trial, 354
    fugue states, 49, 108–9
    general strategies, 132, 139, 151

394